Running a Marathon
FOR
DUMMIES®

by Jason R. Karp, PhD

WILEY

John Wiley & Sons, Inc.

Running a Marathon For Dummies®

Published by
John Wiley & Sons, Inc.
111 River St.
Hoboken, NJ 07030-5774
www.wiley.com

Copyright © 2013 by John Wiley & Sons, Inc., Hoboken, New Jersey

Published simultaneously in Canada

For general information on our other products and services, please contact our Customer Care Department within the U.S. at 877-762-2974, outside the U.S. at 317-572-3993, or fax 317-572-4002.

For technical support, please visit www.wiley.com/techsupport.

Wiley publishes in a variety of print and electronic formats and by print-on-demand. Some material included with standard print versions of this book may not be included in e-books or in print-on-demand. If this book refers to media such as a CD or DVD that is not included in the version you purchased, you may download this material at http://booksupport.wiley.com. For more information about Wiley products, visit www.wiley.com.

Library of Congress Control Number: 2012949693

ISBN 978-1-118-34308-1 (pbk); ISBN 978-1-118-43207-5 (ebk); ISBN 978-1-118-43210-5 (ebk); ISBN 978-1-118-43211-2 (ebk)

Manufactured in the United States of America

10 9 8 7 6 5 4 3 2 1

WILEY

About the Author

Jason R. Karp, PhD, is a nationally recognized running and fitness coach, freelance writer and author, and exercise physiologist. He owns RunCoachJason.com, a state-of-the-science run coaching and personal training company in San Diego, California. As one of America's foremost running experts and the 2011 IDEA Personal Trainer of the Year (the fitness industry's highest award), Dr. Karp is a trusted source of information. Through his writing, conference presentations, DVDs, and numerous print and television interviews on topics related to running and fitness, he brings the state of the science directly to the public. A sought-after speaker, he is a frequent presenter at national fitness, coaching, and academic conferences. A nationally certified running coach through USA Track & Field, he has also taught USATF's highest level coaching certification and was an instructor at the USATF/U.S. Olympic Committee's Emerging Elite Coaches Camp at the U.S. Olympic Training Center. He also regularly holds clinics for runners, coaches, and fitness professionals.

He is a prolific writer, with more than 200 articles in numerous international coaching, running, and fitness trade and consumer magazines, including *Track Coach, Techniques for Track & Field and Cross Country, New Studies in Athletics, Athletics Weekly, Running Times, Runner's World, Trail Runner, Women's Running, Marathon & Beyond, IDEA Fitness Journal, Shape,* and *Ultra-Fit,* among others. He is also the author of four other books: *Running for Women* (Human Kinetics), *101 Winning Racing Strategies for Runners* (Coaches Choice), *101 Developmental Concepts & Workouts for Cross Country Runners* (Coaches Choice), and *How to Survive Your PhD* (Sourcebooks).

Dr. Karp has coached cross-country and track at the high school, college, and elite club levels. In 1997, at the age of 24, he became one of the youngest collegiate head coaches in the country, leading the Georgian Court University (NJ) women's cross-country team to the regional championship and winning honors as NAIA Northeast Region Coach of the Year. His personal training experience ranges from elite athletes to cardiac rehab patients. As a private coach and founder of *REVO$_2$LT Running Team,* he has helped many runners meet their potential, ranging from a first-time race participant to an Olympic marathon trials qualifier. He has been profiled in a number of publications and is sponsored by PowerBar as a member of PowerBar Team Elite. His popular downloadable training programs are used by runners around the world.

Dr. Karp received his PhD in exercise physiology, with a physiology minor, from Indiana University in 2007; his master's degree in kinesiology from the University of Calgary in 1997; and his bachelor's degree in exercise and sport science, with an English minor, from Pennsylvania State University in 1995. His research includes motor unit recruitment during eccentric muscle contractions, post-exercise nutrition for optimal recovery in endurance athletes, training characteristics of Olympic marathon trials qualifiers, and the coordination of breathing and stride rate in distance runners. His research has been published in the scientific journals *Medicine & Science in Sports & Exercise, International Journal of Sport Nutrition and Exercise Metabolism,* and *International Journal of Sports Physiology and Performance.* Dr. Karp has taught at several universities and currently teaches dissertation writing, a course he designed for doctoral students, at the University of California, San Diego.

Dedication

For my father, Monroe, whose long walking strides through the streets of Brooklyn, New York, caused me to run to keep up. Perhaps it was those fond moments as a kid with my father that planted the seed for me to become a runner. And for my mother, Muriel, who always told me how proud she was of me and who taught me how to endure and "roll with the punches." In her memory, I'm donating 10 percent of my royalty on every book sold to Susan G. Komen for the Cure.

Author's Acknowledgments

This book has been my biggest writing project to date. It couldn't have happened without the support of many people. I'd like to thank the expeditious editorial staff at Wiley, including Stacy Kennedy, Georgette Beatty, and Todd Lothery; Kathryn Born, who created the medical illustrations for the book; and Wiley's graphics department, which created the rest of the illustrations. A well-oiled machine, Wiley published this book faster than a dummy can run a marathon!

I'd also like to thank my twin brother, Jack, for inspiring me to be as good a writer as he is and for not making nearly as many jokes as he could have about me writing a book for dummies; my hard-working agent, Grace Freedson, who made this book possible and who thankfully understands my perfectionism; Traci Cumbay, who helped with the initial "dummifying" of my writing; photographer Maurice Roy, for his great photographs that beautifully illustrate my text; models Martha Carbajal Moreno, Natalie Jill, and Pedro Molina, who made the photographs pop off the page; and my parents, who left this world much too early but who are with me with every word I write and every step I run.

Publisher's Acknowledgments

We're proud of this book; please send us your comments at http://dummies.custhelp.com. For other comments, please contact our Customer Care Department within the U.S. at 877-762-2974, outside the U.S. at 317-572-3993, or fax 317-572-4002.

Some of the people who helped bring this book to market include the following:

Acquisitions, Editorial, and Vertical Websites

Senior Project Editor: Georgette Beatty

Acquisitions Editor: Stacy Kennedy

Copy Editor: Todd Lothery

Assistant Editor: David Lutton

Editorial Program Coordinator: Joe Niesen

Technical Editor: Patricia Heniff

Editorial Manager: Michelle Hacker

Editorial Assistant: Alexa Koschier

Art Coordinator: Alicia B. South

Cover Photo: © Maurice van der Velden / iStockphoto.com

Cartoons: Rich Tennant (www.the5th wave.com)

Composition Services

Project Coordinator: Katherine Crocker

Layout and Graphics: Carrie A. Cesavice, Jennifer Creasey, Corrie Neihaus, Brent Savage

Proofreaders: John Greenough, The Well Chosen Word

Indexer: Galen Schoeder

Photographer: Maurice Roy Photography

Illustrator: Kathryn Born, MA

Special Help Traci Cumbay

Publishing and Editorial for Consumer Dummies

    Kathleen Nebenhaus, Vice President and Executive Publisher

    David Palmer, Associate Publisher

    Kristin Ferguson-Wagstaffe, Product Development Director

Publishing for Technology Dummies

    Andy Cummings, Vice President and Publisher

Composition Services

    Debbie Stailey, Director of Composition Services

Contents at a Glance

Table of Contents

Chapter 8: Making a Plan as a Beginner Runner 121

Chapter 9: Prepping for Your Next Race
as an Intermediate Runner 133

Introduction

*T*o paraphrase the ancient Chinese philosopher Confucius, "A journey of 26.2 miles begins with a single step." From the time the ancient Greek runner Pheidippides ran from Marathon to Athens in 490 BC to announce the Greeks' victory over Persia in the Battle of Marathon, humans have had a compelling interest in taking that single step, and many more after that.

Humans have repeatedly tried to push the limits of running endurance, which have been nothing short of remarkable: 50 marathons in 50 days and 300 miles of nonstop running by Dean Karnazes of the United States, and the current world records in the marathon, which equal an average marathon pace of 5 minutes and 10 seconds per mile by England's Paula Radcliffe and 4 minutes and 43 seconds per mile by Kenya's Patrick Makau.

So when people, upon finding out what I do for a living, tell me they can't run, I have to smile to myself. Of course they can run. And you can, too. Running is in your DNA. As long as you train your body properly, it has a remarkable capacity to adapt and endure. Whether you want to run a marathon just for the thrill of it or qualify for the Boston Marathon, it all starts with a single step, which leads to another step, and then another, and then another. When you put all those steps together and they cover 26.2 miles, you become a marathoner.

This book is all about getting you to become a marathoner, whether it's your first one or fastest one. As the famous Czech runner Emil Zátopek, who won five gold medals in two Olympics, once said, "If you want to win something, run 100 meters. If you want to experience something, run a marathon."

The marathon truly is different from any other running race. It unites people. When you're in the race, it doesn't matter what your income is or how beautiful or handsome you are or what your ethnicity is or what type of car you drive; everyone has 26.2 miles to run. And that's not easy for anyone.

The marathon changes people's lives. And it will change yours.

About This Book

Much like the marathon itself, *Running a Marathon For Dummies* is a journey — it took just as long to write as it takes to train for a marathon! This book is for anyone who wants to run a marathon, and it covers everything you need to know about the marathon, and then some. Within it, you find information on

- ✔ Preparing to run a marathon
- ✔ Choosing the right running gear
- ✔ Proper running form
- ✔ Different training strategies and workouts
- ✔ Training programs for beginner, intermediate, and advanced runners
- ✔ Diagnosing and preventing injuries
- ✔ Racing strategies and tips
- ✔ Destination marathons
- ✔ Frequently asked questions about the marathon
- ✔ And so much more!

In contrast to the marathon itself, in which you can't run mile 24 without first running miles 1 to 23, you don't need to read this book from start to finish (although I put a lot of time into it, so I hope you read the whole thing). You can pick and choose the topics you want to read about and then set the book aside until you need it again. Using this book is that simple.

Conventions Used in This Book

I use the following conventions throughout the book to make things consistent and easy to understand:

- ✔ New terms appear in *italic* and are followed by a definition. I also use italics for emphasis.
- ✔ **Bold text** highlights the action parts of numbered steps and the keywords in bulleted lists.
- ✔ All web addresses appear in `monofont`.

When this book was printed, some web addresses may have needed to break across two lines of text. If that happened, rest assured that I've added no extra characters, such as hyphens, to indicate the break. So when using one of these web addresses, simply type in exactly what you see in the book as though the line break doesn't exist.

What You're Not to Read

As a writer, I believe every word I write is important. But I understand that not every word between the covers needs to be read. After all, the more time you spend reading, the less time you have to run! The skippable material in this book includes the following:

- ✔ **Text in sidebars:** The sidebars are shaded boxes that appear throughout the book. They contain information that's interesting but not critical to your understanding of a particular marathon-related topic.

- ✔ **Text next to the Technical Stuff icon:** I went to college for 13 years to study the science of exercise and to understand how to make runners run better. I love physiology and love applying that physiology to a training program. However, I know that many runners just want to know what to do and don't care why they're doing it. So you don't *have* to read the information marked by the Technical Stuff icon, but I hope you do. Like the text in sidebars, the text with this icon is interesting but not crucial to the goal of running a marathon.

- ✔ **The stuff on the copyright, dedication, and author's acknowledgments pages:** Seriously. There's nothing there that can help you run a marathon. Unless you want to know the Library of Congress info, whom I dedicated the book to, or how I thanked my twin brother for his jokes about me writing a book for dummies, just skip these pages.

- ✔ **The about the author page:** You don't need to know who I am to know that this is the best book on running a marathon out there. After all, all *For Dummies* authors are considered experts in their fields. But feel free to take a peek to satisfy your curiosity. It may impress you.

Foolish Assumptions

In writing this book, I had to make some assumptions about you (please forgive me). I assume that you

- ✔ **Know how to run:** Though it may seem hard to do at times, running is in your genes. Although some people are more graceful and efficient runners than others, I assume you know the basic idea of how to run, even if your tongue is hanging out and you don't look pretty doing it.

✔ **Are in good health and are physically capable of undertaking the training to run long distances:** The marathon is a big physical challenge, so if you have any health issues or are older than 40, consult your doctor before training for a marathon.

✔ **Are a little crazy:** You have to be a little crazy to run a marathon. It's a long way to run.

✔ **Know that a marathon is 26.2 miles:** If you didn't know that before picking up this book, you do now. (I hope you'll still read it.)

✔ **Are ready to run your first or fastest marathon:** This book is for first-timers as well as those who have some marathon experience and want to run the marathon again — and better than ever.

How This Book Is Organized

Running a Marathon For Dummies is divided into five parts, each of which contains several chapters. If you've never run a marathon before, you may want to start at the beginning. If you have run a marathon, feel free to skip around to chapters that address your needs. The upcoming sections are a guide to what you find in each part of the book.

Part 1: The Basics of Running a Marathon

In this part, I give you an overview of running a marathon, including some insight into its growing popularity, the expected time commitment you need to prepare for it, unique aspects of the marathon, and directions for getting started.

Because marathon running literally starts with your feet, I also give you information on how to pick the right shoes. With all the different types of running shoes and the bells and whistles on them, how do you know what you need or whether you need shoes at all?

In addition, I talk about other running gear, I show you correct running technique to keep you moving without injury, and I tell you all about the elegant changes your heart, blood, and muscles make so that you can run 26.2 miles without falling over!

Part II: Creating Your Own Marathon Training Plan

In this part, you get all the training information you need, whether you're a newbie runner or an experienced marathoner looking to run your best race yet. I give you the thorough information that gets you from point A to the finish line. I show you how training works, including how many miles to run, how to get the most out of your long runs, and how to improve your fitness with tempo training and interval training.

I also give you 20-week plans for beginner, intermediate, and advanced runners, laid out in an easy-to-follow, calendar-style format that includes each day's specific training.

Part III: Going Above and Beyond to Stay Strong and Healthy

Training for a marathon can and should be about more than just running. This part is about everything non-running that keeps you healthy and strong — strength training, cross-training with non-running activities, stretching, and recovery.

Because the last thing you want is to get injured while training, I also give you a detailed guide to common running-related injuries, including the secrets of preventing them!

Part IV: Gearing Up for Race Day (And Beyond)

You do so much to prep your body for the marathon, and you also want to prep for the big day by easing your jitters and increasing your odds of running a good race.

In this part, I talk about the marathon taper — your time to slow down and give your body a much-needed rest in preparation for the big effort to come. I give you tips for getting your mind (and gear) ready for the race, and I take you through a race so that you're armed with all the knowledge that my years of coaching and running have taught me.

Part V: The Part of Tens

Want to know what to do on marathon race day? What about how to avoid the most common training errors? Want to run a marathon while on vacation? From helpful and sometimes humorous race day tips to the best destination marathons in the world to frequently asked questions about running a marathon, you find quick bits of juicy information about marathons in this part.

Icons Used in This Book

Every *For Dummies* book has little pictures in the margins — *icons* — to help direct your attention to certain kinds of information. *Running a Marathon For Dummies* is no exception. I use the following icons to categorize the information in this book.

Some points are worth returning to again and again. This icon highlights important concepts and ideas that you're likely to want to flip back to quickly.

In some instances, I go deeper into the physiology of running than you may be interested in. I'm a big fan of this kind of information and think it helps you understand the *what* and *why* of training. But I also know that I'm a rare bird, so feel free to skip this info. You can run a marathon just fine without it.

Whenever I provide information that saves you time or frustration or clues you into a more efficient training process, I highlight that text with this icon.

You can train smart and still get injured. If you follow bad training advice, you're even more likely to end up hurt. Whenever I discuss something you should be careful about or a misguided notion that can leave you limping or otherwise inhibit your training, I mark it with this daunting icon.

Where to Go from Here

You can start *Running a Marathon For Dummies* with any chapter you like. That's the beauty of this book — you don't have to read it cover to cover (unless you really want to).

If you're a beginner runner, I recommend that you start by reading Chapters 1 and 2 so you can get an overview of the journey you're about to take. If you've run a marathon before, I recommend that you start by reading Chapter 3 — which covers the physiology behind the training so that you can train smarter and run your next marathon better — and Chapter 4, just to make sure you have the proper running technique. Or you can just jump in and start reading wherever you land! Good luck!

Part I
The Basics of Running a Marathon

In this part...

It's time to get moving! This part gives you an overview of running a marathon, including the expected time commitment to prepare for it, unique aspects of the marathon, and directions for getting started.

I also give you information on how to pick the right shoes and gear to run in different climates so you start off your training on the right foot . . . literally.

I also devote a chapter to the basic physiology of running a marathon and all the changes your heart, blood, and muscles make with training that allow you to run 26.2 miles successfully (or faster than you've ever run before!). Finally, I show you correct running technique so you can begin training!

Chapter 1

Training for the Big Race: An Overview

When Pierre de Coubertin from France founded the modern Olympic games that were first held in Athens, Greece, in 1896, he decided to include a long running race. Being the sentimental guy that he was, he named the race a *marathon* after the Greek town where the ancient Greek runner Pheidippides's legendary run began. Little did he know how popular his little footrace would become.

With nearly 500 marathons in the United States each year and half a million people running them, saying that running a marathon is a big deal is an understatement. It has become a popular item on people's bucket lists. It may even be on yours. Perhaps that's because people recognize the truth in what running philosopher George Sheehan once said: "The marathon is an adventure into the limits of the self, a theater for heroism, where the runner can do deeds of daring and greatness." And it gives you really nice legs!

Running a marathon is a huge undertaking. There's a lot to know after you decide to do it. Where do you begin? In this chapter, I give you an overview of running a marathon, including the expected time commitment to prepare for it, ways to get started, and potential challenges.

Why Run a Marathon?

Before you start preparing to run a marathon, you should know why you're doing it. After all, deciding to run a marathon isn't like deciding what to eat for dinner or what to order at your favorite coffee shop. It's a pretty big decision that requires commitment. So why you're doing it is an important first question to ask yourself. You may want to run a marathon for many reasons:

✔ **To get fit:** Training for a marathon is a great way to improve your aerobic fitness (not to mention get a great butt). Nothing gets you fit like running. Because running involves your whole body, it trains all your muscles. It also drives your heart rate up higher than any other activity, which is a powerful stimulus to improve your cardiovascular fitness.

✔ **To lose weight:** Running is one of the best ways to lose weight because it burns more calories than just about every other activity. And because training for a marathon means a whole lot of running, that's quite a lot of calories. Most people, even seasoned runners, drop at least a few pounds during marathon training.

✔ **To challenge yourself:** Humans often like to undertake difficult endeavors — to set tough goals and go after them. What better way to challenge yourself than to run 26.2 miles? Doing so is both a physical challenge and a test of your mental strength.

✔ **To accomplish something and improve your self-esteem:** Trying — and better yet, succeeding at — something you think is difficult feels good. It feeds your ego and makes you feel better about yourself. Even though running a marathon is becoming more popular, those who do it are still the minority.

✔ **To bond with your friends and family:** Running a marathon can be very social, as you and your friends and family can share the experience together. Many people train for and run marathons together. The support (and the shame factor when you flake out of a group training run) can provide a lot of motivation, and those long runs offer plenty of time to catch up with your fellow runners.

✔ **To raise money for charity:** Running a marathon is a great way to raise money for a good cause. When you run for charity, you're not just running for you anymore; you feel a measure of responsibility. You're running for kids with leukemia or for your mom with cancer. You're doing something good for yourself *and* others.

✔ **To assuage your midlife crisis:** Getting your mind off your age is actually a very common reason to run a marathon. Lots of people make big decisions and like to shake things up a bit when they hit those milestone birthdays, like 40 or 50 (or 60 and beyond). Doing something challenging is a great distraction from those creeping anxieties about aging. The amazing benefit of running a marathon as a distraction is that it has the power to make you feel younger.

✔ **To cross it off your bucket list:** The marathon has become a popular bucket-list item, one of those things to do before you, well, kick the bucket. A lot of people want to experience the challenge of training for and running 26.2 miles just for the sake of doing it. It's right up there with skydiving (only safer).

Making the Time to Train for a Marathon

Some things you can do at the last minute, like picking up dinner at a fast-food restaurant, mailing your taxes on April 15, and sending your twin brother an e-card because you failed to remember his birthday until 9:54 p.m.

Didn't expect to see "training for a marathon" on that list, did you? I hope not; training for a marathon is a huge endeavor that normally takes months and that you need to take seriously. For many reasons, it's not something you can do (or should try to do) in a few weeks, and risk of injury is probably the major reason to take your time. The biggest risk of injury comes when you run too much too soon, before your bones, muscles, tendons, and ligaments are able to completely adapt. (I tell you more about common running injuries in Chapter 13.)

Great strides: The growth of the marathon

The marathon has grown faster than a bodybuilder on steroids. According to MarathonGuide.com, 299,000 people completed a marathon in the United States in 2000, growing to 503,000 in 2010. In 2000, 62.5 percent of marathoners were male, and 37.5 percent were female. In 2010, 58.8 percent were male, and 41.2 percent were female.

Many popular marathons are held in the United States, which hosted a whopping 483 of them in 2010. The largest marathon in the United States is the ING New York City Marathon, which boasted 44,704 finishers in 2010. The next five largest marathons (by number of finishers in 2010) are the Bank of America Chicago Marathon (36,159), the Boston Marathon (22,540), the LA Marathon (22,403), the Marine Corps Marathon (21,874), and the Honolulu Marathon (20,169).

The amount of time to prepare for a marathon varies from person to person, according to circumstances, goals, and a lot of other things, including

✔ Your prior running experience

✔ How many days per week you plan to run

✔ How quickly your body adapts to training and how much recovery time you need, which influence your risk of injuries

✔ How fast you want to run the marathon

If you're a new runner, I recommend running a few days per week for at least a year before running a marathon. Run some other races, like 5Ks and 10Ks, and work your way up to the half-marathon and marathon. That's the safest way to do it. The marathon requires maturity, in terms of both training and experience. Trying to run a marathon without first becoming a runner is like trying to earn a PhD without first earning a bachelor's degree. You increase the risk of injuries and of making training and racing mistakes.

The exact amount of time you need to train for a marathon depends on how long and how often you've been running:

✔ If you've been running up to 20 miles per week for at least a year but have never run a marathon before, give yourself eight to ten months to prepare for it.

✔ If you've been running for a few years and have run a marathon before, give yourself six to eight months to prepare.

✔ If you're one of those speedy types who runs every day, sleeps with your running shoes on, and makes running a marathon as much a habit as eating pasta and soaking your legs in cold water, give yourself enough time to fully recover from your last marathon and to ramp your mileage back up before attempting another one. Typically, that means about four to six months, especially if you want to run your next marathon faster.

Depending on your level and goals, you can run a marathon on 5 to 15 hours of training per week. That includes the (increasingly) long run you'll do each week.

Training for a marathon isn't just a time commitment for you; it's a time commitment for your family, too. So unless you're single with no responsibilities other than yourself, you need to let your family know how important running a marathon is to you so they can be supportive. Someone has to watch the kids when you're out running for three hours on Sunday morning!

How did the marathon become 26 miles, 385 yards, anyway?

Ever wonder how the marathon became the distance it is? Don't you wish it was shorter? The seemingly arbitrary distance of 26 miles, 385 yards (26.2 miles or 42.2 kilometers) has a long history. For the first modern Olympic games in 1896, the founder of the Olympics, Pierre de Coubertin, included a running race that was 25 miles (40 kilometers), approximately the distance of the legendary run that the ancient Greek soldier Pheidippides took from the Greek town of Marathon to Athens to announce the Greeks' victory over Persia in the Battle of Marathon. For the next couple of Olympics, the race distance was changed. In preparation for the 1908 Olympics in London, the International Olympic Committee and the British Olympic Association agreed to include a marathon of 25 miles. Logistical problems with the layout of the course caused organizers to revise it, which lengthened the route, as did plans to make the start line 700 yards from Queen Victoria's statue by Windsor Castle. Organizers planned for the runners to enter the Olympic stadium through the royal entrance, run one lap of the track and, at the request of the royal family, finish in front of the family's viewing box. This made the race 26 miles, 586 yards, and 2 feet. However, this distance was changed yet again after running a trial marathon before the Olympics, with the start line being moved to the private east terrace of Windsor Castle to avoid interference with the public at the start line, making the final distance 42.195 kilometers, or 26 miles, 385 yards. What a headache!

For the next Olympics in 1912, the length was changed to 25.0 miles (40.2 kilometers), and it was changed again for the 1920 Olympics to 26.56 miles (42.74 kilometers). In 1921, the International Amateur Athletics Federation (now the International Association of Athletics Federations), the international governing body of track and field, irrevocably fixed the marathon at the 1908 Olympic distance of 42.195 kilometers. And that's who we have to thank for that!

 If running a marathon were easy, everyone would do it, and it wouldn't be a big deal. Anything worth accomplishing in life is difficult. Running a marathon is a huge undertaking, but it's also very rewarding. As you plan your schedule to prepare for your marathon, take your time and do it the right way.

Starting to Prepare for a Marathon

Assuming you've made the decision to run a marathon (which is why you're reading this book), how do you begin to prepare for it? Do you just go out and run 20 miles? No, please don't. Building up to that distance takes time. Here's what you need to do to start preparing:

✔ Read this book so you can find out as much as you can about training for the marathon.

✔ Get your head in the game. Many beginning runners are timid about running, but it's really not that hard — you start by putting on a pair of comfortable running shoes and going out the door to run, even if it's only for a few minutes. You'll huff and you'll puff and you may even blow your house down, but that's okay. Being out of shape turns into being in shape pretty quickly if you stick with it.

✔ Decide whether you're going to train on your own, with a group, or with a friend. (I discuss these options later in this chapter.)

✔ Make sure you have a good pair of running shoes — not the dusty pair of 10-year-old Converse sneakers sitting in the back of your closet. I tell you about choosing the equipment you need in Chapter 2.

✔ Tell your friends and family you're going to run a marathon. Your commitment to accomplish something is greater when you announce it to others who are important to you.

✔ Mark the marathon date on your calendar so it becomes something real rather than just an idea.

✔ Find a good training plan that progresses slowly and systematically. (I give them to you right here in this book, of course, and they're tailored to your running experience. Flip to Chapters 8, 9, and 10 to take a peek.)

✔ Learn proper running form. I teach you all about that in Chapter 4.

✔ Surround yourself with people who support your goals and with other runners. The energy and motivation that come from other runners is contagious.

✔ Evaluate your current fitness. Knowing where you are helps get you where you want to go. If you can run 13 miles, you're halfway to the marathon already. If you huff and puff after running three steps, you may want to spend a couple of months running and improving your fitness before training for a marathon.

✔ Check with your doctor. This sounds like one of those disclaimers you read in fitness magazines and other books on the subject, but getting checked out by your doctor is a good idea, especially if you have any existing medical issues or are over 40.

✔ Cut back on the alcohol. Alcohol dehydrates you, and with all the sweating you'll do, you need to hydrate as much as possible.

✔ Start eating better. Marathon training requires certain nutrients, like complex carbohydrates and protein, to recover after those long runs. So clean out your fridge and replace the processed food with fruits and vegetables, just like your mother told you. (You can keep the chocolate; the sugar in chocolate is good energy for your muscles.)

✔ Figure out safe places to run in all weather. If you're unfamiliar with your neighborhood, now's a good time to make sure that where you're planning to run is safe — from animals *and* humans.

✔ Start believing that you can run a marathon. Success always begins with a belief, no matter how small. So believe in yourself and your abilities and keep repeating to yourself, "I can do this."

Running through Basic Marathon Training Strategies

When it comes to running a marathon, there's more than one way to train. However, there are ways to train and then there are smart ways to train. Training must be systematic and progressive.

✔ *Systematic* means that the training isn't arbitrary, with a smattering of workouts here and there; that it doesn't include abrupt changes in mileage or intensity; and that each cycle of training builds on what came before so that the entire program is seamless.

✔ *Progressive* means that the training stress increases over time — the weekly mileage gets higher, the long runs get longer, and the workouts get faster. I've seen many runners run the same five-mile route day after day. Humans, and especially runners, are creatures of habit. They do the same thing over and over, and though they may not always expect a different result, they certainly hope for one. To improve your fitness and performance, your training must be progressive.

To train smart, you need to optimize your training and train at more effective levels of effort to get the best results. Smart training sets you up for success. Although you can achieve running success through many different paths, you can also train incorrectly.

For example, one of the biggest mistakes runners make is thinking that to run faster in races, they need to run faster in workouts. So they run their workouts faster than their current fitness level dictates. I once coached a college runner who ran around 19 minutes for a cross-country 5K and told me she wanted to be trained like a 17:30 5K runner. So I told her to run a 17:30 5K and then I'd train her like a 17:30 5K runner.

Races, which tell you your current level of fitness, dictate your training pace, not the other way around. As a marathon runner, you don't do workouts to practice running faster. You do workouts to improve the physiological characteristics that enable you to run farther and hold a faster pace for longer (see Chapter 3 for details). Think of an assembly line: If you want to make more products, increasing the number of workers (physiological characteristics) so you have more assembly lines to do the work is a better strategy than increasing the speed at which the assembly line workers work. The goal of training is to obtain the greatest benefit while incurring the least amount of stress, so you should run as slow as you can to obtain the workout's desired goal. Running faster than you need to only increases fatigue without any extra benefit.

Because the marathon is *aerobic* — that is, the activity requires that your muscles use oxygen — your training should focus on your body's ability to use more oxygen. For most people, the key is the weekly mileage and long runs. Unless you're an advanced runner with years of running behind you, your marathon training program shouldn't include a lot of *interval training* — periods of faster running interspersed with short recovery intervals. Initially, your main focus is to become as aerobically developed as possible to improve your endurance. I talk about how to do that in Chapter 5.

As an experienced runner who wants to get better, your training matures, growing from a basic outline of mileage and long runs to more mileage, tempo runs that train you to hold a faster aerobic pace, and interval training to boost your speed (see Chapter 7 for more about interval training). You progress from higher volume and lower intensity to lower volume and higher intensity, although you must always pay attention to the volume of training given the importance of mileage for the marathon. If this sounds complicated, you're right, it is. Even if you've run a marathon before, it can be daunting. I tell you how to mix training components together in a training plan in Chapters 8, 9, and 10 (for beginners, intermediate runners, and advanced runners, respectively).

No plan is ingrained in stone. You must always leave room for adjustment based on things like how much time you have to train, how much recovery you need, how fatigued you are, and so on. For women, the ever-changing hormonal environment and menstrual cycle issues also come into play, so a woman's program should always be open to change.

Training is complicated, sure, but some basic concepts underlie a solid marathon training program. Here are a few basic, but very important, points of training:

- ✔ **Balance training with recovery.** All the adaptations you make that enable you to run farther and faster occur when you're not running, so take recovery as seriously as you take your training. I talk more about recovery in Chapter 12.

- ✔ **Mix up your paces.** If you run slow all the time, you'll just become a slow runner. Train using the whole continuum of paces, from very slow to very fast, to enhance both your endurance and your speed. I talk more about improving your speed in Chapter 7.

- ✔ **Respect the distance.** Twenty-six miles is a long way to run. Respect the distance by preparing adequately for it. Don't take a nonchalant approach to the marathon. Confidence comes from being prepared, so prepare yourself.

- ✔ **Run a lot.** There's no way around the fact that running a marathon requires a lot of preparation. Although you don't have to run more than 100 miles per week like the best marathon runners in the world, you still have to run a lot. Training is the key to running the marathon successfully. You must run at least a few times during the week in addition to your long run on the weekend.

- ✔ **Run long.** You need to do many long runs to prepare for the marathon. Your longest run should fall somewhere between 20 and 24 miles, or three to three and a half hours, whichever comes first. If you're an advanced runner, you may run longer than 24 miles before the marathon. I talk about long runs in Chapter 6.

As you train for your marathon, take a few risks, and gain strength and momentum from your running to help you see those risks through. Remember that though there may be a chance of failing, people take risks because the chance of failing makes success taste even sweeter.

Considering the Challenges of Marathon Preparation

Running a marathon takes a long time, even for those who do it extremely well. Because you'll be running for so long, you run into some challenges that don't play a major role in shorter races.

Coping with increased body temperature

The air temperature can dramatically change the way your body copes with all that running. When you run for a long period, your body temperature rises because your muscles produce heat when they contract. So when it's hot outside, your body temperature rises even more, sometimes to dangerous levels.

You naturally slow down when you experience increased body temperature, called *hyperthermia.* Blood flow to your active muscles decreases as more blood goes to your skin to help your body cool itself. Given a choice between maintaining a nine-minute-mile pace in the marathon and trying to lower your body temperature so you don't die of heat exhaustion, your body chooses the latter (and thank goodness for that).

The increase in body temperature also affects your cardiovascular system. Your heart rate drifts upward in an attempt to maintain *cardiac output* (the volume of blood your heart pumps each minute) and blood pressure. The increase in heart rate when your running pace hasn't increased is called *cardiac drift.*

As you might imagine, the combination of hyperthermia and cardiac drift is very stressful to your body. If the marathon is on a hot day, you need to train your body to handle that stress. A good way to do that is to run in hot weather. Integrate running in the heat slowly by going for some of your shorter runs (anything shorter than 10 miles) in the heat before attempting your longer runs. However, avoid running any distance in extremely high temperatures (more than 95 degrees) unless you're an experienced hot weather runner.

Maintaining your pace while your muscles lose fuel

A significant aim of your training is to teach your muscles to do a better job of using fuel so you can maintain your pace. Your muscles store carbohydrates that they use for fuel when you run. That stored fuel is called *glycogen,* which is a branched chain of glucose (sugar) molecules. You have enough stored glycogen in your muscles to last slightly more than two hours of sustained running at a moderate pace. So unless you run a marathon as fast as the best runners in the world, you're going to run out of fuel. When your muscles have no glycogen left, that's called *glycogen depletion,* and that's no fun. Glycogen depletion and the accompanying low blood sugar coincide with hitting the infamous marathon wall — your legs feel heavy, you feel lethargic, and you want to stop running. So you want to delay glycogen depletion for as long as possible.

Running for long periods increases how much fuel your muscles store and also forces your muscles to rely more effectively on fat for fuel, which delays your muscles' use of carbohydrates. In Chapter 3, I tell you more about the elegant physiological adaptations that your body makes in its use of fuel when you run long — adaptations that help you maintain your pace in the marathon. In Chapter 6, I tell you more about fueling your long runs.

Avoiding dehydration

Water is the largest component of your body. It's vital for many chemical reactions that occur inside your cells, including the production of energy for muscle contraction. So when you lose water, you experience some harsh consequences. When you sweat a lot, you become dehydrated, which causes a decrease in blood volume, decreasing the amount of blood your heart pumps with each beat. Oxygen flow to your muscles is then compromised, and your pace slows. Dehydration also causes an increase in body temperature while you run. Running performance declines with only a 2 to 3 percent loss of body weight due to fluid loss.

 Consuming fluids when you run can help delay dehydration. Because most runners lose water through sweating faster than what they can replace by drinking while they run, nearly every runner is dehydrated at the end of a marathon. Your goal is to delay dehydration for as long as possible. During your marathon, drink at every aid station.

 You need to stay hydrated during training, too, because your level of hydration affects your workouts. Drink fluids that contain sodium, which stimulates your kidneys to retain water (see Chapter 6 for details). When you're not running, you can tell whether you're hydrated by the color of your urine (don't try to determine this while you're running). The lighter your urine, the more hydrated you are. Your urine should look like lemonade rather than apple juice.

Joining a Marathon Training Group

Most runners like to train with others. After all, humans are social animals. Group training can help you become a better runner because pushing yourself is easier when someone is running right next to you. Group training also offers camaraderie, accountability, encouragement, motivation, and a network for information about all things running.

Before searching for a group to run with, decide which type of group you want to join. Many options are available, from small, informal groups that meet in front of a running shoe store and include runners of all levels to large, competitive, fee-based clubs that meet at a track for coach-led formal workouts and long runs, fully staffed with volunteers and aid stations.

With the marathon's growing popularity, many national and local marathon training groups exist to help you accomplish your marathon goal. Many large marathons, like the New York City Marathon and the Chicago Marathon, partner with national or local charity organizations that offer training programs and group training. Check the marathon's website for a list of participating charities.

 The following national, coach-led groups have local chapters in nearly every major U.S. city. Check online for the chapter in your area:

- ✔ **Joints in Motion** (www.arthritis.org/joints-in-motion.php): A charity-based, 18- to 20-week program that raises money for the Arthritis Foundation.

- ✔ **Team Challenge** (www.ccteamchallenge.org): A charity-based, 16-week program that focuses on half-marathons and raises money for the Crohn's & Colitis Foundation.

- ✔ **Team In Training** (www.teamintraining.org): A charity-based, 16-week program that raises money for the Leukemia & Lymphoma Society.

- ✔ **USA Fit** (www.usafit.com): A fee-based, 24- to 28-week program.

Most formal marathon training groups offer the following:

- ✔ **Aid stations:** During long runs, volunteers typically hand out water, sports drinks, and carbohydrate gels so you stay hydrated and fueled.

- ✔ **Educational clinics:** Want to know which shoes to get or what to eat to fuel your muscles? How about some mental tricks for the marathon? Many groups offer clinics, usually held before or after the long run.

- ✔ **Mapped-out long runs:** Don't worry about getting lost on long runs. Groups provide you with a map and directions.

✔ **Pace groups:** Smaller groups based on your current abilities or goal marathon pace enable you to stick with other runners who run the same pace as you.

✔ **Snacks:** Many groups offer post–long run snacks to replenish all the carbohydrate you used during the run.

✔ **Training program:** Whether online or on paper, a plan that outlines your marathon preparation is standard issue for training groups.

✔ **T-shirt:** Oh, the coveted T-shirt! Runners collect running T-shirts like bees collect honey. And long gone are the days of cotton — you get to enjoy lightweight *technical T-shirts,* which are made of fancy fabric that wicks moisture away from your skin.

Do an online search or check with your local running shoe stores to find out about marathon training groups in your area.

Working with a Coach

If you've never run a marathon before and haven't been running for long, consider working with a coach. Although most running groups have coaches, you won't get the hands-on attention that you get with a personal coach. A knowledgeable coach is the greatest asset you can have as a runner. A coach designs a training program for you, monitors what you're doing, and motivates and inspires you to do things that you never thought possible. You see much better results with a coach than you do training on your own.

Having an outside pair of eyes is important. Wanting to challenge yourself is fantastic — it's one of the great opportunities of the marathon — but when you try to coach yourself, you're too close to your situation to see what's really going on. I've coached many runners who want to run even when they're sick because they don't want to lose fitness and feel guilty by missing a run. You need a coach who can see the whole picture and tell you when to push and when to back off and recover.

Check online to find a coach in your area. Some coaches write a training program for you that you can follow on your own, some coach you by e-mail, and some meet you for workouts. The choice comes down to how much hands-on guidance you want. Coaches range in price from $50 to $300 per month.

Just as when choosing other professionals for a service, make sure the coach has the proper credentials before hiring him. Most running coaches don't have any credentials other than being runners themselves. Here are some factors to help you narrow down your choice of a coach:

- ✓ **Does the coach have an exercise science or related degree or a coaching certification?** You'd be surprised how many coaches don't have education in the field.

- ✓ **Is coaching the person's profession or does he do it as a hobby?** Although many coaches aren't full-time coaches, you want to work with someone who's at least serious about coaching and doesn't just do it as a hobby. Keep in mind that you're spending money on this person, just like you would for any other professional.

- ✓ **Do you feel comfortable with this person?** The final decision of whom you choose to coach you often comes down to how well you get along with him. If you don't feel comfortable talking to your coach, you're less likely to communicate with him, which hurts you in the long run. The more feedback you give your coach, the more he can help you. So you need to feel comfortable providing that feedback. Feel free to interview coaches before choosing one.

Don't underestimate the value of a good coach. A coach can be a trainer, motivator, teacher, and source of inspiration. He can guide you to achieve a level of success that's hard to obtain on your own.

Going It Alone (With the Help of This Book)

Much has been written about the loneliness of the long-distance runner. Through my hours alone on roads and trails, I've discovered how to become my own psychologist — how to "work in" rather than "work out." Running gives you a chance to work through your personal issues and to search for answers. It may sound hokey, but the time spent running alone is a great chance to think, to problem-solve, to wonder what can be.

You don't have to train as part of a group or with a coach to run a marathon. Many people like running alone. Running alone for most of my adult life, I know firsthand its many advantages:

- ✓ **You can save time.** When I've been part of a school team or run with a group as an adult, I'm always amazed at how much time a run takes compared to running alone. Between driving to the group's location, the time waiting for everyone to gather, announcements, socializing, stretching, the post-run socializing, and driving back home, a five-mile run that would take 40 or 45 minutes from your front door turns into almost two hours!

✔ **You determine your own schedule of when to run.** Want to run when you first get out of bed? How about after work? Or, perhaps, if you're like me and are lucky enough to work for yourself, whenever you want? Running alone gives you the flexibility of running at any time of the day. If the weather forecast calls for rain beginning in the evening (when most training groups meet during the week), you can change your schedule and run in the morning.

✔ **You can tune out the world.** When you run alone, you don't feel obligated to hold a conversation with someone else. You can listen to music, catch up on audiobooks, or listen to your favorite podcast.

✔ **You can run wherever and however fast you want.** Want to run at the beach or a nearby park? Okay! Want to change your route at the last minute? No problem! Feeling frisky and want to pick up the pace? Go for it! When you run alone, the possibilities are endless.

✔ **You can be alone.** Don't underestimate solitude. Running may give you the only chance you have all day to be alone with your thoughts and emotions. It can be an opportunity for meditation and for great exploration of who you are and what you want to become.

Training by yourself isn't all rosy, however. It also has major downsides, such as

✔ **The feel of being alone:** Training for a marathon is a big deal that requires a big commitment. Unless you don't mind running by yourself every day, you may feel lonely in the process.

✔ **The lack of accountability:** Left to their own devices, many people won't get out the door and run on a regular basis. The temptation not to run when you perceive other things getting in the way is always there. If you're one of those people who needs to be held accountable, training alone is not for you.

✔ **The lack of camaraderie:** When training alone, you're, well, alone. You have no one to talk to about how your training's going, brag to about your kid acing his history test, or complain to about your in-laws visiting for the weekend.

✔ **The lack of external motivation:** Training by yourself means the motivation to run has to come from within. You won't have a cheering squad on the side of the road, waiting for you to run by during your 20-miler, or even anyone to say, "Good job! You're looking great!"

If you choose to train for the marathon alone, I don't suggest you try to climb this mountain completely on your own. Everyone needs help to accomplish great things. That's why I've written this book. You have all the information you need right here between the two yellow-and-black covers, so use the information to guide you. May your marathon journey bring you memorable runs and the chance to become the runner and the person you want to be.

Chapter 2

Getting a Leg Up with the Right Running Gear

- -

In This Chapter

▶ Determining your arches and pronation

▶ Understanding different types of running shoes

▶ Putting orthotics to use

▶ Buying running shoes

▶ Selecting other running gear

- -

*Y*ou take approximately 26,000 steps with each foot to run a marathon (26.2 miles), so you want every one of them to be as comfortable as possible. With all the different types of running shoes on the market and all their bells and whistles, how do you know what you need or whether you need shoes at all?

This chapter is your guide to choosing the running shoe that's right for you. It also includes information on other running apparel — including socks and running bras — and advice on how to dress for different types of weather.

Evaluating Your Feet

Your feet aren't necessarily like your sister's or your best friend's or marathon superstar Ryan Hall's. That doesn't mean you can't run the heck out of a marathon, but it does mean you need to evaluate your feet so that you can match them with the shoes that will most comfortably take you the distance. Which shoes do the trick depends on the shape of your foot and how you use it.

How high is your arch?

Before buying shoes, you need to know what type of feet you have. The easiest way to determine this is to make a footprint. Stand with wet feet on a surface that leaves a footprint, like a brown paper bag or colored paper. Check the shape of your feet to see whether you have a normal arch, a high arch, or a low arch (see Figure 2-1). Also check the width of your feet to see whether they're narrow or wide, which you can later match up with sizing for different widths of shoes.

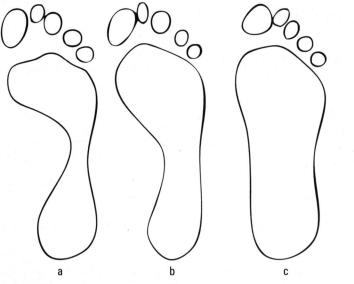

a   b   c

Illustration by Wiley, Composition Services Graphics

Figure 2-1: Check your footprint to figure out whether your arch is high (a), normal (b), or low (c).

Though your arch's height influences how much arch support you need in a shoe, the main effect of your arch is its influence on how much your foot *pronates,* or rolls inward, when your foot lands on the ground. Pronation is the main factor that dictates what type of shoe you need. I talk more about pronation and the selection of shoes in the following sections.

How much do you pronate?

Your foot type influences how much or how little you pronate. If you're like most runners, when your foot lands, the outside part of your heel contacts the ground first. Your foot then rolls inward until it's in contact with the ground to optimally distribute the forces of impact. With your whole foot on the ground through the stance phase, you use the entire ball of your foot to push off.

If you're an *overpronator,* your foot rolls inward more than is ideal because your foot and ankle can't adequately stabilize your leg. Because your ankle collapses inward, more of your weight is on the inside part of your foot, and you push off the ground using your big toe and second toe rather than distributing the force evenly across the ball of your foot. (Overpronation is a major cause of running-related injuries. For more information on injuries, stride on over to Chapter 13.)

If you're an *underpronator,* your foot doesn't roll inward enough after the outside of the heel lands. Consequently, the outside of your foot takes the brunt of the impact. Because your foot remains on its outside edge, you push off the ground using the smaller toes on the outside of your foot rather than distributing the force evenly across the ball of your foot.

If you have a normal arch, chances are you pronate normally. If you have flat feet, you probably overpronate. If you have high arches that look like the McDonald's sign, you probably under-pronate. You can check out normal pronation, overpronation, and underpronation in Figure 2-2.

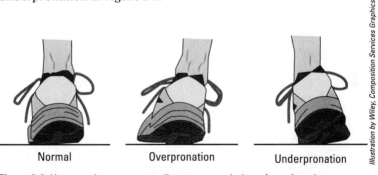

| Normal | Overpronation | Underpronation |

Illustration by Wiley, Composition Services Graphics

Figure 2-2: How much you pronate dictates your choice of running shoes.

If you already have running shoes that you've been running in, look at their soles to see the wear pattern. What part of the shoes has the most wear? If you land on the outside of your heel like most runners, that part of the shoe will show the most wear. If your foot overpronates, the back of the shoe will be caved in when you view the shoes from behind.

I talk about how pronation relates to your choice of running shoes in the next section.

Comparing Different Types of Running Shoes

Two of the most common questions I'm asked are, "What's the best running shoe?" and "What shoes should I get?" Well, there's no best running shoe. (Thought you were going to find out some secret, huh? Sorry.) The best pair of shoes for you comes down to what feels comfortable, how much support you need, and how much your foot pronates (see the preceding section for an explanation of pronation).

When you walk into a running shoe store, the array of shoes can be dizzying. Despite the large selection, there really aren't as many shoes as it seems. Fewer types of shoes exist than do types of toothpaste. (You should have more trouble choosing toothpaste.) And depending on the way you run and the surface you run on, you can discount at least two-thirds of the options right out of the gate.

Running shoes have specific combinations of support and stability designed for different running gaits. Shoes are divided into three major categories — cushioning/neutral, stability, and motion control. Other shoes are designed for specific running conditions, such as trail running and racing. When you know which category you need, you can start looking for the shoes that feel comfortable right out of the box.

Cushioning/neutral shoes

Cushioning shoes (sometimes called *neutral shoes*) allow you to pronate naturally to absorb shock upon landing. They're best suited for runners with normal to high arches. They have minimal *medial* (arch-side) support, which you can see by the shoes' curved *last* — the mold around which a shoe is constructed. Cushioning shoes are distinguishable by the rubber on the medial side; it's compressible and is usually white. If you have a normal arch and don't overpronate or underpronate (not common, but it happens), get cushioning/neutral shoes.

Stability shoes

Stability shoes allow only limited pronation while retaining some cushioning characteristics. They're best suited for runners who have normal to low arches and mild to moderate pronation. You can tell a stability shoe by its added material on the medial side, which is firmer to the touch. If you have a normal or low arch and overpronate slightly, get stability shoes.

Motion-control shoes

Motion-control shoes do exactly what their name implies — they control your foot's motion. They're best suited for runners with flat feet and severe overpronation. They have a straighter last than cushioning and stability shoes and contain a harder material on the medial side that's usually of a darker color than the rest of the rubber cushioning. If you have a very low arch (flat feet) and your foot rolls inward so much that it looks like it's about to fall sideways off a cliff, get motion-control shoes.

Trail shoes

Trail shoes are specifically designed for running on trails. They have more support than road-running shoes and greater traction on the sole, and they're a darker color given how dirty they get when you run on trails. Almost all trail shoes fall in the stability shoe category.

Because most marathons are on the road, stay away from trail shoes for most of your runs, especially the long runs, unless you're planning to run a trail marathon. However, if you plan to run some of your weekly runs on trails, get trail shoes as a secondary pair.

Racing flats

Racing flats are very lightweight cushioning shoes made for racing on the road. Although the best marathoners in the world wear racing flats for running a marathon, I wouldn't recommend wearing them for a race that long unless you're light on your feet, you have an efficient running style with normal pronation, and you've trained substantially in them. Because racing flats have little support, wearing them for a long race like the marathon can really beat up your legs.

Minimalist shoes and barefoot running

I wouldn't normally talk about *minimalist shoes* — shoes that contain very little cushioning — and barefoot running in a book about the marathon, but this issue has attracted so much press lately that I think it's a good idea to address it before somebody influences you to go run down the street barefoot.

In response to the observation that many of the world's best runners grow up in poor countries running barefoot and the growing popularity of the argument that shoes themselves cause injuries to runners because they force you to land on your heel, shoe companies have started developing minimalist shoes. Some people argue that minimalist shoes decrease the risk of injury by altering your foot-strike pattern and reducing your contact time with the ground. Regular cushioning shoes have a lot of padding in the heel, which promotes a heel-strike pattern of running. This is different from how you run when barefoot like your ancient ancestors. With minimalist shoes, you land more toward your forefoot than on your heel and spend less time on the ground. Although minimalist shoes do change how you run, whether they actually reduce injuries in runners is still up for debate.

Minimalist shoes can be beneficial because they force your feet to do more work, which can strengthen your feet and ankles. However, training for a marathon requires a lot of running, so unless you're an efficient runner to begin with, training in minimalist shoes may not be a good idea. If you're a beginning runner, stick with running shoes. If you want to give minimalist shoes a try, use them to strengthen your feet by running only a few minutes in them a few times per week.

Considering Orthotics

Have you ever cringed at a runner who looks like she's going to get injured if she keeps running like that? Some runners have such aberrant biomechanics that shoes alone don't do a good enough job to prevent improper mechanics that can lead to injuries. If that sounds like you, you may need *orthotics* — custom-made shoe inserts that conform to the shape of your foot and realign it into its correct position to alleviate pain and prevent injury. Orthotics adjust the angle at which your foot strikes the ground.

If you have a history of running injuries, you may be a candidate for orthotics, but they should be a last resort — something to use only after you've tried to correct the issue with proper shoes, efficient running mechanics, and smart training. Over-the-counter insoles, like Dr. Scholl's or Superfeet, which are sold at many sporting goods and running shoe stores, may provide enough support. Alternating between different pairs of shoes may also alleviate the stress that's causing problems. When in doubt, see a podiatrist or a sports-medicine physician to determine whether you need orthotics.

Shopping for Running Shoes

As you've probably heard, running is the only sport that you can do with just a pair of shoes. No racquets, no shin guards, no swimming pool — all you need is good shoes and motivation. Buying that one piece of equipment is important, and it's fun, too. It's an investment in your future and a vote of confidence that you'll stick with running and meet your goals.

In the following sections, I list common places to shop for shoes, and I provide some handy guidelines for making your purchase.

Surveying some shopping spots

Where should you shop for running shoes? A few options exist:

- **Running shoe stores:** If you're a beginning runner and have no idea which shoes to get (although you'll know more after reading this chapter), go to a store that specializes in running shoes and apparel. These stores usually have trained staff to help you find the right shoes. Many stores have treadmills that you run on so the staff can evaluate your running mechanics and tell you the type of shoes you need.

- **Sporting goods stores:** If you already know which type of shoes you need, you can save money by buying your shoes at a general sporting goods store instead of a specialty running shoe store. Sporting goods stores may not have as extensive a selection as specialty running shoe stores, but the shoes are significantly cheaper.

- **The Internet:** Nowadays, you can order shoes online at shoe companies' websites or on general retail websites like Amazon.com.

    Because you never want to buy a pair of running shoes without first trying them on and running in them, I suggest buying shoes online only if you get the same pair of shoes you currently have.

Making the big buy

Keep these tips in mind when shopping for shoes:

- Don't be influenced by the price. More expensive doesn't necessarily mean better. A higher price can mean that the shoe has more technology or it can simply mean that it's a flashy new model with a high markup cost. Most runners don't require all the bells and whistles found in fancy styles.

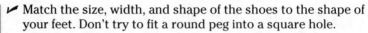

✔ Match the size, width, and shape of the shoes to the shape of your feet. Don't try to fit a round peg into a square hole.

✔ Make sure the shoes don't cause pressure points or squeeze your toes. Wiggle your toes in the shoes to make sure you can move them around. You don't want shoes that compress your toes and don't allow for freedom of movement. Pressure can lead to blisters, and as I can tell you from some painful experiences, you don't want to get blisters while you're running.

✔ Buy shoes later in the day, when your feet are slightly swollen. Your feet also swell slightly when you run for a long time, so buying shoes later in the day (and even after you've run) more closely mimics the condition of your feet while you run.

✔ Try on both shoes. Believe it or not, not all right and left feet are created the same. Your feet may be slightly different sizes, and one foot may pronate more than the other.

✔ Wear the same type of socks that you run in. The more similar you can create your running conditions, the better fit you'll get in the shoes.

✔ Run in the shoes while you're still in the store. Shoes often feel very different when walking around the store for a few steps versus actually running in them. You may feel things when you run that you don't feel when you walk. Many stores even have a policy that allows you to run in the shoes after you buy them and return them if they don't feel right. If the store has that policy, take advantage of it (just don't run in the mud before bringing them back).

✔ Make sure you have a finger-width distance between your toes and the end of the shoe. Keep in mind that your feet swell slightly when you run. Your toes should never touch the top of the shoes.

✔ Buy shoes that are breathable. Sweaty feet don't just make your shoes smell — they can also give you hot feet, which can cause blisters and is uncomfortable.

✔ Wear the shoes only to run. No matter how proud you are of your new sneaks and your commitment to train for a marathon, don't wear them out on the town or to a cocktail party. Your shoes will last longer (and you won't embarrass yourself or your mother) if you reserve them only for their intended purpose.

✔ Buy a couple of pairs of shoes and alternate wearing them. Doing so lengthens the life of your shoes, and your feet don't get accustomed to just one pair. When you buy new shoes, keep your old ones and wear them on rainy days.

✔ Change your shoes after 300 to 500 miles because they lose their shock-absorbing abilities.

Choosing Other Running Apparel

Although shoes are the most important piece of clothing you need as a marathon runner, you can't just run down the street in shoes and nothing else. (Well, you can, but you'd get a lot of stares and a possible citation for indecent exposure.) Especially when running on hot or cold days, you need to wear specific clothes that keep you comfortable.

 Shoe retailers won't like me saying this, but if you want to save money, don't buy your clothes in specialty running shoe stores, because they're more expensive. Go to general sporting goods stores instead; they usually have just as large a selection as specialty running shoe stores without the hefty price tags.

Hot weather gear

Running in the heat can be a challenge if you're not prepared for it. The most important consideration is to choose clothes that allow heat to dissipate. Dress in light-colored clothes made from lightweight fabrics like polyester or Coolmax, which wick moisture away from your skin. Here are some guidelines:

- ✔ **Shorts:** A few types of running shorts exist, including *compression shorts,* which are like bicycle shorts without the padding; *V-notch shorts,* which have a continuous outside seam notched in a V-shape at the bottom; and *split shorts* and *half-split shorts,* which don't have a continuous seam but instead have a slit on the side, making the front panel overlap the back panel. Split shorts give you the most movement flexibility when you run. Many shorts also include a liner for support. Whichever shorts you decide on, make sure they're made from a lightweight, flexible material that wicks away moisture.

- ✔ **Socks:** Stay away from cotton socks; they hold sweat and make your feet hot. And no tube socks (you'll just look silly). When cotton gets wet, it stays wet, and that's not fun when you're running for two or three hours. Go for thin Coolmax socks that wick away moisture and fit your feet like a glove. You don't want socks bunching up between your toes while running 26.2 miles. Can you say blisters?

- ✔ **Sports bras:** Look for a bra that provides support, stability, and comfort. Choose fabrics like spandex, which provides stretch where needed, and breathable materials like Coolmax and Supplex that wick away moisture and keep you dry. If you have small- to medium-sized breasts, get a compression sports bra, which holds your breasts close to your chest, restricting their movement when you run. If you have large breasts, select an encapsulation sports bra that limits the motion of your breasts by closely surrounding and separating each breast. Try on several sizes to find the one most suited to your body. Specialty stores now offer bra fittings for women with special needs.

A bra with wide straps and a wide bottom band won't dig into your skin, provides the best support, and minimizes bounce as you run. A racerback- or T-back-style bra provides maximum freedom of movement. Avoid bras with inside seams that can make you chafe.

- **T-shirts:** Throw away the 1980s cotton T-shirt and go for a moisture-wicking shirt instead — such as a Nike Dri-Fit T-shirt — which wicks away moisture from your skin and keeps you cool. When it's really hot, wear a light-colored shirt that reflects the sun.

Cold weather gear

Running in the cold can be very invigorating if you dress for it. The most important thing is to dress in layers so that you trap in body heat when you most need it and you can peel clothes off as you warm up.

- **Gloves:** Your hands can get cold easily, so keep them warm with form-fitting gloves. On really cold days (below 20 degrees), opt for mittens, which keep your hands even warmer.

- **Hat:** You lose a lot of heat through your head, so wear a ski hat to cover your head and ears on cold days.

- **Long-sleeved T-shirts:** Unless it's really cold, a long-sleeved T-shirt may be the only upper body garment you need. Wear polyester or a polyester-Lycra blend.

- **Running jacket:** When it's very cold or raining, you may need something more than a windbreaker. Polyester or Gore-Tex running jackets are typically thicker and have an inner lining.

- **Socks:** To keep your feet warm in the winter, wear thicker polyester or Coolmax socks than in the summer. Never wear cotton, especially if it's raining.

- **Tights or running pants:** When the temperature drops below 45 or 50 degrees, it can be too cold for shorts (although I've known some runners who wear shorts until it's below freezing!). Tights made from Lycra or running pants made from a polyester-Lycra blend allow you to move naturally while keeping your legs warm.

- **Windbreaker:** When it's cold and windy, you need something that blocks the wind and traps in body heat. Look for a windbreaker with a hood and zippered sleeves that you can remove to create a vest.

Extra gear that isn't necessary (but is nice to have)

You don't need anything fancy to start training, but you can find a lot of nice extras if you want them. If you have money and interest, there's almost no end to the types of gear for runners that can enhance your experience, including the following:

- **Fuel belt:** If you need to fuel on long runs and you don't have any easily accessible pockets or don't want to hold your carbohydrate gels, fuel belts are a hands-free way of storing small packets of carbs and flasks of fluid.

- **GPS watch:** If a stopwatch and heart rate monitor aren't enough for you, a GPS watch has it all and then some — stopwatch, timer, heart rate monitor, instantaneous and average pace per mile, and distance covered. Some models come with a computer connection that allows you to upload the data from your workouts onto your computer, where you can generate graphs of all the numbers.

- **Heart rate monitor:** Checking your heart rate is a great way to determine whether you're running at the right intensity. Heart rate monitors come in a variety of styles. Some give you only your average heart rate for the whole run; some give you the high, the low, and the average; and others allow you to set a target heart rate range and beep when you go below or above that range. This latter option is great for beginners who need extra guidance on how fast to run.

- **MP3 player:** If you can't stand the thought of running for three hours alone or while listening to your running partner drone on about his kids, you can run with an MP3 player and listen to just about anything you want — music, a podcast, a favorite movie or radio program, or an audio book.

- **Running hat or visor:** To keep the sun off your face and head, wear a light-colored running hat or visor made from Coolmax or polyester.

- **Running watch:** If you want to run a specific distance in a specific time or just know the elapsed time of a run, get a watch with a stopwatch and a rubber or Velcro band that stands up to sweat.

- **Sunglasses:** To protect your eyes from the sun, wear lightweight sunglasses with UV protection. Choose glasses that don't bounce or put pressure on your nose.

Chapter 3

Understanding the Physiology of Marathon Running

*R*unning is pretty simple: You put one foot in front of the other. After you put one foot in front of the other for 26.2 miles, you've run a marathon.

Running is also extremely complex. It includes a beautiful integration of cardiovascular, muscular, and metabolic systems operating together to influence the transportation of oxygen, the extraction and use of that oxygen, and the use of the muscle fuels of fats and carbohydrates.

If you run with a group of other runners, you may notice that some of them run like the wind. They look like they were born to run. Well, they were. Many runners run fast because they have genes that enable them to do so. You can't change your genes, so all you can ask of yourself is to run the best *you* can with what *you* have.

When you understand why you should train for your marathon a certain way, you become invested in the process. You can run a better marathon because you understand *why* a specific strategy leads to a specific result. That's a higher level of understanding than simply knowing *how*. This chapter delves into the science of marathon running, explaining the physiological factors that influence your marathon performance and set the stage for smarter training.

Getting to the Heart of Running

Your heart is your most extraordinary muscle. It has the unique ability and responsibility of delivering the most important chemical — oxygen — throughout your body to sustain life. Oxygen also sustains your marathon pace, keeping your legs moving for 26.2 miles.

The following sections explain how your heart cycles blood through your body and describe some heart-related measurements that are important for runners — namely, heart rate, stroke volume, cardiac output, and aerobic power.

Discovering how your heart pushes blood through your body

Located just beneath your ribs under your left breast, your heart is composed of four chambers: the left and right atria and the left and right ventricles. The left ventricle is the largest and most important chamber because it's responsible for sending blood to your entire body except your lungs. Blood moves through a circuit, like this (see Figure 3-1):

1. **The left ventricle pumps oxygen-rich blood through the aorta, your body's largest artery.**

2. **Blood then travels through the arteries, the small arterioles, and finally the very small capillaries that surround your muscle fibers.**

3. **Your muscles extract however much oxygen they need, and the blood, which is now low in oxygen and high in carbon dioxide from the chemical reactions of your muscles' metabolism, travels back to the heart, first through the capillaries, then the small venules, then the big veins, and finally through the vena cava, your body's largest vein.**

4. **From the vena cava, the blood enters the right atrium.**

5. **As the right atrium fills with blood, it contracts, pumping the blood through the tricuspid valve and into the right ventricle.**

6. **When the right ventricle contracts, the blood is pumped through the pulmonary artery and into the lungs, where it discards the carbon dioxide and picks up the oxygen that you inhale from the air.**

7. **The oxygenated blood then travels through the pulmonary vein and enters the left atrium.**

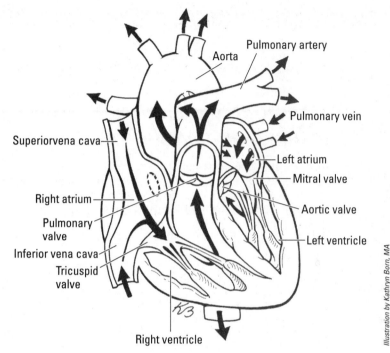

Figure 3-1: The circuit of blood through your body.

Illustration by Kathryn Born, MA

> **8. As the left atrium fills with blood, it contracts, sending the blood through the bicuspid (mitral) valve and into the left ventricle. Then the cycle starts all over again.**

After the blood leaves your heart, its flow to your muscles depends on a number of factors:

- ✓ **Redistribution of blood away from other, less important organs to the active muscles:** When you're running, you want as much blood as possible going to your muscles so your muscles can get more oxygen.

- ✓ **Resistance of blood flow through your blood vessels:** The more dilated your blood vessels are, the less resistance there is, making it easier for blood to flow through.

- ✓ **Ability to transport oxygen in your blood:** *Hemoglobin* is a protein inside your red blood cells that carries oxygen. The more red blood cells and hemoglobin you have, the more oxygen your blood can carry.

- ✓ **Ability to transport oxygen in your muscles:** *Myoglobin* is a protein that carries oxygen inside your muscles. After hemo- globin carries oxygen to your muscles, it hands off the oxygen to myoglobin, like a relay baton pass.

✔ **Density and volume of capillaries around your muscle fibers:**
Capillaries are the small blood vessels within your muscles.
The more capillaries surrounding your muscle fibers, the
faster oxygen travels deep within your muscles. (I talk about
capillaries in more detail later in this chapter.)

Zeroing in on heart rate, stroke volume, and cardiac output

As you run, your heart has to work hard to ensure enough oxygen
gets to your muscles. As you find out in the following sections, the
rate at which it beats and the amount of blood it pumps increase
dramatically to ensure the supply of oxygen meets your muscles'
demand.

Heart rate

Your heartbeat — the split-second sequence of contractions of
your heart's four chambers — is responsible for sending blood
and oxygen to your muscles and other organs. Your *heart rate* is
the number of times your heart beats per minute. While sitting
and reading this book, your heart beats about 70 to 80 times per
minute. (Unless you're really excited about what you're reading, in
which case it's higher!)

The fitter you are, the lower your resting heart rate is. When you
run, your heart rate increases a lot, but in a predictable way.
Depending on how fast you run, your heart rate can climb all the
way up to about 200 beats per minute, depending on your age. The
older you are, the lower your maximum heart rate is.

Stroke volume

Heart rate isn't the only variable that dictates the flow of oxygen to
your muscles. Every time your heart contracts, a specific volume
of blood is pumped out of the left ventricle, which is responsible
for sending blood and oxygen everywhere in your body except
your lungs. (The right side of your heart handles the lungs.) The
volume of blood pumped out of the left ventricle with each beat is
called the *stroke volume.*

Your stroke volume is determined by

✔ **The volume of blood returning to your heart through the
veins:** When your heart pumps blood, it travels through the
arteries to get to your muscles. Then the blood travels back to
your heart through the veins. The amount of blood that travels
back to your heart is called the *venous return.* The greater the

venous return is, the greater the stroke volume is, because your heart has more blood it can pump with the next beat.

✔ **The heart's ability to contract quickly and forcefully:** Like other muscles, your heart produces more force and pumps more blood when it contracts strongly, a measurement called *contractility.*

✔ **The amount of pressure in your heart's left ventricle:** When blood enters the left ventricle from the left atrium, it pushes against the left ventricle's walls, creating pressure in that chamber. This pressure is called the *preload.* When a large volume of blood dumps into the left ventricle and pushes against its walls, the walls actively stretch. The left ventricle, like skeletal muscles, contracts more strongly when actively stretched immediately before contracting, ejecting more blood out of the chamber and thus increasing the stroke volume.

✔ **The amount of pressure in your aorta:** When blood is ejected from the left ventricle, the first place it goes is the aorta. Like a narrow hose that shoots out a lot of water, there's a pressure head at the front end of the aorta, creating resistance to blood flow. This pressure is called the *afterload.* The smaller the afterload is, the less resistance there is for blood to flow through the aorta, and the greater the stroke volume is.

✔ **The size of your heart:** Size matters when it comes to your heart. A large heart pumps more blood with each beat because the left ventricle can hold more blood.

Cardiac output

Multiply your heart rate by your stroke volume and you get the volume of blood that your heart's left ventricle pumps per minute, called the *cardiac output.* Cardiac output is extremely important for running a marathon because the more blood your heart pumps each minute, the more oxygen gets to your muscles and the faster pace you can run.

When you're sitting comfortably reading this book, your cardiac output is about 5 liters of blood per minute, give or take, depending on how big a person you are (and therefore how much blood you have). Resting cardiac output is about the same for everyone, regardless of how fit you are. What's different is resting heart rate — unfit people achieve their resting cardiac output by having a high heart rate and a low stroke volume. Fit people achieve their resting cardiac output by having a low heart rate and a high stroke volume. That's why your resting heart rate is lower when you're fit — your stroke volume is greater, so your heart doesn't have to pump as many times each minute to send out the same volume of blood.

The marathoner's lungs

When you first start training for a marathon, you may notice that you have trouble breathing. Many new runners complain that they can't breathe as soon as they start running around the block. Indeed, getting enough air is foremost on their minds. Beginning runners seem to get frustrated with their lungs because they perceive them as limiting their ability to continue running. Even trained runners sometimes feel this way.

At first glance, marathon running seems to have everything to do with big, strong lungs. After all, you get oxygen through your lungs. If the size of your lungs mattered, you'd expect the best marathon runners to have large lungs that hold a lot of oxygen. However, the best marathon runners in the world are comparatively small people, with characteristically small lungs. Total lung capacity, which is the maximal amount of air your lungs can hold, is primarily influenced by body size; bigger people have larger lung capacities. Despite what you may think or feel when you're just beginning to run, your lungs don't limit your ability, especially if you're not an elite runner. Breathing more deeply to try to get more oxygen doesn't make running easier, because oxygen input doesn't limit your ability to run. That limitation rests on the shoulders of your cardiovascular and metabolic systems, with blood flow to and oxygen use by your muscles the major culprits. There's no relationship between lung capacity and how fast you run a marathon.

Unlike your cardiovascular and muscular systems, your lungs don't adapt to training. Therefore, the lungs may limit performance only in elite runners who've developed the more trainable characteristics — cardiac output, hemoglobin concentration, and mitochondrial and capillary volumes — to capacities that approach the genetic potential of the lungs to provide for adequate diffusion of oxygen into the blood. In other words, the lungs *may* limit performance in elite runners by lagging behind other, more readily adaptable characteristics. But this is only a problem when those other characteristics have been trained enough to reach their genetic potential.

The main stimulus to breathe (at sea level) is an increase in your blood's carbon dioxide content, not a need for more oxygen. The reason you breathe more when you run fast is because carbon dioxide is produced in your muscles from metabolism and needs to be expelled through your lungs. Oxygen is all around you and has no problem diffusing from the air into your lungs. Even when you run as fast as you can, the hemoglobin in your blood is nearly 100 percent saturated with oxygen. If you run at a high altitude, however, you do breathe more to get more oxygen into your lungs to compensate for your blood being less saturated with oxygen.

Training your cardiovascular and metabolic characteristics improves your ability to transport and use oxygen, making you feel less out of breath. So the next time you're running up a hill or finishing a hard run and you're thinking, "I can't catch my breath," don't blame your lungs.

Maximum cardiac output, however, which occurs when your heart's working as hard as it can, is very different among people — the fitter you are, the greater your heart's maximum ability to pump blood is. As a point of reference, the maximum cardiac output of a sedentary person is about 20 liters of blood per minute, while that of an elite marathoner is nearly 40 liters per minute! That means the heart of an elite marathoner pumps over 10½ gallons of blood every minute. No wonder elite runners have such big hearts!

Because men typically have larger hearts than women, men have a greater maximum stroke volume and cardiac output to send more blood and oxygen to the muscles. That's one of the reasons why men generally run faster marathons than women.

Your cardiac output when you run at your heart's maximum capability to pump blood is extremely important for your success as a marathon runner and is one of the key traits you want to improve. Although you may never achieve the heart size and maximum cardiac output of an elite marathoner, specific training can make your heart larger and increase your stroke volume and cardiac output. To see how, stride on over to Chapter 7.

Focusing on your aerobic power (VO₂max)

Getting blood from your heart to your muscles is only half the story. After blood is delivered to your muscles, they extract from the blood however much oxygen they need to maintain the pace you're running.

Together, the maximum cardiac output (the volume of blood and oxygen sent to the muscles from the heart) and the amount of oxygen your muscles extract and use determine your *aerobic power,* or *VO_2max* — the maximum volume of oxygen your muscles consume per minute.

VO_2max is an important physiological variable for marathon runners because it represents your ability to consume and use oxygen. VO_2max is the best single indicator of your aerobic fitness. It was first measured in humans in the 1920s and has become one of the most often measured physiological variables in the field of exercise physiology. There's a lot riding on it — the faster your muscles consume oxygen, the better you run.

There are some clever ways to increase your VO_2max, such as aerobic training and interval training. To find out how, flip to Chapters 5 and 7.

Knowing How Your Muscles Carry You 26.2 Miles

Even though your heart is very important (as you discover earlier in this chapter), it's your legs that run 26.2 miles. So they need to have some specific machinery to handle that job. How do your legs use all that oxygen that your heart sends to them? Find out in the following sections.

Mitochondria: Your muscles' aerobic factories

As you first learned in high school biology class, *mitochondria* are microscopic, energy-producing factories deep inside your muscles. They aerobically burn fat and carbohydrates.

The more mitochondria you have in your muscles, the more aerobic energy your muscles can produce. Inside the mitochondria are enzymes, which catalyze (speed up) chemical reactions. (Figure 3-2 shows you a mitochondrion and its enzymes.) The number of mitochondrial enzymes is important because enzymes, through their catalyzing effect on chemical reactions, control the rate at which energy is produced. Like bees in a beehive, enzymes are the factory workers inside the mitochondria. The more factory workers there are, the quicker the work gets done. Training increases the number of mitochondria and mitochondrial enzymes in your muscles. I tell you more about this topic in the section "Becoming a better aerobic machine: More mitochondria and enzymes," near the end of the chapter.

 Mitochondria are unique in that they have their own specific DNA. You inherit your mitochondria from your mother because the mitochondria from your father's sperm, which is contained in the tail that powers the sperm's movement, never enter your mother's egg. Only the head of the sperm, which contains the DNA for everything else, enters the egg. So the only mitochondrial DNA that's passed on to you comes from your mother's egg.

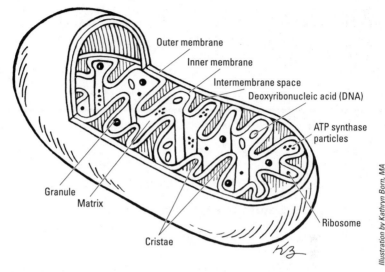

Figure 3-2: A mitochondrion and its enzymes produce energy.

Capillaries: Your muscles' highway system

When I first moved to San Diego, I was amazed at how many highways the city has. (They call them freeways there, but being from the East Coast, I call them highways.) The great thing about a lot of highways is that you never have to drive very far on local roads to get to your destination. You get off the highway at one of its many exits, and boom — you're close to where you need to go. If I had to drive on local roads all the time, it would take much longer to get anywhere.

Capillaries, the smallest of blood vessels, are your muscles' highway system. They surround and traverse your muscle fibers like a spider web, leading to places deep inside the muscles. Oxygen molecules in the blood "drive" along the capillaries, waiting to take an exit.

If you have only a few capillaries around your muscle fibers, the oxygen molecules have to drive a far distance from an exit to get to their destination — the mitochondria. But if you have a lot of capillaries, oxygen molecules don't have to drive very far to get to the mitochondria. The larger the spider web of capillaries surrounding your muscle fibers, the shorter the distance oxygen must travel from the capillaries to the mitochondria. And the faster that oxygen can get inside the mitochondria, the better you'll run. You build your network of capillaries through training, which I discuss in the later section, "Delivering oxygen to your muscles with greater capillary density."

Muscle fibers: Your muscles' power generator

When I was a kid, I used to show girls my biceps. (Boys do silly things to impress girls.) As adults, both men and women search for countless ways to make their biceps, and the rest of their muscles, look appealing to themselves and to one another. To most people, muscles are external structures, admired from the outside. But what lies within a shapely bicep is a wonderfully complex structure responsible for everything from metabolism to movement.

Muscles are very organized. Each of your more than 600 muscles is made up of bundles of compartments, or *fascicles*. Each fascicle is made up of discrete bundles of *fibers*. Each fiber is made up of bundles of *myofibrils*. Each myofibril is made up of bundles of microscopic proteins that interact with one another in a unique way to contract your muscles. This organization (see Figure 3-3) permits an enormous diversity of movements, from threading a needle to running a marathon.

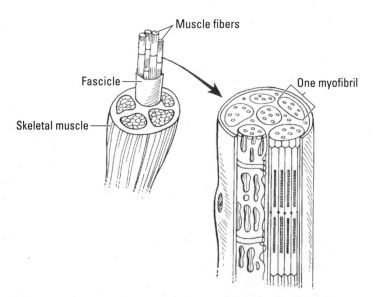

Muscle fibers

Fascicle

One myofibril

Skeletal muscle

Illustration by Kathryn Born, MA

Figure 3-3: The detailed organization of muscles enables a huge variety of movements.

Of all the muscle's compartments, the fibers are the ones that are different among people. The following sections describe different kinds of muscle fibers and how you use them when you run.

Distinguishing types of muscle fibers

You have three different types of muscle fibers (as well as gradations among them), the percentages of which are genetically determined.

- **Slow-twitch (ST) fibers:** You use these fibers for aerobic activities like walking, maintaining posture, and running a marathon. Most of your activities of daily living use ST fibers. They're not very strong or powerful, but they can keep contracting for long periods. To be a good marathon runner, you need a lot of ST fibers, which take a long time to fatigue. Fat is the major stored fuel of ST fibers (I talk more about fuels later in this chapter). ST fibers have many characteristics needed for endurance, including a lot of

  - Capillaries to supply oxygen

  - Myoglobin to transport oxygen

  - Mitochondria to use oxygen

  - Enzymes to speed up the chemical reactions of the aerobic energy pathways

- **Fast-twitch A (FT-A) fibers:** You use these fibers for faster-paced running and when the ST fibers start to fatigue. These fibers contain both endurance and power characteristics. They have fewer mitochondria and capillaries than the ST fibers. Glycogen is the major stored fuel of FT-A fibers.

- **Fast-twitch B (FT-B) fibers:** You use these fibers for short, intense sprints and when the FT-A fibers start to fatigue. These fibers are very strong and powerful, but they fatigue very quickly. To be a good sprinter, you need a lot of FT-B fibers, which are *anaerobic* — they don't use oxygen. They have few mitochondria and capillaries but a lot of enzymes that speed up the chemical reactions of the anaerobic energy pathways. FT-B fibers use glycogen and *creatine phosphate* as fuels. (Creatine phosphate is used for quick bursts of energy, like sprinting and jumping.)

Although it's easy to speak of muscle fibers as three discrete types, your fibers really exist on a continuum based on a combination of the preceding characteristics.

You can see the difference between the fiber types when eating a turkey dinner — the dark meat of your turkey, so colored because of its myoglobin content, is ST fibers and the white meat is FT fibers. But if you want to run a great marathon, don't reach for the dark meat too quickly. Unfortunately, the type of meat you eat has no impact on your endurance or sprinting ability.

Using muscle fibers when you run

When you run, you recruit your muscle fibers along a gradient, which is dictated by the size of the neuron that supplies the muscle fibers. ST muscle fibers, which are the smallest muscle fibers and have the smallest neuron connected to them, have the lowest firing threshold and are recruited first. Recruiting increasingly larger muscle fibers meets demands for larger muscle forces or faster speeds. FT-B fibers, which are the largest muscle fibers and have the largest neuron connected to them, have the highest firing threshold and are recruited last.

Regardless of the pace you run, you always recruit ST muscle fibers first. When you run at a slow pace, ST muscle fibers may be the only ones that you recruit. When you run fast, you recruit ST muscle fibers first, followed by FT-A fibers and, if needed, FT-B fibers. You also recruit FT fibers to pick up the slack of fatiguing ST fibers, even when you run at a slow pace. When you run long distances, ST fibers are initially the only fibers you recruit. But run long enough and your ST fibers eventually fatigue, forcing you to recruit FT fibers to continue running. Thus, you have two ways of training your FT fibers: run fast or run long.

To hold a faster pace in your marathon, you have to make your ST fibers better at handling a faster pace, because the sooner you start recruiting your FT-A and FT-B fibers, the sooner you start to show signs of fatigue. To find out how to train your ST fibers to handle a faster pace, stride on over to Chapter 5.

Running economy: Making muscles more efficient

As I explain earlier in this chapter, your VO_2max represents the size of your aerobic engine — how fast your muscles consume oxygen when you're running at 100 percent of your maximum heart rate. Your VO_2max is your aerobic ceiling. It's very different among runners, and that difference often determines who gets to the finish line first. But if you and your running partner have the exact same VO_2max, that doesn't necessarily mean the two of you will cross the finish line together. Huh? Why not?

How do muscles contract?

Apart from thinking, every human activity requires a muscle action, called a *contraction.* The contraction is initiated by impulses, called *action potentials,* which are conveyed by a neural cell called a *motor neuron.* (If you're a woman who's given birth, you know all too well what a contraction is. Labor pains are the contractions of the smooth muscles of the uterus.)

In 1957, Nobel Prize winner Andrew Huxley discovered that skeletal muscles contract and produce force through the interaction of two microscopic proteins: *actin* and *myosin.* Myosin, which looks like an oar with its paddle at an angle, attaches to actin, which looks like two strings of pearls twisted together. The paddle portion of myosin binds to actin and pulls it so that actin slides past myosin. The mechanism is much like the movement of a rowboat's oars, except that the water (actin) moves past the stationary boat (myosin). This movement happens among millions of actin and myosin proteins within each fiber, with all the actin proteins from opposing sides moving closer together, causing the entire muscle to shorten. The more actin and myosin proteins you have in your muscles, the more force they can produce. A boat with eight oars stroking the water is stronger and more powerful than a boat with two.

Aside from the exception of smooth muscles, your muscle fibers either contract or they don't. There's no such thing as a partial contraction. Like a light, fibers are either on or off. You vary the amount of muscle force by varying the number of muscle fibers you contract and the frequency with which your central nervous system recruits those fibers, not by varying their degree of contraction. (*Smooth muscles,* on the other hand — which line blood vessels and your gastrointestinal and urinary tracts and which are involuntary — can contract partially. They have a dimmer on their light switch, called tone. This characteristic comes in handy when trying to do such things as regulate blood pressure, which your body elegantly accomplishes through subtle alterations in the dilation and constriction of blood vessels.)

Muscles contract and produce force in three ways:

✔ When pushing off the ground, your muscles shorten in a *concentric contraction.*

✔ When your leg lands on the ground, your muscles lengthen in an *eccentric contraction.*

✔ In the short time between your leg landing on the ground and your leg pushing down and back against the ground, your muscle fibers remain the same length in an *isometric contraction,* which stabilizes your leg.

To visualize the three contractions, think of lifting weights: Lifting a weight is a concentric contraction, lowering a weight is an eccentric contraction, and trying to lift a weight that you can't or pushing against something immovable is an isometric contraction. Of the three contractions, eccentric contractions are the strongest and cause the most muscle damage and soreness, as the myosin is pulled apart from its binding site on actin. That's why running downhill makes your muscles sorer than running uphill.

People use different amounts of oxygen when running at the same submaximal speeds, and this difference explains why runners with the same VO_2max can have very different race performances. This difference in oxygen use is called *running economy* — the volume of oxygen (VO_2) that muscles consume to run at submaximal speeds. So, while VO_2max explains what happens at the upper limit of oxygen use, running economy explains what happens at levels below that upper limit. In advanced, well-trained runners who have already reached the VO_2max limit, the only way to make a difficult task — like running a marathon — easier is to improve running economy.

To understand why running economy is so important, imagine that you and your running partner have the same VO_2max, but you use 70 percent of that VO_2max and your running partner uses 80 percent while running at a 9-minute-per-mile pace. The pace feels easier for you because you're working at a lower percentage of your maximum to maintain the pace. In other words, you're more economical. If you were to run at 80 percent of your VO_2max just like your running partner, you'd be running faster than your partner. Therefore, you can run at a faster pace before feeling the same amount of fatigue as your partner.

To run a good marathon, you need a low energy cost to run at a particular speed. Although VO_2max gets most of the attention among runners, I'd go as far to say that running economy is more important — it exerts a much greater influence on your ability to run a marathon successfully because you run the race at a submaximal pace. Running economy is influenced by many internal and external characteristics; I describe both types in the following sections.

Knowing how economical you are is difficult because finding out exactly how much oxygen you use to run at specific paces takes some sophisticated laboratory equipment. Unless you're lightweight, an experienced runner, and were born with a lot of ST muscle fibers and mitochondria, you're probably not very economical. Only very talented runners are economical from the time they start running. But running economy is very responsive to training because running builds more mitochondria, makes you a smoother runner, and helps you lose weight. Better and more experienced runners have better economy.

Internal characteristics

The internal characteristics that affect your running economy include

- **Ability of tendons to store and use elastic energy:** Like a rubber band when stretched, your Achilles tendon, which connects your calf muscle to your heel bone, stores energy when your foot lands on the ground and gives back that energy when you push off, helping to propel you forward. Long, thin Achilles tendons are good at storing energy with each step. They make your legs work like springs, which is very economical.

✔ **Amount of mitochondria:** More mitochondria mean more aerobic factories to spread around the work, which makes you more economical. (I talk about mitochondria in more detail earlier in this chapter.)

✔ **Biomechanics:** Your running mechanics influence your economy because any unnecessary movements (and therefore unnecessary muscle contractions) increase the amount of oxygen your body consumes to maintain your pace. The more optimal your mechanics are — including proper foot placement on the ground with just the right amount of pronation to absorb shock upon landing, correct arm swing, minimal vertical movement (bouncing) of your center of mass, and so on — the more economical you are. Chapter 4 tells you about running mechanics.

✔ **Body weight:** The less you weigh, especially from the waist down and even more so from the knee down, the less work your body needs to do to transport your weight as you run. Slim legs make you more economical because they require less energy to lift off the ground. Adding weight, particularly at the end of a long lever, requires more energy to move the lever and makes the work harder.

✔ **Muscle fiber recruitment:** You want as little muscle recruited as possible to run at the desired pace. Any extra muscle activity reduces economy because more muscle activity means you're using more oxygen.

✔ **Number of slow-twitch muscle fibers:** Slow-twitch fibers are made for aerobic activities like running a marathon. They're much more efficient than your fast-twitch muscle fibers, which are made for sprinting. (See the earlier section "Distinguishing types of muscle fibers" for more info.)

External characteristics

The external characteristics that affect your running economy include

✔ **Shoe weight:** Lightweight shoes that still provide you with enough cushioning improve your running economy. You don't want big clunkers on your feet that make it sound like Godzilla is running down the street. (Flip to Chapter 2 for more about shoes and other running gear.)

✔ **Training:** Training is the biggest factor that affects your running economy. Increasing your weekly mileage, adding faster-paced running to a base of mileage, and doing strength training all improve running economy. (See Chapters 5 and 11 for more about these types of training.)

✔ **Wind:** Running into the wind decreases your economy because you have more air resistance to overcome. That's why drafting behind other runners during the marathon is such a good idea. I talk more about how to save energy by drafting in Chapter 16.

Making Sense of Metabolism

Your marathon performance isn't just about your cardiovascular system and your muscles; it's also about *metabolism* — the chemical reactions that control how your muscles use their energy pathways to convert fat and carbohydrates into energy for muscle contraction. In the following sections, I explain two facets of metabolism that affect marathon runners: acidosis threshold and the use of carbohydrates and fats.

Acidosis (lactate) threshold: Your fastest sustainable speed

To run a good marathon, you have to hold a hard aerobic pace for a long period. The *acidosis threshold* is the fastest pace you can hold and is a bit faster than the pace you can sustain for a marathon.

Lactate (a chemical produced in your muscles) is a byproduct of the metabolic pathway called *anaerobic glycolysis* — the breakdown of glucose (sugar) without oxygen. At slow running speeds, you use glycolysis only a little, and your muscles produce only a little bit of lactate. As you pick up the pace, you use glycolysis more because your muscles begin to rely more on carbohydrates for fuel. If you keep picking up your pace, you get to a pace at which you rely on glycolysis so much that lactate begins to accumulate in your muscles and blood. While lactate accumulates, hydrogen ions also accumulate in your muscles, lowering the pH of your muscles and making them more acidic, a condition called *metabolic acidosis.*

Acidosis is a big reason why your pace slows down, mostly because the enzymes that control the rate of chemical reactions don't work as well in an acidic environment. It's like asking factory workers to work just as fast in sweltering conditions. The acidosis threshold (AT) — more commonly called *lactate threshold* — is the pace above which lactate begins to accumulate in your muscles. I tell you more about the difference in terminology in Chapter 5.

The AT signifies the transition between running that's almost purely aerobic and running that includes significant anaerobic (oxygen-independent) metabolism. (All running speeds have an anaerobic contribution, although when running below the AT, that contribution is negligible.) Thus, the AT is an important determinant of your marathon performance because it represents the fastest pace you can sustain without a significant anaerobic contribution (and therefore the development of metabolic acidosis).

As long as you run below your AT, everything is cool and comfortable — you can maintain your pace for a while. Run faster than your AT and you'll start feeling fatigued, and you won't be able to hold the pace for very long. Because the marathon is a long race, you run the entire marathon below your AT. The more you can raise your AT — that is, the faster your AT pace — the faster the pace you can sustain.

Want to know how to increase your AT pace? Check out Chapter 5.

Using your fuels — carbohydrates and fats — effectively

The amount of carbohydrate (glycogen) stored in your skeletal muscles strongly influences your ability to perform prolonged endurance exercise. Get low on glycogen and fatigue sets in. The infamous marathon wall you've undoubtedly heard about coincides with low glycogen and the low blood sugar (hypoglycemia) that goes hand in hand with it.

Although carbohydrate is your muscles' preferred fuel when you run, your muscles' ability to metabolize fat also influences your marathon performance because your muscles have only a limited store of carbohydrate. That store of carbohydrate provides enough energy for only about 100 minutes of marathon running.

By contrast, humans' store of fat is virtually unlimited, with enough to fuel about five days of marathon running, or about 1,000 miles of walking for a 145-pound person with 18 percent body fat. At slow running speeds, some of carbohydrate's metabolic responsibility for providing energy is relieved by fat, in the form of free fatty acids in the blood and the stored fat inside muscles. Even with fat helping to delay the depletion of glycogen, you can sustain a moderate running pace for just two to three hours. One of the things that makes the marathon unique from other races is that you run out of carbohydrates during the race because of its duration.

One of the keys to the marathon is to teach your muscles how to use fat more effectively so you conserve your glycogen stores for when you really need them late in the race. That's one of the reasons for practicing very long runs — to literally run out of glycogen so your muscles are forced to rely on fat, which makes them better at using fat for energy. To find out more about long run strategies, stride on over to Chapter 6.

Although women can't pump as much blood from their hearts as men can, they seem to have a greater capacity to metabolize fat and conserve glycogen, which may give them an advantage for very long races, longer than a marathon (if you can imagine running longer than 26.2 miles!). In many of these very long races, called *ultramarathons,* women often place very high. In 2002 and 2003, ultramarathon runner Pam Reed beat all the men at the 135-mile Badwater Ultramarathon.

Seeing How Your Body Adapts to Marathon Training

Your body's structure and function match the demands you put on it, so if you increase the demands, you increase the amount of change that takes place to keep pace with the increased demands. When you apply stress through marathon training, your body adapts and even overcompensates so that if you encounter that same stress again, it doesn't cause the same degree of physiological disruption. In other words, your body adapts to handle the stress by making specific changes so it can handle more work.

Adaptation is a process during which you respond to the repeated stress of training over time. Many aspects of your physiology improve from marathon training, as you discover in the following sections. With the right stimuli, muscle fibers increase their mito-chondria and cardiac muscle grows larger (among other things). Think of these stimuli as small threats to your body's survival and adaptation as your body making specific adjustments to assuage those threats.

Sizing up your heart

When I speak at conferences, I often make the joke that, as a distance runner, I have a great capacity to love because I have a large heart. That one-liner always produces a few laughs from the audience (but has seldom helped me get a date).

One of the most elegant adaptations your body makes to endurance training is an increase in the size of your heart's left ventricle as a way to increase your stroke volume and pump more blood. The larger your left ventricle is, the more blood it can hold; the more blood it can hold, the more blood it can pump to the muscles you use to run.

Imagine what your heart goes through during training. After you complete a difficult workout, your heart says, "Geez, Jason is running hard workouts on a regular basis that cause me to reach my maximum capability to pump blood. If he keeps doing this and I don't do something, I'm not going to be able to survive." Thus, in response to the imposed threat of running at your heart's maximum ability to pump blood, your heart responds by increasing its pumping strength and by enlarging its most important chamber so that it can send more blood and oxygen to the working skeletal muscles. Pretty elegant, huh? An enlarged heart is so characteristic of individuals who do a lot of endurance training that scientists and doctors have given it the medical term, *athlete's heart.*

A larger heart increases the maximum amount of oxygen you consume per minute (VO_2max) because it gives you a larger max stroke volume and cardiac output. (I describe these terms in the earlier section "Getting to the Heart of Running.")

Moving oxygen where you need it

One of the first changes that occurs inside your body from marathon training is an increase in your blood volume. More blood means your heart pumps a greater volume with each beat, which increases your stroke volume. More blood also means you have more red blood cells and hemoglobin to carry oxygen to the muscles you use for running.

Overall, a greater blood volume increases your ability to transport oxygen to your muscles.

Becoming a better aerobic machine: More mitochondria and enzymes

Given how important mitochondria are in giving you aerobic energy (as I note earlier in this chapter), it should come as no surprise that marathon training increases the amount of mitochondria in your muscles. Mitochondria increase both in number and size, giving you more and larger power plants to run aerobically. More and bigger mitochondria in your muscles means

✔ **You can run farther and faster.** With more mitochondria comes a greater use of oxygen, which increases your VO_2max.

✔ **You can use fuel more quickly.** More mitochondria mean more enzymes, which speed up the chemical reactions that break down carbohydrates and fat for energy.

✔ **You use more fat at the same running pace.** Training enhances your muscles' ability to use fat for fuel at the same pace, which spares your limited store of carbohydrates. This steering in fuel use to a greater reliance on fat at the same running pace is one of the hallmark adaptations to aerobic training. In effect, you become a better fat-burning machine.

Together, more mitochondria and capillaries also improve your running economy by decreasing the energy cost of running at a particular pace. To find out how to increase your mitochondria and capillaries, flip to Chapters 5 and 6.

Delivering oxygen to your muscles with greater capillary density

In response to the constant "push" of oxygen into the muscles from running long distances, marathon training increases the number of capillaries surrounding your muscle fibers and expands old capillary beds, creating a greater highway system for delivering oxygen to the muscles.

With more capillaries, oxygen has less distance to travel to get inside the mitochondria, where it's used. A greater capillary density improves your ability to run more comfortably at a given pace and increases your VO_2max because more oxygen is delivered to your muscles. Overall, blood and oxygen circulation throughout your body is improved.

Altering your muscle fibers

Although you can't change your muscle fibers from one type to another — an ST fiber can't become an FT fiber or vice versa — endurance training can change the characteristics of the FT fibers, increasing their aerobic capacity and enabling them to support the workload of the ST fibers. (For an explanation of these fibers, see the earlier section "Distinguishing types of muscle fibers.")

Training can also change the amount of area that the fiber type takes up in the muscle. For example, say a muscle has a 70/30 mix of ST/FT fibers. Because ST fibers are smaller and therefore take up less space than FT fibers, 55 percent of that muscle's area may be ST and 45 percent may be FT. With aerobic marathon training, the *number* of ST and FT fibers remains the same (still 70/30), but the ST fibers get bigger and start taking up more space in the muscle. The FT fibers get smaller because you're not using them as much. The area of the muscle, which began at 55 percent ST and 45 percent FT before training, may change to 65 percent ST and 35 percent FT following training. The muscle's endurance capabilities increase and its strength and power decrease because endurance training interferes with strength gains.

As a normal process of training, your muscle fibers experience microscopic damage, especially when you run for long periods. During recovery, the fibers heal and even grow back stronger, becoming more resistant to the fatigue that occurs from the constant pounding of your legs against the hard ground. That's why training on asphalt is so important — you have to give your muscles a chance to adapt to the same conditions they experience in the marathon.

Storing more fuel in your muscles

Repeatedly running for long periods presents a threat to your muscles' survival by depleting their storage of carbohydrates, which is their preferred fuel. If you run out of fuel, your muscles say, "Hey, Johnny is running for so long that I don't have any more fuel. If he keeps this up, I won't be able to survive. If this activity is going to be Johnny's regular habit, I need to do something clever to protect myself. I know — I'll make more fuel!"

So, guess what happens? When you consume carbohydrates following your long run, you respond to the empty tank by synthesizing and storing more glycogen than usual in your skeletal muscles, thus increasing your storage of fuel (and therefore your endurance) for future efforts. Imagine if your car did that. Imagine if you kept driving your car until the gas tank was empty and your car responded to that threat by making its tank bigger so it could hold more gasoline. Pretty elegant.

Chapter 4

Starting Off with Proper Running Technique

• •

In This Chapter

▶ Knowing how to move your feet and arms while you run

▶ Practicing running drills to improve your form

▶ Making your stride more fluid

• •

1 see a lot of runners, and I see a lot of them running badly. Many of these runners run marathons, and many of them get injured training for marathons. One reason they get injured is because they haven't learned *how* to run before attempting to train for a marathon. That's like playing in a tennis tournament before learning how to hit a backhand, or entering a golf tournament before learning how to swing a golf club, or participating in a triathlon before learning how to swim. Or . . . you get the idea.

Learning how to run correctly helps prevent injuries and enables you to tolerate more training because you do the training with the proper skill. If you want to be a better runner, start by running better.

Running has an under-recognized neural component. Just as the repetition of walking movements decreases the jerkiness of a toddler's walk to the point that it becomes smooth, the repetition of specific running movements makes you a smoother runner. Extraneous movements, unnecessary muscle contractions, and an inefficient absorption of force when your feet strike the ground increase your use of oxygen to maintain a given pace, making your running uneconomical. With countless repetitions of helpful exercises, though, your running movements and the specific ways you use your muscles to run become ingrained, allowing for smoother running mechanics and a more efficient application of muscular force.

After you learn and ingrain proper running mechanics, you're better able to handle — and even thrive off of — your marathon training. This chapter walks you through correct running technique with the use of specific drills.

Running Right with Proper Mechanics

Most people training for a marathon walk out the door and start running. They never pay any attention to how they run. Proper running technique is the first step in preparing for a marathon so you can avoid injury and handle the training that enables you to be successful. The following sections go over the correct foot placement and arm movement to use when you run.

Focusing on foot placement

There seems to be a lot of commotion lately in the running world about heel striking and landing on your midfoot. Runners sometimes mistakenly devote attention to exactly how their feet land on the ground, but whether you land slightly on your heel first or on your midfoot isn't as important as where your foot lands in relation to your body. The faster you run, the more you naturally land toward the forefoot.

When you run, keep these points in mind:

- ✔ Place your foot on the ground directly underneath your hips so that you roll into the next stride. Your foot should already be moving backward relative to the ground as it lands so that you make a smooth transition into the next step.

- ✔ Don't overstride by landing sharply with your heel and your leg out in front of your body. This causes you to decelerate.

- ✔ Make a conscious effort to run as lightly as possible, springing off the ground with each step.

- ✔ Run tall, with your hips directly over your legs.

See Figure 4-1 to get an idea of how your body should align during each stride.

Figure 4-1: Your foot should land under your hips during a proper running stride.

Swinging your arms

What about your arms? Are they important when you run? I'm glad you asked. Yes, your arms are important, because they balance your legs. As Isaac Newton discovered a long time ago, every action has an equal and opposite reaction. Quick, powerful arm movements mean quick, powerful leg movements. If you move your arms the wrong way, your legs move the wrong way. After you practice how to move your legs and how to land with your feet directly beneath your hips (see the preceding section), add the motion of your arms.

Hold your arms close to your body and swing them back and forth from your shoulders like a pendulum, with your forearms swinging at a slight angle toward your body rather than directly forward and backward like a robot. Good form for arm movement should also include the following (see Figure 4-2):

✔ **Keep your elbows bent at 90 degrees or slightly less.** When your arms flare open, you lengthen your levers, which makes swinging your arms more difficult.

✔ **Don't allow your arms to cross over the midline of your chest.** Direct all your effort into moving your body forward; when your arms cross your chest, your torso starts twisting and you add undesirable sideways movement.

✔ **Keep the palms of your hands facing your body and cup your hands like you're gently holding a potato chip.** Relax your hands and arms so you don't create tension in your upper body.

✔ **Swing your arms with quick, compact movements.** Your legs do what your arms do, so quick arms mean quick legs.

✔ **To run faster, increase the cadence of your arms.** Move your arms back and forth faster, but keep the movements controlled and compact.

Photograph by Maurice Roy Photography

Figure 4-2: Swing your arms like a pendulum as you run.

Improving Your Form with Running Drills

Like any other skill, from playing the piano to riding a bicycle, running expertise comes through constant repetition. Drills that specifically target each part of the running motion help improve your running mechanics and coordination as the movements are ingrained in your central nervous system. Drills also increase flexibility because their dynamic action moves your joints through an exaggerated range of motion.

Do everything you can to ensure that your form is good while you perform running drills so you're not wasting your time. Not doing the drills at all is better than doing them with improper form because improper form only creates and ingrains bad habits. So make sure that you

- Recover for a minute or two between each set and each drill to ensure you're using proper form and avoiding fatigue.

- Are deliberate about all the movements.

- Execute the drills on either your midfoot or the ball of your foot.

You must master the drills in the following sections and the proper running technique they aim to produce before you can train effectively and prepare for a marathon. I can't emphasize this enough. During all your runs, practicing correct technique is vital. It must become automatic. Do these drills a few times each week before you run, using crisp, sharp motions with a springiness to your legs.

The high-knee walk

This drill trains your *hip flexors* (the muscles in front of your hips) to lift your legs and drive them forward.

Start marching by bringing your hip to 90 degrees so that your thigh is parallel to the ground. Create 90-degree angles at your knee and ankle, as Figure 4-3 shows.

Bring your legs down directly underneath your center of gravity and land on your midfoot. Use quick, sharp movements. Horizontal movement across the ground isn't as important as the proper movement of your arms and legs (see the earlier "Swinging your arms" section). Stand tall and keep your support leg straight.

Photograph by Maurice Ray Photography

Figure 4-3: Aim for 90-degree angles when you practice the high-knee walk.

March in a high-knee walk for about 30 meters, rest, and then repeat. Do two to four sets.

The high-knee skip

This drill is similar to the high-knee walk in the preceding section, but the drill progresses as a skip so that you learn proper form with faster movements. Focus on three 90-degree angles — at your hip, knee, and ankle.

Skip across the ground, driving your knee up using your hip flexor muscles. Bring your legs down directly underneath your center of gravity and land on your midfoot, as you see in Figure 4-4. As you drive the other leg up, hop slightly off the ground with your support leg. Use quick, sharp movements. Horizontal movement across the ground isn't as important as the proper movement of your arms and legs (see the earlier "Swinging your arms" section). Stand tall and keep your support leg straight. Do two to four sets of 30 meters.

Photograph by Maurice Roy Photography

Figure 4-4: Focus on three 90-degree angles during the high-knee skip.

The high-knee run

This drill is similar to the high-knee walk and skip in the preceding sections, but here you progress to a run, which makes this drill more difficult. Going from a walk to a skip to a run teaches you how to do the movements correctly because you move slowly through the range of motion. Adding speed makes the drill more closely resemble actual running. Like any other skill, you must do the movement slowly before doing it quickly.

You cover horizontal distance slowly, but you emphasize moving your legs vertically as fast as you can, like a piston or sewing machine. You don't run across the ground but rather move your legs up and down, almost running in place. Think of the ground as hot coals, and pick up each leg as soon as it touches the ground.

Bring your legs down directly underneath your center of gravity, as Figure 4-5 shows. Remain on the ball of your foot. Run tall and don't lean back. Use quick, sharp movements and keep your support leg straight. Think, "Toe up, knee up." Do two to four sets of 30 meters.

Photograph by Maurice Roy Photography

Figure 4-5: Stay on the balls of your feet during the high-knee run.

Butt kicks

This drill concentrates on what your foot does after it lands on the ground and before it swings forward. In addition, this drill trains your *hamstrings* (the muscles on the back of your thighs) to contract quickly to bend your knee.

As you run 30 meters, focus on flexing your knees and flicking the back of your butt with your heels, as Figure 4-6 shows. Move your legs fast but cover horizontal distance slowly, at a jogging pace (or even do the drill running in place). Bring your legs down directly underneath your center of gravity. Remain on the ball of your foot. Use quick, sharp movements. Do two to four sets of 30 meters.

Photograph by Maurice Roy Photography

Figure 4-6: Bring your heels to your butt as you run to train your hamstrings.

The running leg cycle

All the drills in the preceding sections come into play in this drill, which takes your legs through the entire running cycle, ingraining the whole circular movement of your legs.

Face a fence or pole and lean forward slightly with your hands on the fence or pole. While standing in place, move your leg through the entire running cycle. Start with your foot on the ground (see Figure 4-7a), extend your leg at the hip and sweep your leg back (see Figure 4-7b), bend your knee and pull it to the front of your body until your hip is at 90 degrees (which also creates 90-degree angles at your knee and ankle; see Figure 4-7c), and then lower your leg to the ground under your center of gravity and repeat. Think, "Land, push off, pull through; land, push off, pull through." Do two to three sets of 20 reps with each leg.

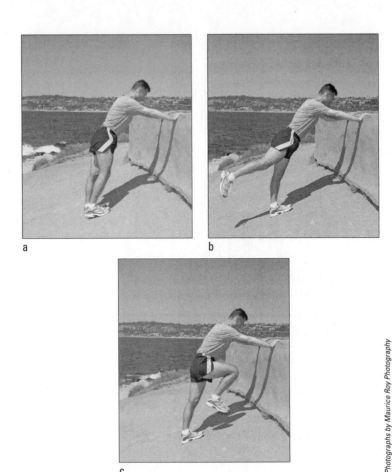

a   b

c

Photographs by Maurice Roy Photography

Figure 4-7: While leaning against a tree or wall, cycle your legs for the running leg cycle drill.

Strides

Strides are short, controlled sprints that integrate all the preceding form drills. Although you don't need much sprint speed for a marathon, strides help you work on your running mechanics, improving your coordination and your running form.

When doing strides, keep your attention on your arms and legs, just as you do in the preceding drills. Keep your knees high, actively flex your knees with your hamstrings, and swing your arms powerfully from your shoulders, with your elbows at a 90-degree angle. Paw at the ground with your feet and push the ground behind you. Aim for a fast, smooth feeling. Keep your head up, looking at the horizon. Figure 4-8 shows how your form should look.

Photograph by Maurice Roy Photography

Figure 4-8: When doing strides, focus on correct movement of arms and legs.

Do strides on flat ground for 50 to 150 meters (10 to 25 seconds). Repeat four to eight times, with full recovery between each.

TIP

Don't muscle through the strides or sprint all-out; they shouldn't feel difficult. Relax, move your legs fast to increase your cadence, and extend your legs behind you from the hip to increase your stride length.

Adding Fluidity to Your Stride

After you're comfortable with the drills in the preceding section, you can focus on adding fluidity to your stride by practicing the exercises in the following sections.

Your stride has two components: *stride rate,* which is the number of steps you take per minute, and *stride length,* which is the distance of each step. Running speed equals stride rate times stride length. To get faster, you must increase stride rate, stride length, or both.

Lungs and legs: Coordinating breathing and stride rate

For my doctoral dissertation, I studied the relationship between runners' stride rates and their breathing rates, and I found something very interesting: Trained runners coordinate their breathing to their stride rate, typically taking three or four steps per breath when running slowly and two steps per breath when running at a 5K-race pace. Coordinating the breathing rhythm to the stride rhythm is linked to running experience, with more fit and experienced runners exhibiting more coordination. With many miles of training, runners seem to subconsciously learn how to most effectively ventilate their lungs, possibly to minimize how much oxygen the breathing muscles use, which may improve running economy.

During your training, practice coordinating your breathing to your stride rate, taking three or four steps per breath during slower running paces and two steps per breath at faster running paces, always exhaling as your foot lands on the ground. Coordinating your breathing and stride rate helps make you a more economical runner and also gives you something to focus on during your long runs.

With many miles of training and faster-paced running to work on technique, your body adopts the best combination of stride rate and stride length to make you a more economical, fluid runner, giving new meaning to the phrase *poetry in motion*.

Increasing your stride rate with sprints

Although stride rate varies considerably among runners, aim for 80 to 90 steps per minute with each leg. To calculate your stride rate while you run, simply count how many times your right foot hits the ground in one minute. If your stride rate is less than 80, you'll likely benefit from increasing your cadence. With a slightly faster stride rate, you take lighter steps and spend less time impacting the ground, which reduces your chance of injury.

Stride rate is influenced by the number of fast-twitch muscle fibers you have and the ability of your central nervous system to recruit muscle fibers and move your legs quickly. Fast running is the simplest way to increase stride rate because it trains your central nervous system to recruit those fast-twitch muscle fibers.

After a thorough warm-up of easy running for about 10 minutes, gradually accelerate to full speed and then hold your maximal speed without straining for about five to ten seconds before decelerating. Because your arms and legs move in sync, you can increase your stride rate by pumping your arms more quickly. Remember to remain relaxed through the sprint. Do five to ten sprints a couple of times per week.

Lengthening your stride

Have you ever run with someone much taller than you and noticed that she takes longer strides? Despite what you may think, little correlation exists between a person's height and stride length or between a person's leg length and stride length. Taller runners don't always take longer strides than shorter runners. Surprised, huh?

Of the two components of your stride, stride length is more important than stride rate. When you increase your pace from a jog to a run to a hard run, your stride length increases more than your stride rate.

Stride length explains much of the difference in speed among runners. The subconscious manipulation of stride length and stride rate at different speeds may be governed by what is most economical for runners; that is, at each pace you run, you may have a stride length that's most economical for you to use, while staying at a specific stride rate (or within a narrow range of stride rates) may be what's most economical for all your running paces.

Stride length is influenced by your range of motion at the hip — specifically, your hip extension — and the amount of force your muscles produce against the ground as you push off. As you become a better runner, your stride length naturally gets longer, but you can also do specific training exercises to increase the strength and power of the muscles you use for hip extension and for pushing against the ground. For strength and power workouts to increase your stride length, stride on over to Chapter 11.

To increase your pace, increase your stride length by pushing the ground behind you with the ball of your foot. Never reach your leg out in front of your body, which causes braking.

Part II

Creating Your Own Marathon Training Plan

The 5th Wave

By Rich Tennant

"I used to think 'running for the endorphins' was a charity race for an endangered sea mammal."

In this part...

After you decide to run a marathon, you need all the planning help you can get. This part gives you all the marathon training information you need. I include advice on the total weekly distance you should run, long runs, tempo training to improve your max aerobic pace, interval training to improve your speed, and other training principles, guidelines, and instructions to guide you along your journey.

I also provide specific 20-week marathon training plans for beginner, intermediate, and advanced runners so you know exactly what to do every day!

Chapter 5

Aerobic Training: The King of Marathon Preparation

In This Chapter

▶ Prepping for a marathon with many miles each week
▶ Running hills
▶ Mastering your marathon pace
▶ Discovering how to do tempo workouts

A nd so it begins. Your journey to the marathon starts with going out the door to take your first steps. One run, then two, then three, until you've completed so many runs that they all blend together to create a huge body of aerobic work.

Any race that takes longer than three minutes is primarily influenced by your muscles' ability to produce energy aerobically. The marathon is obviously much longer than three minutes. For even the best runners in the world, the marathon takes more than two hours to finish. The average marathon time for men and women combined is four and a half hours, so aerobic training is extremely important. This chapter shows you how to train aerobically to handle 26.2 miles on race day by running many miles each week, working out on hills, practicing your marathon pace, and using tempo training. (Long runs and interval workouts also count as aerobic training; see Chapters 6 and 7, respectively, for more details.)

Running Mileage: The Key to Marathon Success

The number of miles (or amount of time) you run each week, every week, is the most important part of your marathon preparation. I can't emphasize this enough. Every time I ask runners how many miles they're running in preparation for their marathon, they always tell me about their weekly long run. They never mention anything else (like their weekly mileage and tempo and interval workouts), as if the long run is the only thing they do to prepare for the marathon. Training for a marathon is not just about one long run each week; it's about the total amount of running — and therefore the total aerobic training — you do.

Many marathon training groups and programs available on the Internet shorten preparation time, promising the whole kit and caboodle on as little training as possible. This is a recipe for failure and teaches you nothing about the value of commitment, discipline, and hard work.

Running a lot makes you a lot fitter, burns a ton of calories, helps you lose weight, and prepares you for a marathon. It also allows you to see and experience places and things you wouldn't otherwise see and experience and gives you a chance to discover things about yourself, such as discipline, courage, and the ability to meet a challenge.

In the following sections, I describe the benefits of running a lot, help you figure out the right weekly mileage for your level of running experience, and explain how to increase your weekly mileage as you continue to train.

Whether you're a beginner runner training for your first marathon or one of the world's best runners training to win the Olympics, how much you run is the key to your success. That's why I suggest you become a runner first before setting your sights on the marathon. Many people who've never run a step in their lives decide they want to run a marathon in six months. You can do that, but if you start running first and focus on becoming a runner, your marathon experience and your chances of success are a whole lot greater.

Discovering the benefits of running many miles

Nothing takes the place of running to train for a marathon. Running a lot of miles stimulates many physiological, biochemical, and molecular adaptations:

- ✔ **Better fuel storage:** Running lots of miles stimulates the storage of more fuel (glycogen) in your muscles and increases your body's use of fat so that your muscles spare your reserved glycogen.

- ✔ **Improved ability to produce energy:** Through the complex activation of gene expression, running increases how many mitochondria you have in your muscles and the number of aerobic enzymes contained within them. That combination increases your muscles' capacity to produce energy aerobically so you can keep running.

✔ **An increase in blood volume:** A greater amount of blood circulating in your body means a greater number of red blood cells, which transport oxygen. Inside the red blood cells is a protein called *hemoglobin,* which carries oxygen to your working muscles. These changes to your blood improve your blood vessels' ability to transport oxygen.

✔ **More efficient transport of oxygen:** When you run a lot, your body creates more capillaries surrounding your muscle fibers. More capillaries mean more rapid diffusion of oxygen into your muscles.

These specific adaptations, combined with increases in your bone density and your muscles' ability to adapt to the muscle fiber damage from repeatedly pounding the pavement, go a very long way (pun intended) toward preparing you to run a marathon. The volume of training you do induces the biological signal for adaptation and dictates your performance. Think of these adaptations as your body's attempt to cope with the demand you place on it by running on a regular basis. (Flip to Chapter 3 for full details on these and other physiological adaptations.)

Running a lot of miles also makes you a more economical runner. The countless repetitions your arms and legs go through have a very important neural effect, as your central nervous system becomes better at recruiting muscle fibers, making you a smoother runner. (If you have children, you can appreciate the effect of what running a lot does to your running form. The process is very similar to what happens when a toddler takes his first steps — the toddler's initial movements are jerky and uncoordinated, but after much practice, they become smooth and controlled.) Running also burns lots of calories, which helps you lose weight and so also improves your economy.

Knowing how many miles to run

So how many miles do you really need to run to prepare for a marathon? That's a tough question to answer, but the short answer is "a lot." The exact number of miles you run depends on many factors, including

✔ **The amount of mileage you can psychologically handle:** People can handle only so much running before getting burned out. You don't want running to become a chore; you want to look forward to your daily runs. Ask yourself how much running you can handle before you feel like it's becoming too much.

- ✔ **The amount of mileage you'll physically adapt to:** Though running more miles typically makes you a better runner, more isn't always better; more is only better if you continue to adapt to more. Knowing what your strengths and weaknesses are as a runner and combining that knowledge with trial and success, you can find out how much mileage will continue to make you a better runner.

- ✔ **The amount of time you have to train:** Running a lot of miles takes up a lot of time, so you need to look at your schedule and decide how much time you have to prepare. If you have a full-time job, a spouse, four kids, and two dogs, you're not going to be able to run as much as someone who has fewer responsibilities.

- ✔ **Your marathon goals:** Do you simply want to finish the race or do you want to shoot for a specific time? In general, the better marathon you want to run, the more miles you need to run.

The more untrained you are, the more you can expect to improve by increasing your mileage. However, you don't keep getting better indefinitely. The more miles you run, the less you keep improving by the same amount. For example, when you initially go from 20 miles of running per week to 30 miles per week, you'll notice a big difference in your aerobic fitness and running performance. Going from 70 miles per week to 80 miles per week, however, gives you a smaller return on your investment. Depending on your goals, you have to decide at what point the small return on your investment is worth the extra commitment. Are you happier running a 3-hour marathon on 50 miles per week or would you rather run 2:55 on 60 miles per week?

The main difference between Olympic athletes and everyone else is that Olympic athletes continue to make physiological adaptations with more and more training, even when they run more than 100 miles per week. Most people stop adapting far short of 100 miles per week. The key is finding out how many miles work for you, keep you healthy, and keep you going out the door the next day for more. I've coached marathon runners who run anywhere from 40 to 100 miles per week. Some thrive off of more miles; some thrive off of less. The upcoming sections offer some general weekly mileage guidelines for different levels of runners.

Although most runners plan their training based on miles, the amount of time you spend running is actually more important than the number of miles you run. A faster runner covers more miles than a slower runner in the same amount of time. For example, a runner who averages a 7-minute mile pace for 40 miles per week runs the same amount of time as a runner who averages a 10-minute mile pace for 28 miles per week and therefore experiences the same amount of stress. And that's what matters — the stress. The slower runner may run fewer miles, but the time spent running — and therefore the stimulus for adaptation — is the same.

If a slower runner tries to run as many miles as a faster runner, the slower runner experiences more stress — because he's taking more steps and enduring more landing impact — and therefore puts himself at a greater risk for injury. The slower runner also has a greater chance of becoming dehydrated from sweating and because his body temperature is increased for a longer time. Your body has no comprehension of what a mile is or what 26.2 miles are; it only knows how hard and how long it's working.

Beginners

If you're a beginner runner who has never run a marathon before, starting slowly is important. Try starting with 10 to 15 miles per week and maxing out at 30 to 35 miles per week, with three to four days of running per week (Chapter 8 has a specific training plan for beginners to follow). If you have more than five or six months to prepare, you can increase your mileage even more.

If you've never run before, you may have to start by mixing periods of running with periods of walking — such as alternating five minutes of walking with three minutes of running — which allows you to run for longer periods of time. As your running fitness improves, you can decrease your walking time and increase your running time. As you adapt to the training, you'll find that you can run longer before taking a walking break.

On the days you don't run, do some cross-training with other types of cardiovascular exercise (elliptical, bike, swim, and so on) to increase your overall cardiovascular fitness. (For more on cross-training, see Chapter 12.)

Intermediate runners

If you're an intermediate runner who runs regularly and may or may not have run a marathon before, try ramping up your mileage from what you're currently used to running. Start with about 30 to 35 miles per week and max out at 45 to 50 miles per week, with four to six days of running per week. Every few weeks, decrease your mileage by about a third for a recovery week. (Chapter 9 features a specific training plan for intermediate runners to follow.)

Advanced runners

If you're an advanced and competitive runner who has run a few marathons before and wants to improve your marathon performance, then the sky's the limit when it comes to how much you run, as long as you train smartly so you don't get injured.

Becoming an athlete: Running as training

I wish I had grown up when it was chic to gulp down a dozen raw eggs first thing every morning, followed by a run up the bleacher steps with a towel around my neck at the local high school. That wasn't exercise; that was *training*. Wearing old, generic gray sweats dug out from the bottom of my closet, I would ascend the steps one by one, then two by two, maybe even doing some one-legged hops up them. The cool morning air, drying the thin layer of sweat on my forehead, would feel refreshing entering my lungs. I'd hear the chirping of a bird and look up to see it fly across the sky, reminding me that, no matter how high I got up these steps, something would always be higher.

Now the in thing is to become a member of the local fitness center and take cardio kickboxing classes with hip-hop music and bubbly instructors wearing pink scrunchies in their hair. Exercise now happens assembly-line style, with stair-climbing machines on which the steps move instead of us — all lined up in rows, each person side by side, only a few precious inches separating one another's sweaty T-shirts.

Although I run for a variety of reasons, I admit that fitness isn't one of them. For me, it's simply a welcome benefit. The low percentage of body fat, toned muscles, and low blood pressure have nothing to do with why I run. I don't go to the fitness center myself to work out, to wring a few extra pounds off my waistline, to manufacture a body as if it were a product on the assembly line. By focusing too much on the product, you forget about the process. You get caught up in pounds to lose, muscles to look toned, or fitting into skinny jeans or a bikini in the summertime. Running is more than that.

Most runners have one thing in common: They're always *in process.* They're always looking for ways to improve, avenues to explore, means not simply for justification of the ends but for the means themselves. They're only as good as their last race, their last long run, their last interval workout. Even most Olympic champions say it's not the gold medal itself that means so much but the process they went through to obtain it.

Athletes become so wrapped up in the activity for other reasons that fitness becomes little more than a byproduct. Their activity becomes a sport, they go from being exercisers to being athletes, and their exercise becomes *training.* I see myself first as an athlete, a role that gets lost in our society somewhere between the Little League baseball field and the cluttered desk at the office. But everyone, including you, should strive to become an athlete. You're training for a marathon, after all. Whether you're a beginner, intermediate, or advanced runner, whether you've run zero marathons or 20, approach your running as an athlete approaches training for his sport, because the lessons of sport and athletic training are many. Sport engages. Sport teaches. Sport empowers. Sport reveals. Sport allows us to become athletes — to train rather than run.

Try starting with 50 to 60 miles per week and maxing out at 70 to 80 miles per week, with six to seven days of running per week. Every few weeks, decrease your mileage by about a third for a recovery week. (Chapter 10 has a specific training plan for advanced runners to follow.)

Many advanced runners even run twice per day to maximize their mileage. When all your runs become longer than an hour each, you may want to break up some of the runs into two separate runs as a way to spread around the stress and get in more mileage.

Increasing your weekly mileage

Throughout your marathon training program, you need to increase your weekly running mileage. Doing so provides the biggest impact on your ability to run a marathon and, if you've run a marathon before, on your ability to run it faster. How you increase your mileage is important; the major reason runners get injured is because they increase their mileage too quickly for their bodies to adapt.

Always increase your running mileage systematically and with reason behind it, and be careful — you can easily get injured if you increase your weekly mileage too quickly.

Here are some guidelines:

✔ Increase your mileage by no more than 1 mile per day per week. For example, if you currently run 20 miles in four days per week, run no more than 24 miles the next week by adding 1 mile to each of the four days. Don't run 24 miles the next week by adding all 4 miles to only one day of running. Many books and articles quote the 10 percent rule of increasing mileage, but I've found nothing special about 10 percent, and you can often increase by more than that if you're smart about how you do it.

✔ If you're a highly trained runner, you may be able to get away with adding more miles more quickly, especially if you have experience running more miles. For example, if you've run 60 miles per week in the recent past and now you're training for your fifth marathon and building your mileage, you don't necessarily have to go from 40 to 45 to 50 to 55 to 60 miles per week over a couple of months. You may be able to make bigger jumps in mileage because your legs already have experience running 60 miles per week. However, if 60 miles per week is brand-new territory for you, then you do need to increase your mileage in smaller increments. If you're a new runner, an older runner, or are prone to injury, run the same mileage for three to four weeks before increasing it. Give your legs a chance to adapt to each level of running before increasing the level.

If you run less than 30 to 40 miles per week, it's best to run just once per day. Running 5 miles all at once is better than running 2 miles in the morning and 3 miles in the evening. Longer single runs build endurance and make you a better runner (plus, you get to see more of your surroundings!).

When your daily runs start averaging an hour or more, it's best to run twice per day at least a couple of times per week rather than extend the length of all your runs. Of course, running twice per day takes more time out of your day and makes it more difficult to recover between runs, so you'll need to factor that in, too.

The biggest advantage of doubling up is that it allows you to increase your training load while minimizing stress on your body and reducing recovery time. Both physically and psychologically, it's easier to run 4 miles in the morning and 6 miles in the evening than it is to run 10 miles (or even 8 miles) all at once.

Proper nutrition after your first run, including carbohydrate and protein, is important so you can recover quickly between runs. Consume 200 to 400 calories of carbohydrate and protein immediately after your first run so you can recover faster, and spread your two runs at least six hours apart.

As you increase your weekly mileage, give yourself time to recover and run slowly on easy training days. The following sections give you some handy pointers on performing these tasks; see Chapters 8, 9, and 10 for training plans that put these pointers to use.

Taking time to recover

Whether you run the same mileage for a few weeks or increase the mileage slightly for a few weeks, decrease the distance by about a third for one recovery week before increasing your mileage. Doing so gives your legs a chance to absorb and recover from the training you've done and make the necessary adaptations. For example, if you've been running 30 miles per week for three weeks, back off to 20 miles for one week before increasing above 30 miles for the next week.

Think of this strategy as taking one step back at the end of each training cycle so you can take two steps forward during the next one. Over time, your weekly mileage progression will look something like this:

- ✔ **Weeks 1–4:** 30-30-30-20 miles
- ✔ **Weeks 5–8:** 35-35-35-23 miles
- ✔ **Weeks 9–12:** 40-40-40-26 miles

As you can see, you increase your weekly mileage over time, but you do it systematically, without any abrupt changes, which is key for enabling your body to adapt and for preventing injuries.

Pulling back on easy days

The single biggest mistake runners make is running too fast on their easy training days. Doing so adds unnecessary stress to your legs without any extra benefit and keeps you from getting the most out of your harder days. Easy runs, which make up the majority of your marathon training — and possibly all your marathon training if you're a beginner — must remain easy.

Because many of the cellular adaptations associated with aerobic training are volume-dependent rather than intensity-dependent, the pace of your easy runs isn't as important as their duration. (See the earlier section "Discovering the benefits of running many miles" for more on these adaptations.) The slower you run, the longer you can go and the more miles you can run each day. Running slow during your easy runs has at least three benefits:

- ✔ It decreases the chance of injury.
- ✔ It enables you to get more out of your harder days of training because your legs aren't as fatigued.
- ✔ It enables you to increase your overall weekly mileage.

If you have a heart rate monitor, aim for 70 to 75 percent of your maximum heart rate for your easy aerobic runs (see Chapter 7 for info on how to accurately determine your max heart rate). Your heart rate fluctuates with the terrain, fatigue, and the weather, but your runs should still feel comfortable. You should be able to hold a lengthy conversation with someone while you run. Your breathing will be elevated but still very comfortable and rhythmic.

Including Hills in Your Weekly Runs

Hills are often a big part of marathon courses, so you have to prepare for them. You don't want all your runs to be on flat ground or you'll be in for some big surprises on marathon race day, like labored breathing, burning quads, and greater fatigue as you climb the hills.

Hills add variety to your aerobic training. The feeling of your heart pounding and your shortness of breath at the top of a hill attests to the great workout hills provide for your cardio-respiratory system. But hills also provide a great workout for your skeletal muscles. Hill training does many things. It

- ✔ Increases your leg muscle power.

- ✔ Strengthens your Achilles tendon, protecting you from injury.

- ✔ Transitions you into more formal speed training, like tempo and interval training.

- ✔ Improves your heart's ability to pump blood and oxygen because your heart rate easily climbs up to its maximum when you run up a hill.

- ✔ Uses your leg, arm, and trunk muscles in ways that are different from flat running, making you a powerful hill runner.

Even though running uphill seems harder, running downhill is actually tougher on your legs. Most runners underestimate down-hills, generally because they don't present much of a challenge. But running downhill requires the muscles to lengthen, using *eccentric* muscle contractions that cause microscopic tears in the muscle fibers and generate more force than muscle contractions associated with running uphill or on level terrain. Also, the faster you move, the harder each foot strikes the ground, and the more pounding your muscles endure. Because gaining momentum on a steep descent is easy, you can easily overdo it and suffer later on as a result. Running downhill carries a greater risk of overuse injury than uphill or flat running.

The good news is that, with a little practice, you can build the strength you need to weather the downhills and learn to manage the descents with more control, which helps you gain speed later in the run and bounce back sooner from the efforts. Damaging muscle fibers by running downhill makes them stronger. You can expect your muscles to be sore after the first time you run down-hill, but subsequent downhill workouts will cause less soreness because running downhill protects you from future muscle damage and soreness.

The following sections provide some hill workouts you can incorporate into your aerobic training, along with some important pointers.

Up and down: Hill workouts to try

Try incorporating these hill workouts into your weekly running. Be sure to warm up and cool down for about 10 to 15 minutes before and after each workout. To warm up, start with a slow jog and finish with some strides, as I describe in Chapter 4.

If you live in a place that doesn't have hills or you're training during the winter, when it's too cold or icy to run hills outside, use a treadmill at a gym for these hill workouts.

Try one of these hill workouts each week. If your marathon has hills, choose the workouts that most closely mimic the hills on the marathon racecourse.

- ✓ **Hill accelerators:** Run a 200- to 400-meter hill, running the bottom of the hill at 5K race pace effort (leading into the hill from a 200-meter flat section at 5K race pace effort) and accelerating the last 50 meters of the hill and 100 meters after you get to the top, with a jog back down as recovery. The focus of this workout is the acceleration at the top of the hill, which is opposite to the recovery that runners naturally want to take at the top of a hill. When you get to the top of the hill, remind yourself to pump your arms to help you accelerate and lengthen your stride, which shortens on the hill. Run four to eight repeats.

  If you don't know what your 5K race pace is, run hard enough that you're breathing very hard, but not so hard that you can't repeat the hill when you get back down to the bottom. The effort should feel like an 8 or 9 on a scale of 1 to 10.

- ✓ **Hill run:** Run 4 to 8 miles at an easy effort on rolling terrain that includes hills of varying lengths and grades. Like with most of your easy runs, the pace isn't as important as the effort. This run simply gets your legs used to navigating hills as part of a normal, everyday run.

- ✓ **Long hill repeats:** Run a half-mile uphill (5 to 8 percent grade) at 5K race pace effort with a jog back down as recovery. Run five to six total repeats.

- ✓ **Short downhill repeats:** Run 100 meters nearly all-out downhill (2 to 3 percent grade) with a walk/jog back uphill as recovery. Run eight to ten total repeats.

- ✓ **Short hill repeats:** Sprint 100 meters uphill (15 to 20 percent grade) with a jog back down as recovery. Run eight to ten total repeats. Exaggerate your arm swing, lean into the hill, and focus on pushing off with the ball of your foot.

- ✓ **Uphill/downhill repeats:** Run a half-mile uphill and a half-mile downhill (2 to 3 percent grade) at 5K race pace effort with 3 minutes of jog recovery. Run four total repeats.

Guidelines for hill training

Hill training requires some strategies that are different from running on flat ground. When running hills, follow these guidelines:

✔ **Add downhills to your training a little at a time.** Start with a short, gradual slope of about 2 to 3 percent and progress to steeper and longer downhills as you get more comfortable. If possible, train on a soft surface like grass before moving on to the road. Treat downhill workouts as hard sessions and take time to recover with two to three days of rest or easy running afterward.

✔ **Aim for a specific effort rather than a specific speed.** Because uphill running uncouples the effort from the speed — you're running relatively slowly even though you're working hard — the exact pace you run isn't as important as your effort. Watching your heart rate with a heart rate monitor is a great way to make sure you're working hard enough.

✔ **Back off of the hills in the final couple weeks before the marathon.** Because hill running causes fatigue, make sure you back off before the big day so you feel rested.

✔ **For the longer hill repeats, use a hill that takes at least 3 minutes to climb to boost aerobic fitness.** Doing so gives your heart rate enough time to rise to its maximum.

✔ **Shorten your stride when running downhill to prevent over-striding and to emphasize quicker leg movement.** Shorter strides keep your momentum going forward. You can easily overstride when running downhill, which only makes you land harder, wears you out sooner, and makes you more vulnerable to injury. Running downhill should feel like controlled falling.

Practicing Marathon-Pace Runs

When I was in elementary school, I acted in a couple of plays. That's the extent of my acting career. Even though one of my roles was a tree, the teachers knew that we had to rehearse our lines and actions so we didn't make fools of ourselves (and of them) in front of the parents. So we rehearsed over and over again until we felt comfortable (or until we ran out of time before the play began). The marathon is no different.

Doing some of your miles each week at your projected marathon pace helps you practice and ingrain the pace so that on race day, you're familiar and comfortable with it. The more you practice running at marathon pace, the better you'll be at holding the pace in the marathon. Running at marathon pace also builds confidence. Knowing you can hold your marathon pace for 16 miles in training gives you a ton of confidence for race day.

Because marathon-pace runs qualify as easy running (after all, they represent the pace you can hold for a few hours), they don't take too much out of you until they become long. But when they do become long (10 miles or longer), you have to treat them as harder workouts and take a recovery day the next day.

In the following sections, I show you how to calculate your marathon pace and provide tips for working out at marathon pace.

Determining your correct marathon pace

I know a lot of runners who say they want to run a specific time for the marathon despite not having the skills or the training to run it. You can't just decide you want to run a three-hour marathon or qualify for the Boston Marathon unless that's realistic based on your current fitness, the times you've run in the past, and the aggressiveness of your training.

You can't fake a marathon. The sad truth is that most runners cross the marathon finish line in a time that's slower than what they hoped for. That happens for many reasons, but one of them is because runners often choose a time that they *want* to run, not a time that they *can* run. You have to be honest with yourself.

For most average runners, marathon pace is only a little faster than the pace of regular easy runs, if any faster at all. If you're a beginning runner who hasn't run a marathon before, figuring out the pace you can sustain for a marathon can be difficult, but it's likely very close to the pace of your easy runs. Remember, marathon pace is the pace you can hold for a *few hours,* so it's unlikely you run slower than that pace for an hour run on Tuesday. The better runner you are, the greater the difference between your easy running pace (the pace you run for your regular runs when you're not pushing yourself) and your marathon pace.

To estimate your marathon pace, follow these guidelines:

- ✔ Beginning runners (>4:30 marathon):
  - 0 to 30 seconds per mile faster than easy running pace
  - 70 to 75 percent of max heart rate (you can use a heart rate monitor to estimate this number or do the max heart rate test I give you in Chapter 7)
- ✔ Recreational (intermediate) runners (3:30 to 4:30 marathon):
  - 30 seconds to 1 minute per mile faster than easy running pace
  - 75 to 80 percent of max heart rate

✔ Competitive and highly trained runners (2:30 to 3:30 marathon):

- 1 to 1½ minutes per mile faster than easy running pace

- 80 to 85 percent of max heart rate

- 15 to 45 seconds per mile slower than half-marathon pace

Running marathon pace workouts

One of the best ways to do marathon-pace runs is to run them as part of a longer race. Find a half-marathon that you can run at marathon pace or a full marathon that you can run part of at marathon pace (plan this ahead and have someone pick you up at a predetermined place on the course). You get accurately marked miles and aid stations on the course, so you can practice the hydration and fueling strategies that you'll use in the marathon (see Chapter 16 for details). Use these runs as your dress rehearsal. (I include races in each of the training plans in Chapters 8, 9, and 10.)

You have many ways to do marathon-pace runs. Here are a few:

✔ 10 miles easy plus 5 miles at marathon pace

✔ 2 miles easy, 10 miles at marathon pace, and 2 more miles easy

✔ A half-marathon (13.1 miles) at marathon pace

✔ 2 miles easy plus 13 to 16 miles at marathon pace, starting at the slower end of the pace range listed in the preceding section and progressing toward the faster end every few miles, until you're running at the fastest end of the pace range for the last few miles

These workouts go from easier to harder, so start with the first one and progress to the last one.

In these workouts, as in the marathon itself, try to control the pace so that it fluctuates very little. The most efficient way to run the marathon is with a steady, even pace throughout. These marathon-pace runs are a great chance to practice running at an even pace.

Improving Your Max Aerobic Pace with Tempo Training

Improving your max aerobic pace improves your ability to endure — to hold a faster pace for a longer time. Whether you're training for your first marathon or your 50th, improving your max aerobic pace makes you fitter and faster.

When you exceed your max aerobic pace, the demand for oxygen from your muscles is greater than its supply from your cardiovascular system. Thus, your muscles begin to rely more on *anaerobic glycolysis* — the breakdown of glucose (sugar) without oxygen — and along with this process comes the accumulation of lactate in the muscles and blood. The technical term for your max aerobic pace is the *lactate threshold* (also known as *acidosis threshold,* or AT), an important physiological marker that indicates the pace at which your muscles begin to rely on *anaerobic metabolism* — the production of energy without oxygen — which causes a drop in your muscles' pH, a condition called *acidosis.* Acidosis negatively affects how your muscles contract and is a major reason why you fatigue and why your pace slows down.

The lactate threshold is so-named because scientists measure the amount of lactate in the blood. I coined the term *acidosis threshold* because it's the acidosis rather than the lactate that contributes to fatigue.

Your AT signifies the transition between running that's almost purely aerobic and running that includes significant anaerobic metabolism. (All running speeds have an anaerobic contribution, although when you run slower than your AT pace, that contribution is negligible.) Therefore, your AT represents the fastest speed that you can sustain aerobically — your max aerobic pace. It's a great physiological predictor of marathon performance.

Imagine running with a faster-running friend at an 8-minute-mile pace. You're huffing and puffing to keep up, feeling out of breath and wondering when the torture is going to stop. Your friend is moving along comfortably, even having a conversation with you as he runs (don't you hate people like that?).

Now imagine six months later, you go for another run with your friend and you're able to keep up with him at that 8-minute-mile pace. Your breathing is much more controlled and you can contribute to the conversation instead of just listening to him speak. That's what training your AT does — it increases your max aerobic pace, which enables you to run faster before you begin to feel and show signs of fatigue. Think of it as taking what was once an anaerobic pace and making it high aerobic.

The best way to improve your max aerobic pace and thus your aerobic endurance is with runs at a specific pace or tempo that corresponds to your acidosis threshold. The following sections help you figure out your tempo pace and provide different tempo workouts.

Getting some upfront guidance

As you progress with your tempo workouts, increase your training load by increasing how much you run at tempo pace in a single workout or by adding a second tempo workout each week. Although you may be tempted to try to beat your time from last week in the same workout, you improve your max aerobic pace by progressively increasing the amount of training you do at tempo pace, not by trying to force the pace to get faster by running faster workouts.

Think of your acidosis threshold as the ceiling of steady-state aerobic running; the more you keep running at the ceiling, the more likely you are to make physiological adaptations that raise that ceiling. Increase the pace of the workouts only when

- ✔ You run your races faster than usual, which shows your fitness level is higher.

- ✔ Your heart rate is lower than it usually is when you run at your tempo pace, which indicates your fitness is improving.

- ✔ Your tempo pace begins to feel much easier than it used to.

Tempo running is hard but controlled aerobic running. The length of the workouts, rather than the pace, is what fatigues you and prepares you for the marathon. So don't push the pace. Run at your correct tempo pace and try holding that pace for longer periods of time.

Determining your correct tempo pace

Tempo runs are runs that you do at AT pace. Tempo pace, AT pace, and max aerobic pace all refer to the same pace. A tempo run should be a lot faster than your normal easy running pace and a bit faster than your marathon pace, but not so fast that you can't keep going. It should feel comfortably hard. I've noticed that tempo runs are the most difficult type of workout for most runners to run at the correct pace — especially those who are young or inexperienced with these workouts — because they require you to hold back a bit and not push the pace. That comfortably hard feeling requires practice to attain and hold.

For beginner and recreational/intermediate runners, tempo pace is

- ✔ About 10 to 15 seconds per mile slower than 5K race pace

- ✔ Equal or very close to 10K race pace (if you're slower than about 53:00 for 10K, your tempo pace will be slightly *faster* than 10K race pace)

> ✔ 80 to 85 percent of max heart rate (you can use a heart rate monitor to estimate this number or use the max heart rate test I give you in Chapter 7)

Tempo pace for competitive and highly trained runners is

> ✔ About 25 to 30 seconds per mile slower than 5K race pace
>
> ✔ About 15 to 20 seconds per mile slower than 10K race pace
>
> ✔ 85 to 90 percent of max heart rate

If you're still unsure at what pace to run your tempo workouts, don't sweat (pun intended) — I've taken the liberty of using the preceding pacing guidelines and developed a table of tempo training paces based on your 5K and 10K times (Table 5-1). Simply find your 5K or 10K race time from the table and find your corresponding tempo pace. If you don't have a recent 5K or 10K race for reference, use a combination of effort (comfortably hard) and heart rate to run the right pace.

Table 5-1	**Tempo Workout Paces**	
5K	**10K**	**Tempo Pace (Pace per Mile)**
30:00	62:03	9:50–9:55
29:40	61:24	9:44–9:49
29:20	60:43	9:37–9:42
29:00	60:04	9:31–9:36
28:40	59:23	9:25–9:30
28:20	58:44	9:19–9:24
28:00	58:03	9:12–9:17
27:40	57:14	9:07–9:12
27:20	56:37	9:01–9:06
27:00	55:54	8:55–9:00
26:40	55:17	8:49–8:54
26:20	54:37	8:42–8:47
26:00	53:57	8:37–8:42
25:40	53:11	8:30–8:35

(continued)

Table 5-1 *(continued)*

5K	10K	*Tempo Pace (Pace per Mile)*
25:20	52:31	8:24–8:29
25:00	51:51	8:18–8:23
24:40	51:09	8:12–8:17
24:20	50:25	8:05–8:10
24:00	49:48	8:00–8:05
23:40	49:05	7:54–7:59
23:20	48:25	7:47–7:52
23:00	47:45	7:42–7:47
22:40	47:05	7:35–7:40
22:20	46:25	7:29–7:33
22:00	45:45	7:23–7:28
21:40	44:57	7:17–7:22
21:20	44:13	7:10–7:15
21:00	43:36	7:05–7:10
20:40	42:59	6:58–7:03
20:20	42:19	6:52–6:57
20:00	41:39	6:46–6:51
19:40	40:52	6:40–6:45
19:20	40:13	6:34–6:39
19:00	39:33	6:28–6:33
18:40	38:51	6:22–6:27
18:20	38:20	6:15–6:20
18:00	37:30	6:10–6:15
17:40	36:53	6:03–6:08
17:20	36:12	5:57–6:02
17:00	35:33	5:52–5:57

5K	10K	Tempo Pace (Pace per Mile)
16:40	34:52	5:45–5:50
16:20	34:13	5:39–5:44
16:00	33:28	5:33–5:38
15:40	32:51	5:27–5:32
15:20	32:08	5:20–5:25
15:00	31:31	5:15–5:20
14:40	30:52	5:08–5:13
14:20	30:10	5:02–5:07
14:00	29:33	4:55–5:00

Running tempo workouts

Each of the following tempo workouts gives you something different, and each is designed to get you to your acidosis threshold.
They're all very rhythmic. You can do these workouts almost
anywhere, but your best bet is to do them on a track, a measured
bike path, or some other flat ground, where you know the distance.
After you've run a few weeks of easy mileage, add one tempo workout each week. (Check out Chapters 8, 9, and 10 for specific training plans that feature tempo workouts.)

Tempo run

Run 2 to 6 miles (from 15 to 20 minutes to about 40 to 45 minutes)
continuously at tempo pace. This is the most basic of tempo workouts, but it's very effective for improving your acidosis threshold.

Keep your pace as steady as possible during this workout, with
little to no fluctuation. The point is to reach your AT and then hold
it there for the workout's duration.

Long tempo run

Run 6 to 10 miles (45 to 60 minutes) at 10 to 20 seconds per mile
slower than tempo pace. This is a continuous run that's a bit longer
than the tempo run at slightly slower than tempo pace. When preparing for a marathon, you often benefit from running a bit slower
than tempo pace to accommodate a longer distance, which comes
with the psychological demand of holding a comfortably hard pace
for an extended time. This run, while challenging, really prepares
you for the marathon, so bring your A game to this workout.

Tempo intervals

Here are two ways to do tempo interval workouts:

- ✔ Eight reps of 800 meters (½ mile) to 1,200 meters (¾ mile) at tempo pace with a 1-minute rest between reps

- ✔ Three to five reps of 1 mile at tempo pace with a 1-minute rest between reps

These workouts break up the continuous tempo run into short runs at tempo pace with short rest intervals. This makes the tempo run both physically and psychologically easier and increases the distance you can run at tempo pace in a single workout. The second workout is more difficult than the first because the work periods are longer (1 mile versus ½ mile to ¾ mile), so try the first workout first.

Although you may be tempted to run faster when the work periods are shorter, the purpose of this workout is the same as that of the continuous tempo runs in the preceding sections — to increase your acidosis threshold. Therefore, make sure you don't run any faster when you do tempo intervals than when you do tempo runs. Run at your correct tempo pace, and run each repetition at exactly the same pace.

Tempo+ intervals

Here are two ways to do tempo+ interval workouts:

- ✔ Five reps of 800 meters (½ mile) at 5 to 10 seconds per mile faster than tempo pace, with 45 seconds rest between reps

- ✔ Two sets of three to four reps of 800 meters (½ mile) to 1,000 meters at 5 to 10 seconds per mile faster than tempo pace, with 45 seconds rest between reps and 2 minutes rest between sets

This version of tempo intervals, which is geared toward intermediate and advanced runners, is slightly faster than tempo pace (hence the plus sign) with very short rest intervals. Do this workout only after you complete a number of tempo runs and tempo intervals. The second workout is more demanding, so try the first workout first.

Tempo/long, slow distance (LSD) combo run

A twist on the 1970s term *long, slow distance,* which simply refers to running long and slow, this challenging workout, which is geared toward intermediate and advanced runners, is a medium-long distance run (12 to 16 miles) with a portion at tempo pace. Like the long tempo run that I describe earlier, this type of workout prepares you well for the marathon, so make sure you bring your A game.

You can do this workout in any of three ways:

- ✔ 3 to 4 miles at tempo pace, plus 8 miles easy. This workout loads the front end with tempo-paced running.

- ✔ 5 miles easy plus 2 to 3 miles at tempo pace plus 5 miles easy plus 2 to 3 miles at tempo pace. This workout mixes tempo-paced running throughout the whole run.

- ✔ 10 miles easy plus 3 to 4 miles at tempo pace. This workout loads the back end with tempo-paced running, training you to pick up the pace after having run a lot.

Chapter 6

Running Longer, and Longer, and Longer Still

*T*he long run is, unsurprisingly, the key component of marathon training. Of all the different types of workouts you do, the long run most closely simulates the marathon. So runners tend to pay a lot of attention to the long run — and for good reason. Doing so goes a long way toward effecting the physical changes you need to, *ahem,* go the distance.

You can make the most out of long runs with the help of the guidelines in this chapter. Things you need to address include pacing, hydrating, fueling before and during the run, your mental approach, your clothing, and when and how often you take long runs.

 I often get asked if it's okay to break up the long run into two runs on the same day because of lack of time or to reduce fatigue. The short answer is no. Make time in your schedule to always complete your long runs all at once. You benefit from their specific endurance and metabolic aspects only by continuous running.

 Try to do your long runs in the morning, just like the marathon itself. Use the long run as a marathon dress rehearsal. Wear the same shoes, socks, and clothes (yes, even underwear and sports bra) you plan to wear in the race. Practice the same hydrating and fueling strategies, using the same drink and carbohydrate products that you'll use for the race. Practice drinking out of the paper cups they hand out on the racecourse. (It's harder than it looks!)

Becoming tough

One of the runners I used to coach, commenting on why many of the best college distance running teams in the country are in cold climates, used to say that running in cold, icy, snowy weather makes runners tougher. There may be something to that. Distance running is a demanding sport. It's not a sport for high-maintenance or soft people. You have to be willing to be physically uncomfortable. And you have to know how to handle that discomfort. You have to find your inner strength. Marathon running is often used as a metaphor for life because, just as life has moments that are difficult and test your resolve, marathon running (and training) has moments that are difficult and test your resolve. It's a very clear parallel. When the effort becomes uncomfortable, do you back off the pace or stop, or do you push through that discomfort for the self-discovery that lies on the other side? Successful runners have a certain toughness about them, a willingness to be uncomfortable, a willingness to train despite less than ideal climatic conditions. Although that toughness is partially genetic, you can acquire toughness through training, as you become more capable of tolerating high degrees of physical discomfort. Running easy every day is easy, but don't shy away from very long runs and difficult workouts, as they help you develop the toughness you need to run the marathon.

Preparing Yourself to Run Long

Sounds obvious, but the only way to prepare yourself to run long is to run long. Running long gives beginner runners the confidence to complete the marathon. Running long gives advanced runners the chance to get creative and add faster-paced running so they can learn to run hard when fatigued and improve their marathon time. The following sections explain the physical and mental effects of running long and provide some useful preparation tips.

Understanding how running long changes your body and mind

When you run for a long time, a lot of interesting adaptations occur in your body, including

- **Greater fuel storage:** When you run long enough, you deplete (or severely lower) muscle glycogen, your stored form of carbohydrate. Carbohydrate is your muscles' preferred source of fuel, so getting low on glycogen is bad for muscle function. However, your muscles respond rather elegantly to situations that threaten or deplete their supply of fuel: They synthesize and store more glycogen than was previously present, which increases your endurance. Empty a glass and you get a larger refill in its place (much like cocktail parties). The more glycogen you have packed into your muscles, the greater your ability to hold your marathon pace to the finish line.

✔ **Greater psychological strength:** When you run for a long time, your legs aren't the only body parts that get tired. Your mind does, too. This psychological aspect of long runs may be just as important as the physiological reasons for doing them. If the farthest you've ever run is 5 miles, running 10 miles, much less 26.2 miles, may seem overwhelming. But when you add a little stress at a time, you prepare yourself to handle longer and longer runs.

✔ **Greater reliance on fat:** When your muscles run out of carbohydrate, they're forced to rely on fat and so become more effective at using fat for energy. Because the marathon is longer than what you can run on the amount of carbohydrate in your muscles, forcing your muscles to "learn" how to use fat more effectively helps you maintain your pace in the marathon.

✔ **Increased capacity to make more glucose:** Your liver, sensing your low fuel tank, takes things that are not carbohydrate — namely, amino acids and lactate — and converts them into carbohydrate, in the form of glucose, so you have more quick fuel and can sustain your marathon pace. That's called *gluconeogenesis* — literally, the formation of new glucose from non-carbohydrate sources. This process keeps blood glucose levels from dropping too low. Thanks, liver!

✔ **Stronger muscles, bones, tendons, and ligaments:** Running for long periods is tough on your muscles and joints, so they adapt by becoming stronger to handle the stress of pounding the pavement for 26.2 miles.

Adapting physically to long runs

To prevent shocking your legs once a week and to decrease the risk of injury, the long run shouldn't make up more than about a third of your weekly mileage. For example, if you're planning to run longer than 20 miles to prepare for the marathon, ideally, you should run at least 60 miles per week. But unless you're an advanced, competitive runner, you're probably not going to run that much. If you're a beginner or intermediate runner, keeping the long run to no more than a third of your weekly mileage may not be possible if you run low mileage and you run only a few times per week. If your long run is 18 to 22 miles and your peak weekly mileage is 35, you need to be very careful about how you plan the rest of your training so you don't shock your legs each week, running a distance that's much longer than anything else you run during the week. In this case, try running one medium-distance run during the week that's at least half to two-thirds the distance of your long run. (See the later section "Easy long runs" for more information.)

Because most marathons take place on asphalt roads (unless you run a trail marathon), do all your long runs on the road to get your legs used to the pounding of the pavement.

Managing the mental side

Long runs can be pleasurable and invigorating if you're mentally prepared. Try some tricks to get you through long runs:

- ✔ **Divide the long run into sections.** Don't think of your long run as 20 miles. Think of it as 1 mile that you repeat 20 times, or a 5-mile run that you repeat 4 times. Focus only on the current mile.

- ✔ **Listen to music.** Dissociating from the physical work by listening to music makes the time go by much faster. Before you know it, you're at mile 18 of a 20-mile run and you're still waiting for Bruce Springsteen to sing "Born to Run" on your iPod.

- ✔ **Run someplace interesting.** If you run for three hours, choose someplace that captures your interest. Don't run through busy city streets (unless you like that kind of thing). Run on park paths, on country roads, along a canal (all on asphalt), through scenic neighborhoods, or on roads along the ocean. Stay away from power plants, landfills, and the New Jersey Turnpike.

- ✔ **Think positive.** Long runs give you a lot of time to think. When they start to get physically uncomfortable, it's easy to think negatively and doubt whether you can hold the pace. But that kind of thinking isn't going to help you. The things you say to yourself on long runs can be very powerful in determining your success. Any time a negative thought enters your mind during a long run, say, "Stop!" and replace it with a positive thought. Say to yourself, "I'm strong," or, "I'm fast," or, "I can hold this pace." Focus on a specific landmark, like a park or Lincoln Street, and say to yourself, "Just hold the pace until Lincoln Street."

- ✔ **Use other runners.** If you run in a group, the other runners can help you maintain the pace. Don't be afraid or timid to ask them for encouragement if you're not having a good day. Say to yourself, "I can do this. Just stay with Jason for one more mile." If you don't have a group, find a friend to run with.

Energy, endorphins, and flow

Long runs don't just improve your fitness. They can be emotional and spiritual endeavors. Scientists have talked for a long time about *endorphins,* those hormones that the brain releases in response to moderate-intensity exercise. Endorphins are supposed to make you feel euphoric, but I know something more complex than that is happening because in all my years of running, I don't ever recall feeling euphoric. I've never had that "runner's high."

Scientists, and even some runners, often make it seem as if there's an instant in time during the run that this euphoric feeling kicks in. Maybe I'm endorphin-deficient. At times, however, the movements of my run have felt easier and my energy has been higher. I've felt in those moments that my body knows, ahead of my brain, how to perform.

Renowned psychologist Mihaly Csikszentmihalyi calls this experience *flow,* a relaxed state in which you forget about time and feel confident and in control. I can't explain it, but I don't need to. It's as if my body is breaking the first law of thermodynamics and is actually creating energy. I use this energy to formulate ideas that I usually don't have time for. I crystallize my thoughts for the day, sometimes writing some of them in my head. The thoughts don't necessarily have to be profound, although sometimes they are. The energy creates nothing less than a learning experience, a moment during which I can learn about my body and its world in a unique way, a way that's hampered by the rest of my day. I spend the precious time learning about such things as thinking and being, association and solitude, and reality and fiction. What's fiction to everyone else now becomes my reality, just like the characters on the novel's page are real to its author. I'm the author of my body, feeling like I've just created and discovered movement as if for the first time.

The moment of *flow,* like most great moments in life, is fleeting, lasting only a mile or two during my run. Then I return to feeling normal, and the running once again becomes a conscious endeavor. The scientist in me wants to know what causes this feeling, this ease of movement, and why it only happens on certain occasions. Maybe it has something to do with the alignment of the moons. Maybe my Jupiter is not aligned with my Saturn this month. However, the philosopher and the athlete in me don't care at all why this happens and only cares about the moment and the feeling. Maybe someday the science will catch up to the anecdotal evidence. Maybe I have endorphins after all.

Considering the Pace, Time, and Distance of Your Long Runs

Runners ask me all the time at what pace they should do their long runs. The answer depends on your level of experience:

✔ For a beginner or even intermediate runner, the pace of your long runs isn't as important as the time you spend running. So if there's any time when slower is better, the long run is it. Run at a comfortable, conversational pace (about two minutes per mile slower than 5K race pace, or about 70 to 75 percent of max heart rate; see Chapter 3 for more info on this rate). Your breathing, though elevated, should be very comfortable and rhythmic, and you should be able to hold a conversation the entire time, although toward the end of the long run, when it gets very difficult, you may not want to talk to anyone at all!

✔ If you're an advanced runner who wants to improve your marathon time, perhaps even qualify for the Boston Marathon, you need to include some faster-paced running during the long run. Try running a portion of your long run at marathon pace or tempo pace. To find out more about tempo-paced running and for examples of how to add quality to your long runs, see Chapter 5.

In the following sections, I explain how to include easy long runs and long, accelerating runs in your training program.

Easy long runs

Easy long runs are just that — easy. (At least until they get hard, that is.) Their purpose is for all the reasons outlined in the earlier section "Understanding how running long changes your body and mind," all of which prepare you to complete the marathon. Beginners do only this type of long run, but intermediate and advanced runners also need easy long runs in their training programs.

Run from 75 minutes to about 3½ hours over flat or rolling terrain. Do one easy long run each week. The goal is to go longer and longer, so don't worry about your pace; focus on distance. Lengthen your long run by one mile each week for three or four weeks before backing off by a few miles for a recovery week.

If you run more than about 40 miles per week or faster than a roughly 8-minute-mile pace, you can add 2 miles at a time to your long run. If you're a beginner or older runner, you may need to run the same distance for two or three weeks so your legs can fully adapt before increasing the length of the long run.

Because your legs have little concept of distance, only of intensity and time, the amount of time you spend on your feet is actually more important than the number of miles you cover. I recommend capping your long run at about 3½ hours, even if you expect your marathon to take more than four hours, because any run longer than about 3½ hours can make your legs so tired that it can negatively affect your training for the following week.

As the runs get very long, your legs can get pretty trashed, so you have to experiment with how long you can go and still adequately recover for the next week's training. If you want to run longer so you can acquire the confidence that comes from running close to the time you expect to run your marathon, I recommend doing so only every two weeks or so. Give yourself plenty of time to recover from the effort before trying to do other quality workouts.

Most marathon training groups, given their short time frame to train for the marathon, increase the length of the long run every week, which can increase your chance of injury if your bones and tendons aren't strong enough to handle it. Keep adding miles until you reach 21 to 23 (or about 3½ hours, whichever comes first), and do your longest run two to three weeks before the marathon.

During your training program, your weekly long run progression will look something like one of the following plans, depending on your level of running experience. *Note:* The long run lengths in these plans are just examples; for specific training programs for beginner, intermediate, and advanced runners, check out Chapters 8, 9, and 10, respectively.

Beginner

For the beginning runner, the long run progresses slowly for the first three weeks of each four-week cycle, with the same distance repeated twice before increasing the distance and then backing off for one recovery week.

- ✔ **Weeks 1–4:** 5-5-6-4 miles
- ✔ **Weeks 5–8:** 6-7-7-5 miles
- ✔ **Weeks 9–12:** 8-8-9-6 miles

Intermediate

For the intermediate runner, the long run increases by one mile for the first three weeks of each four-week cycle before backing off for a recovery week. The longest run of each cycle repeats in the first week of the next four-week cycle.

- ✔ **Weeks 1–4:** 8-9-10-7 miles
- ✔ **Weeks 5–8:** 10-11-12-8 miles
- ✔ **Weeks 9–12:** 12-13-14-9 miles

The deeper meaning of long runs

You achieve most of the health and physical benefits of running in the first 30 to 60 minutes. It's what comes after that makes running long worth doing.

Physical adaptations aside, running long enough has the power to direct your energy and focus inward. It gives you a chance to think and reflect on things, events, and people in your life. If you're the religious type, you can even have a conversation with God. It can be an emotional experience.

Long runs change how I perceive what I'm doing. Initially, I see and hear everything. My senses are heightened as I follow the white line of the road through neighborhood streets, a nearby park, a bike path. I can hear a single car — even a quiet one — approaching from behind me. I feel the gentle breeze on my face, evaporating my sweat and cooling me. I smell the fresh fabric softener of someone's laundry as I pass by a house. If I run with someone, I listen to my running partner and contribute to the conversation, perhaps even laughing at his dirty jokes. As I begin to fatigue, I go from being aware of my environment and my running partner to being intimately connected to my body. I no longer hear the car approaching or notice the pothole in the street. I feel the effort of each fatiguing muscle, low on fuel, trying to make yet another contraction. I begin to feel alone and vulnerable, each stride drawing me deeper into myself, farther from civilization, closer to discovery. I don't want to talk to anyone.

Through my hours on the road, I become anything or anyone I want. And what I want, more than anything else, is to become a better version of myself. I am a creator, an imaginer, an intellectual, a philosopher, a child, an athlete, an artist. Long runs allow me to become all of these, to become my idealized self. During long runs, I become my own hero. Not a bad way to spend a Sunday morning.

Through attaining a better physical self, I attain a more spiritual self. Running has taught me that. Most people are unaware of this whole life effect of physical training. Running has taught me how to succeed, how to fail, how to win, and how to lose. It has taught me discipline. It has taught me how to strive for the things I want. It has taught me to be patient. It can teach *you* those things, too.

Advanced

For the advanced runner, the long run starts off much longer and increases by one mile for the first three weeks of each four-week cycle before backing off for a recovery week. Each long run is done once before increasing the distance.

- ✔ **Weeks 1–4:** 12-13-14-9 miles
- ✔ **Weeks 5–8:** 15-16-17-11 miles
- ✔ **Weeks 9–12:** 18-19-20-13 miles

If you're an advanced runner who's done a number of marathons before and you have a history of long runs on your legs, going on more long runs isn't going to do much for you; some of your long runs need to be of a higher quality. I recommend alternating a long run (16+ miles) with a medium-long run (12 to 16 miles) that you run a portion of at a faster pace.

Long, accelerating runs

A long, accelerating run is one that starts slow and gets progressively faster every few miles. This run, which is meant for intermediate and advanced runners, prepares your legs to handle fatigue and teaches you how to pick up the pace when you're fatigued.

Run about 75 percent of the distance of your easy long run (8 to 15 miles), with the first quarter at an easy pace, the second quarter at slightly slower than acidosis threshold pace (see Chapter 5 to determine your specific acidosis threshold pace), the third quarter at acidosis threshold pace, and the fourth quarter at faster than acidosis threshold pace. Because this run is pretty demanding, you do it every other week throughout your training program, alternating with the easy long run.

Staying Hydrated and Fueled When Running Long

Keep your runs short and you never have to worry about replenishing fluids and fuel. But the marathon demands quite a bit more: more miles, more time on your feet, more chances of becoming dehydrated or running out of fuel. The following sections explain how to hydrate and fuel your long runs.

Hydrating your long runs

If you run for more than an hour, hydration is very important. Sweating for a three-hour run can easily make you dehydrated. Your ability to run declines with only a 2 to 3 percent loss of body weight from fluid loss. If you lose more than 3 percent of your body weight on your run, you're officially dehydrated, so you need to drink during your long runs to stay as hydrated as you can.

Because you lose body water more quickly than what you can replace by drinking during your run, you can expect to lose some weight after long runs. That's okay — you can get it back by drinking fluids the rest of the day. If you weigh the same after your long run as you did when you started, you're probably drinking too much.

Drink fluid before your long run as well so you're well hydrated before you head out the door. To know how much to drink, follow these guidelines:

- ✔ **Before long runs:** Drink 16 ounces (473 milliliters) two hours before you run.

- ✔ **During long runs:** Drink about 8 ounces (237 milliliters) every 15 to 20 minutes. If you sweat heavily, drink more.

- ✔ **After long runs:** Drink 15 ounces per pound of body weight (or a liter per kilogram) lost during your run.

You probably need to experiment to find out how much fluid you can tolerate without feeling bloated. Drinking fluids with sodium, like sports drinks, stimulates your kidneys to retain water to maintain hydration. Carry fluids on you so you don't have to rely on water fountains; a fuel belt is a great piece of gear to use for this task (see Chapter 2 for more info).

Focusing on fueling

Long runs are your best chance to practice your pre-marathon meal. As your runs get long (more than 15 miles), practice getting up and eating breakfast before you run just as you'll do on marathon race day. Try different foods to see what works and what your stomach can handle.

After you're out the door running, what you eat gets a little trickier. With the popularity of marathon running has also come the popularity of carbohydrate drinks, gels, and bars to replenish blood glucose while running. It seems that everyone now does Saturday or Sunday long runs with a fuel belt around his waist. But do you really need to fuel during your long runs?

Deciding whether to fuel your long runs

Ingesting carbohydrates during long runs maintains your blood glucose level and makes you feel better. However, doing so has the potential to defeat one of the main purposes of the long run, which is to deplete your muscles of carbohydrates. Ingesting carbohydrates during your long runs provides muscles with an accessible fuel, thereby blunting the three adaptations you want to achieve: the depletion and subsequent resynthesis of more glycogen, the muscles' reliance on fat, and the liver's ability to make new glucose (see the earlier section "Understanding how running long changes your body and mind" for details). If you consume carbs during the long run, your liver doesn't have to make new glucose; it can go on vacation, sitting back and watching as glucose enters your blood from what you ingest.

Not consuming carbs during your long runs, though effective for forcing adaptations, isn't for beginner runners or the faint of heart. Running until you've depleted your fuel tank doesn't feel good. Beginner runners just need to get through the long runs, which already provide a stress. If you're a beginner runner and your goal is to finish the marathon without any concern for the time you run it in, feel free to consume carbs during your long runs so you can get through the runs. The carbs can give you both a physical and psychological boost. Ingest simple carbs, preferably glucose, so the sugar can quickly pass through your stomach and get into your small intestine, from where it's absorbed into the blood. Gels, gummy bears, jelly beans, and sports drinks are all good, easily digestible sources of simple carbs.

If you're an intermediate or advanced runner who's run a few marathons before and your goal is to run your next marathon faster, try to go without carbs on some of your long runs so you maximize your physiological adaptations. However, be prepared for the sluggish feeling you're likely to experience toward the end of the run.

Although not fueling your long training runs can help your marathon performance, the marathon itself is another story. In the marathon, you definitely want to consume carbs because maintaining blood glucose levels for as long as you can is important so you can maintain your pace.

Even though you use a different strategy for the marathon than you do for training, you don't ever want to do something in the marathon that you haven't done in training. So don't consume carbohydrates in the marathon if you've never done so during your long training runs. Otherwise, you may end up with some gastrointestinal distress and have to take some trips to the portable toilets along the racecourse! Try to balance the physiological purpose of the long runs with the practical gastrointestinal issue of consuming carbohydrates while running. To attend to both issues, I recommend alternating your long training runs during which you consume and don't consume carbohydrates.

Knowing how much fuel you need

Fueling your long runs is an important part of marathon training, especially if you're a beginner or intermediate runner. Follow these recommendations for how much to fuel before, during, and after your long runs. Advanced runners should follow the advice for before and after long runs but try the strategy of not fueling during the long runs, as I explain in the preceding section.

- ✔ **Before long runs:** Eat 200 to 300 calories 1½ to 2 hours before you run. Your pre-run meal should include carbohydrates and protein, like a bagel with peanut butter. If you run soon after getting out of bed and don't have 2 hours before your run, consume 100 to 200 calories, like a nutrition bar, a banana, and a sports drink.

Stay away from fat and fiber. Fat takes longer to digest, so the carbohydrates and protein in your meal take longer to be absorbed into your blood. Fiber makes you go to the bathroom, which can make your long run very uncomfortable if you have no place to stop.

✔ **During long runs:** Consume 30 to 50 calories of simple carbohydrates every 15 to 20 minutes. Chase the carbs with water so you digest them more quickly.

✔ **After long runs:** To maximize the rate at which you resynthesize and store glycogen, consume about 2 calories of simple carbohydrates like glucose per pound of body weight (or a ½ gram per pound, or a gram per kilogram) within 30 minutes and continue to consume the same number of calories every hour for four to six hours afterward. For a 170-pound male, that means consuming about 340 calories of carbohydrates, which equals about 3½ 8-ounce glasses of chocolate milk (yum!).

Cutting Back on Long Runs before a Race

I once coached a runner who, long before I met him, ran 25 miles a few days before his first marathon so he could feel confident going into the race. Crashing 20 miles into the marathon, he realized that running that long so close to the marathon was a big mistake.

Don't go on a very long run within a couple of weeks of the marathon. All that does is trash your legs for the big day. If you're a beginner, get in at least two long runs of 18 to 20 miles (or about 3½ hours) before the marathon. If you're a more experienced runner who wants to improve your marathon time, try to do as many runs as possible over 20 miles, and make some of your medium-long runs of greater quality by running at a faster pace for a portion of them. In the final two months before your marathon, do four or five long runs, with at least two longer than 20 miles. Although you certainly want to be confident that you can complete the marathon distance, you also need time for your muscles to recover, so do your last long run two to three weeks before the marathon. For more information on tapering before the marathon, stride on over to Chapter 14.

Chapter 7

Getting Faster with Interval Training

. . . .

In This Chapter

▶ Improving aerobic power with interval training

▶ Finding your interval training pace

▶ Doing different interval workouts

▶ Making your interval workouts more challenging

. . . .

Once the training secret of the world's best runners, *interval training* has become the new buzz term among elite and recreational runners alike. Everyone's doing it, from competitive athletes to grandma next door.

During interval workouts, you alternate periods of fast running to get your heart pumping with periods of slow jogging to recover. Interval training is a fast and potent way to get fit because you can accomplish a greater amount of intense work when you intersperse the work with periods of recovery.

For example, you can run $5 \times 1,000$ meters with breaks faster than you can run 5,000 meters continuously; you can run 10×500 meters with breaks faster than you can run $5 \times 1,000$ meters; and you can run 20×250 meters with breaks faster than you can run 10×500 meters. The shorter the distance you run, the faster you can run the total distance of the workout. Sounds obvious, but this simple observation is the basis for interval training and for improving fitness quickly.

This chapter gives you all the details you need to know about interval training — what it is, what it does for you, and how to do the workouts correctly so you can get faster.

Although interval training is a valuable tool that makes you fitter and faster, it can be overused. It causes a lot of fatigue and increases your risk of injury because of its high intensity. Unless you're a very good marathon runner with a solid base of mileage on your legs, use interval training sparingly and only after you spend many weeks running easy miles (see Chapter 5 for details). As a beginning runner, focus on the mileage and on preparing your legs to run long. Intermediate and advanced runners can check out Chapters 9 and 10, respectively, on how to incorporate interval training into specific marathon training plans.

Using Interval Training to Improve Your Aerobic Power

Interval training manipulates four variables:

- Distance (or time) of each work period
- Pace of each work period
- Time of each recovery period
- Number of repetitions

With so many possible combinations of these four variables, you have nearly unlimited potential to vary training sessions. Although runners pay more attention to the pace and distance of each work period, the training stimulus associated with interval training occurs from a combination of work and recovery. That combination is what makes interval training different from continuous running.

In the following sections, I describe the physical effects of interval training on your heart and other muscles, and I show how those effects make you faster.

Understanding the effects on your heart and other muscles

As you train for a marathon, your interval training focuses on your cardiovascular and oxygen-transport systems. (Sprinters and short-distance runners do other kinds of interval training, but that's a whole different book.) One of the best methods to improve your heart's ability to pump blood and oxygen to your muscles is interval training using work periods of three to five minutes and recovery intervals equal to or slightly less than the time of the work periods (I provide specifics on how to do interval training later in this chapter). The work periods are tough — you run at or very close to your maximum heart rate, which also corresponds to your VO_2max, the maximum volume of oxygen your muscles consume per minute. (Chapter 3 has more information on VO_2max and other aspects of running physiology.)

Repeatedly running at your maximum heart rate and cardiac output is threatening to your cardiovascular system. When your body is threatened, it makes adaptations that assuage the threat and ultimately increase its capability. The cardiovascular adaptations associated with interval training, including an enlargement of your left ventricle and a greater maximum stroke volume and cardiac output, increase your aerobic power (VO_2max), giving you greater horsepower for your aerobic engine.

If you're a beginning runner, just running more easy miles per week increases your VO_2max because of all the adaptations that take place in your legs that enable your muscles to use more oxygen. The more trained you are, the more important the intensity of training becomes to improve VO_2max.

 During the recovery interval, your heart rate declines at a proportionally greater rate than the return of blood to the heart. In other words, you have a lot of blood coming back to your heart, but your heart rate drops quickly because you've stopped running fast. The slower heart rate allows more blood to enter the left ventricle and results in a brief increase in your *stroke volume* (the amount of blood your heart pumps with each beat). The increase in stroke volume overloads your heart, making it stronger and enabling your skeletal muscles to be cleared of waste products quickly because of the increased blood flow to your muscles. Because stroke volume peaks during the recovery interval and because interval workouts have many recovery intervals, stroke volume peaks many times, providing a stimulus for improving maximum stroke volume and therefore the capacity of your oxygen-transport system.

Interval training doesn't just train your heart; it also trains your skeletal muscles. Like aerobic training (see Chapter 5), interval training increases the number of mitochondria and enzymes in your muscles, which increases your aerobic capacity. Each work period fatigues you a little more, and repeating the work periods fatigues you many times during a single workout. Interval training improves your muscles' resistance to fatigue by repeatedly exposing them to faster-paced running. As a result, you can sustain a faster pace for a longer period of time, which increases your endurance.

Seeing what happens to the amount of oxygen you consume

Interval workouts are very demanding, but they're the best types of workouts you can do to improve your cardiovascular conditioning. Figure 7-1 shows what happens during an interval workout. During the first hard work period, the volume of oxygen you consume (VO_2) initially rises rapidly and begins to plateau toward the end of the work period. During the recovery period, VO_2 decreases, pretty rapidly at first because you've stopped running hard and, therefore, quickly decreased the demand for oxygen. If the recovery interval is short and active (equal to or less than the time spent running, a 1:≤1 work-to-rest ratio), VO_2 won't decrease all the way back down to what it was when the workout began. That's exactly what you want to happen because the next hard work period then begins with your VO_2 elevated. VO_2 then rises again during the subsequent hard work period, to a point higher than during the first work period.

If planned right, VO_2 reaches VO_2max after a couple of work periods, which is the goal of the workout. These workouts are difficult because your muscles are consuming oxygen as fast as they can and also relying on some anaerobic metabolism to produce energy without oxygen so you can hold the fast pace.

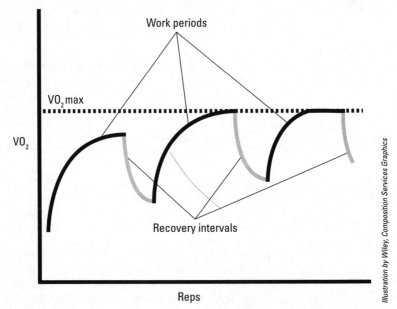

Figure 7-1: The increase in oxygen consumption (VO_2) during an interval workout.

Illustration by Wiley, Composition Services Graphics

A brief history of interval training

Interval training originated in Europe in the 1930s to develop fitness in competitive runners. German coach Woldemar Gerschler and physiologist Hans Reindell of Germany's University of Freiburg studied interval training, focusing on its cardiovascular aspects. They believed that the primary stimulus for cardiovascular improvement occurs during the recovery intervals between work periods rather than during the periods of activity, as the heart rate decreases from an elevated value. Therefore, Gerschler and Reindell placed the emphasis of the workout on the recovery interval, prompting them to call it an *interval workout* or *interval training*. Gerschler and Reindell's original interval training method consisted of running periods ranging from 30 to 70 seconds at an intensity that elevated the heart rate to 170 to 180 beats per minute, followed by sufficient recovery to allow the heart rate to decrease to 120 beats per minute, signifying the readiness to perform the next work period.

Though many athletes used interval training in the first half of the 20th century, the great distance runner Emil Zátopek of Czechoslovakia — the only runner to win the 5,000 meters, 10,000 meters, and marathon in the same Olympics — popularized this method of training in the late 1940s and early 1950s. Also during that time, Hungarian coach Mihály Iglói developed the concept of sets of short distances run quickly to permit a greater total training stimulus. His coaching centered on large amounts of interval training, as he believed that a large amount of speed training also built stamina. This opinion was echoed by Zátopek himself in response to those who told him he was spending too much time training with short distances as if he were a sprinter: "But if I run 100 meters twenty times, that is 2 kilometers and that is no longer a sprint."

It wasn't until the 1960s that famous Swedish physiologist Per-Olaf Åstrand discovered, using a stationary bicycle in a laboratory, what many coaches and runners already knew — that by breaking up a set amount of work into smaller segments, you can perform a greater amount of work at a higher intensity. Runners have been using interval training ever since to get fitter faster.

Determining Your Correct Interval Training Pace

Interval workouts are workouts that you do at VO_2max pace, which is the pace at which you reach your VO_2max — the maximum volume of oxygen your muscles consume per minute. An interval workout should be a lot faster than your acidosis threshold (AT) pace, which is the fastest pace you can sustain aerobically (for more on both VO_2max and acidosis threshold, stride on over to Chapter 3). The pace should feel hard but manageable.

For recreational runners, VO$_2$max pace is

- Between mile and 2-mile (3K) race pace
- About 20 to 25 seconds per mile faster than 5K race pace
- About 40 to 45 seconds per mile faster than 10K race pace
- 95 to 100 percent of max heart rate

VO$_2$max pace for competitive and highly trained runners is

- Equal or very close to 2-mile (3K) race pace
- About 10 to 15 seconds per mile faster than 5K race pace
- About 25 to 30 seconds per mile faster than 10K race pace
- 95 to 100 percent of max heart rate

To find your max heart rate, run one mile (four laps of a standard outdoor track) while wearing a heart rate monitor, starting at a comfortable pace and picking it up each lap until you're running as fast as you can over the final lap. Check your heart rate monitor a few times over the final lap. The highest number you see is your max heart rate.

If you're still unsure at what pace to run your interval workouts, don't sweat (pun intended) — Table 7-1 lists interval training paces based on 5K and 10K times. Simply find your 5K or 10K race time from the table and find your corresponding interval training pace.

Table 7-1		Interval Workout Paces
5K	*10K*	*Interval Training Pace (Pace per Mile)*
30:00	62:03	9:15–9:20
29:40	61:24	9:09–9:14
29:20	60:43	9:02–9:07
29:00	60:04	8:56–9:01
28:40	59:23	8:50–8:55
28:20	58:44	8:44–8:49
28:00	58:03	8:37–8:42
27:40	57:14	8:32–8:37
27:20	56:37	8:26–8:31
27:00	55:54	8:19–8:24
26:40	55:17	8:14–8:19
26:20	54:37	8:07–8:12
26:00	53:57	8:01–8:06

5K	10K	Interval Training Pace (Pace per Mile)
25:40	53:11	7:55–8:00
25:20	52:31	7:49–7:54
25:00	51:51	7:42–7:47
24:40	51:09	7:37–7:42
24:20	50:25	7:30–7:35
24:00	49:48	7:24–7:29
23:40	49:05	7:19–7:24
23:20	48:25	7:12–7:17
23:00	47:45	7:06–7:11
22:40	47:05	7:00–7:05
22:20	46:25	6:54–6:59
22:00	45:45	6:47–6:52
21:40	44:57	6:42–6:47
21:20	44:13	6:35–6:40
21:00	43:36	6:29–6:34
20:40	42:59	6:24–6:29
20:20	42:19	6:17–6:22
20:00	41:39	6:11–6:16
19:40	40:52	6:05–6:10
19:20	40:13	5:59–6:04
19:00	39:33	5:52–5:57
18:40	38:51	5:46–5:51
18:20	38:20	5:39–5:44
18:00	37:30	5:33–5:38
17:40	36:53	5:26–5:31
17:20	36:12	5:20–5:25
17:00	35:33	5:14–5:19
16:40	34:52	5:07–5:12
16:20	34:13	5:01–5:06
16:00	33:28	4:54–4:59
15:40	32:51	4:48–4:53
15:20	32:08	4:41–4:46
15:00	31:31	4:35–4:40
14:40	30:52	4:28–4:33
14:20	30:10	4:22–4:27
14:00	29:33	4:16–4:21

Running Different Interval Workouts

Each of the following interval workouts is designed to get you to your VO_2max. After you run a few weeks of tempo workouts (see Chapter 5), add one interval workout each week. If you're an intermediate or advanced runner and you've been doing two tempo workouts each week, after a few weeks, substitute an interval workout for a tempo workout.

Start with the aerobic power repeats, and as you adapt to the workout, increase the training load by adding more volume (reps or distance of each rep) to the workout. After you do a few aerobic power repeat workouts, incorporate the other types of interval workouts. Exactly which of the following workouts you do each week isn't what's important, although each one gives you a slightly different stimulus. What matters is how you do them and how you progress throughout your training. I've given you different ways of doing interval workouts for variety. Feel free to alternate the different types of interval workouts each week to challenge your body.

Don't run the first work period of your interval workouts so fast that you can't match that pace during the rest of the workout. To improve your VO_2max, running faster than VO_2max pace isn't any better than running at VO_2max pace; doing so just adds more fatigue, causing your next day's run to suffer.

The best place to do these workouts is on a track, where you know the exact distance and can focus on the correct pace. If you don't have access to a track, do the workouts on a bike path or other flat ground and run for time rather than distance.

Aerobic power repeats

An *aerobic power repeat* workout is exactly what it sounds like: You run several work periods of the same distance, with a rest interval between each work period. Here are three ways to do aerobic power repeats:

- Run 800 meters (½ mile) at VO_2max pace four to six times, with a 1:≤1 work-to-rest ratio.

- Run 1,000 meters (⅝ mile) at VO_2max pace three to five times, with a 1:≤1 work-to-rest ratio.

- Run 1,200 meters (¾ mile) at VO_2max pace three to four times, with a 1:≤1 work-to-rest ratio.

Suppose you've run a 5K in 21:42; that's an average pace of 7 minutes per mile. Your VO$_2$max pace is about 6:42 to 6:47 per mile, and the three workouts look like this:

✔ Run 800 meters (½ mile) in 3:17 to 3:20 four to six times, with 2½ to 3 minutes recovery between reps.

✔ Run 1,000 meters (⅝ mile) in 4:07 to 4:10 three to five times, with 3 to 3½ minutes recovery between reps.

✔ Run 1,200 meters (¾ mile) in 4:56 to 5:00 three to four times, with 4 to 4½ minutes recovery between reps.

For these three workouts, the work periods should take 3 to 5 minutes to complete. If you can't complete 1,200 meters in 5 minutes or less when running at VO$_2$max pace, then do 1,000-meter or 800-meter repeats.

When you use shorter work periods, you can accumulate more total distance at VO$_2$max pace in a single workout. However, the greater stress on your cardiovascular system — and therefore the greater training stimulus — occurs with the longer work periods. There's always a trade-off. Which of the preceding workouts you choose depends on how challenging you want the workout to be and how experienced you are with the types of workouts. Each workout is more difficult than the preceding one because the work periods are longer, so try the first workout first before progressing to the second and then the third.

Aerobic power ladders

An *aerobic power ladder* workout mixes the distances (or time) you run in a single workout by increasing the distance (or time) of the work period, like climbing a ladder. To perform this type of workout, run two sets of 800, 1,000, and 1,200 meters at VO$_2$max pace with a 1:≤1 work-to-rest ratio.

Suppose you've run a 10K in 47:05; that's an average pace of 7:35 per mile. Your VO$_2$max pace is about 7:00 to 7:05 per mile, and the workout looks like this:

Run 800, 1,000, and 1,200 meters in 3:30–3:32, 4:22–4:25, and 5:15–5:18, respectively, with 3 to 4 minutes recovery between each rep.

You can also do this workout based on time instead of distance:

✔ Two sets of 3, 3½, and 4 minutes at VO$_2$max pace, with 3 minutes recovery between reps

> ✔ Two sets of 3, 4, and 5 minutes at VO$_2$max pace, with 3 to 4 minutes recovery between reps

Although it's tempting to run faster when the work periods are shorter, run at VO$_2$max pace for all the work periods, regardless of their duration. You increase your VO$_2$max by running *at* VO$_2$max. Running faster than VO$_2$max pace isn't better than running at VO$_2$max pace.

Aerobic power cut-downs

An *aerobic power cut-down* workout mixes the distances (or time) you run in a single workout by decreasing the distance (or time) of the work period. You start off a bit slower than VO$_2$max pace and finish a bit faster than VO$_2$max pace. To perform this type of workout, run one to two sets of 1,600, 1,200, 1,000, 800, and 400 meters, varying your speed throughout. You run at slightly slower than VO$_2$max pace (about 5K race pace) for the 1,600; VO$_2$max pace for the 1,200, 1,000, and 800; and slightly faster than VO$_2$max pace for the 400, all with a 1:≤1 work-to-rest ratio.

The challenge of interval training

The huge physical benefits aside, interval training also gives you a chance to challenge yourself. To put it bluntly, interval training is physically demanding. But something is intriguing about that physical discomfort, about what it allows you to learn about yourself.

I've been doing interval workouts for 28 years, as long as I've been a runner, and I don't plan on ever stopping. I feel that I have to challenge myself on a regular basis to be the runner and the person I want to be. The track has always been a special place for me, and it can be a special place for you, too. It's a place where you're asked to dig deep, to meet the physical challenge head on, to find out who you really are and what you want to become. If going for long runs promotes running within yourself, running on the track promotes running outside of yourself. Your performance on the track tells you the truth, whether or not you want to hear it.

Sigmund Freud once remarked that pure happiness is when you take your foot out from beneath the covers in the middle of winter and then place it back in. To the runner, pure happiness is the exact opposite — taking your foot out from beneath the covers and leaving it out, risking what's uncomfortable. When you do interval workouts, you don't find pure happiness in satisfying comfort; you find it in dealing with discomfort.

Use interval workouts to challenge yourself and to learn how to deal with physical discomfort. It will serve you well, not only in your preparation for a marathon but also in your life.

Suppose you've run a 5K in 20:20; that's an average pace of 6:33 per mile. Your VO_2max pace is about 6:17 to 6:22 per mile, and the workout looks like this:

> Run one to two sets of 1,600, 1,200, 1,000, 800, and 400 meters in 6:33, 4:42–4:46, 3:55–3:58, 3:08–3:11, and 1:31–1:33, respectively, with 3 to 4 minutes recovery between each rep.

You can also do this workout based on time instead of distance: Run one to two sets of 6, 5, 4, 3, and 2 minutes at slightly slower than VO_2max pace (about 5K race pace) for the 6-minute work period, VO_2max pace for the 5-, 4-, and 3-minute work periods, and slightly faster than VO_2max pace for the 2-minute work period, all with 3 to 4 minutes recovery between reps.

Aerobic power pyramids

An *aerobic power pyramid* workout mixes the distances (or time) you run in a single workout, first by increasing and then by decreasing the distance (or time) of the work period. To perform this type of workout, run 800, 1,000, 1,200, 1,000, and 800 meters at VO_2max pace with a 1:≤1 work-to-rest ratio.

Suppose you've run a 5K in 22:20; that's an average pace of 7:12 per mile. Your VO_2max pace is about 6:54 to 6:59 per mile, and the workout looks like this:

> Run one to two sets of 800, 1,000, 1,200, 1,000, and 800 meters in 3:27–3:29, 4:18–4:21, 5:10–5:14, 4:18–4:21, and 3:27–3:29, respectively, with 3 to 4 minutes recovery between each rep.

You can also do this workout based on time instead of distance:

 ✔ 3, 3½, 4, 3½, and 3 minutes at VO_2max pace, with a 1:≤1 work-to-rest ratio

 ✔ 3, 4, 5, 4, and 3 minutes at VO_2max pace, with a 1:≤1 work-to-rest ratio

Progressing with Your Interval Workouts

Think of your VO_2max as the ceiling of how fast your muscles consume oxygen; the more you keep running at the ceiling, the more likely you are to make physiological adaptations that raise that ceiling. Increase the pace of your interval workouts only when

✔ You run your races faster than usual, which shows your fitness level is higher.

✔ Your heart rate is lower than it usually is when you run at your VO_2max pace, which indicates your fitness is improving.

✔ Your VO_2max pace begins to feel much easier than it used to.

You can make all the aerobic power interval workouts that I describe earlier in this chapter — repeats, ladders, cut-downs, and pyramids — more challenging by changing the components. In order of difficulty from hardest to easiest, here's how to make your interval workouts harder:

✔ **Increase the length of each work period.** The most significant way to make an interval workout harder is to increase the amount of time you spend running at VO_2max pace because your body senses how hard and how long it's working.

✔ **Increase the number of repetitions.** Adding more reps increases the total time you spend running at your VO_2max pace.

✔ **Decrease the duration of the recovery intervals.** Shortening how much recovery you take between hard efforts causes you to start each work period more fatigued.

Make the work periods at least 3 minutes because running for shorter than that doesn't give you enough time for your heart rate and VO_2 to reach their maximum. Cap the work periods at 5 minutes because running for longer than that prevents you from repeating the work period more than a couple of times in one workout unless you slow down the pace.

During the recovery intervals of each workout, keep jogging to keep your VO_2 elevated. This helps you reach VO_2max earlier in each work period so that you spend more time running at VO_2max pace. If you can't jog, at least walk fast.

As you progress with your interval workouts, increase your training load by increasing how much you run at VO_2max pace in a single workout or by adding a second interval workout each week. Although you may be tempted to try to beat your time from last week in the same workout, your aerobic power improves by progressively increasing the amount of training you do at VO_2max pace, not by trying to force the pace to get faster by running faster workouts.

Chapter 8

Making a Plan as a Beginner Runner

In This Chapter

▶ Explaining the beginner's marathon training plan

▶ Examining the parts of the workouts

▶ Cycling through your training program

*I*f you're nervous or worried about your first marathon, don't be. I've got you covered. Running your first marathon is all about planning and spending time on your feet, and this chapter has the training plan for you.

Understanding and Using the Beginner's Program

The initial and overall emphasis of the beginner's training program is on improving your aerobic endurance with a steady increase in weekly mileage and long runs. The program, which is made up of six cycles and lasts for 20 weeks (as you discover later in this chapter), slowly increases mileage as you do some quality aerobic running with tempo workouts. I also include races at the end of selected cycles, which you can use to test your progress and to readjust your training paces.

Try to find a half-marathon about four weeks before the marathon (at the end of training cycle 4). Running a half-marathon gives you confidence and a good idea of the pace you can expect to run in the marathon.

Because the beginner program includes four days of running per week, it has inherent flexibility. If your schedule doesn't allow you to run on a specific day, feel free to move runs around to make sure you get in all the runs each week. If your race is on Saturday instead of Sunday, adjust the days of the week accordingly by moving everything up a day.

Although following the plan as closely as you can is best, sometimes, despite your best intentions, life gets in the way and prevents you from running. If you have to miss a run because of work, family commitments, or anything else, don't fret, but don't try to pick up where you left off. For example, if you miss a 12-mile run, don't do the next week's 13-mile run until you complete the 12-mile run. Always keep your training systematic; never make big jumps in mileage, length of long run, or workout difficulty.

Except for long runs, which are supposed to exhaust you, never end a run completely spent. You should always feel in control of the pace and finish the run or tempo workout feeling like you could've run longer.

Breaking Down the Components of the Beginner's Program

To optimize your training so you get the largest return on your investment, stick to the workout descriptions in the following sections. (You can find more detailed descriptions and instructions elsewhere in this book.)

It's not necessary to warm up or stretch before easy runs. The runs are at an easy enough pace that the first few minutes serve as your warm-up. Stretch after your runs. Before more intense workouts like tempo runs and intervals, warm up and do some dynamic stretching. (For specific stretching exercises, stride on over to Chapter 12.) After your workouts, be sure to cool down.

Form drills

Do all the *form drills,* which you use to ingrain proper running mechanics, before the scheduled run for the day so you're fresh and can practice perfect form. For descriptions of the specific form drills — including the high-knee walk, the high-knee skip, the high-knee run, butt kicks, the running leg cycle, and strides — head on over to Chapter 4.

Easy runs

Easy runs make up most of your marathon training. They increase your aerobic fitness by meeting specific weekly mileage totals. They're significantly shorter than your long runs, typically two-thirds of the distance or less.

Unless otherwise noted in the program, do all your runs at an easy, gentle pace. The speed of your easy runs isn't as important as their duration because the goal is to build endurance. The easier you take your runs, the more mileage you can handle each week.

If you're a brand-new runner, you can insert short walking breaks each mile to make the training more manageable and to cover the distance. As you adapt to the training and build your endurance, you'll find that you can run longer before taking a walking break.

If any of the weeks is especially challenging or you feel like the mileage is fatiguing you, repeat a week in the program before moving on to the next week. The program includes recovery weeks every few weeks, but listening to your body is important, so repeat a week if you think it's necessary.

For more details about easy runs, recovery, and building your weekly mileage safely, stride on over to Chapter 5.

Long runs

Run all your long runs slowly enough that you can complete the distance. If you have to stop and walk, then stop and walk. Because long runs are the most beneficial marathon prep for beginning runners, you want to do whatever you have to do to finish, so walk as much as you need to. As the runs get very long (more than 14 or 15 miles), you should feel very tired by the end.

Use the long runs as dress rehearsals for the marathon — wear the same clothes you plan to wear in the marathon, practice consuming carbohydrate gels, and drink the same drinks that they'll have on the marathon race course. (Chapter 2 has details on running gear; Chapter 6 has the scoop on hydrating and fueling.)

For most beginning runners, the long run pace is the same as marathon pace, so the beginner program has no marathon pace runs.

Long runs are scheduled on Sundays, with a rest day the day before and after. If you prefer to do the long run on Saturday, move everything up one day so that the rest days occur on Wednesday, Friday, and Sunday.

Tempo intervals

For *tempo intervals,* you run at *acidosis threshold* (AT) pace for the distance listed, with short rest intervals. The pace should feel comfortably hard and at the upper end of being purely aerobic — a 7 to 8 on a scale of 1 to 10. Run each repetition at exactly the same pace, completing all reps within as close a time to one another as possible. Stand or walk around a bit between each rep. (Find out more about AT pace and tempo intervals in Chapter 5.)

Tempo runs

For *tempo runs,* run continuously at your AT pace for the mileage listed. Run the same pace for tempo runs as for tempo intervals. Keep the pace as steady as possible, with little to no fluctuation. Don't try to run each tempo run faster than the one before it; the goal is to lengthen the amount of time you can hold the pace. (I discuss tempo runs in more detail in Chapter 5.)

Moving through the Beginner's 20-Week Program

The 20-week beginner marathon program outlined in the following sections begins with 15 miles per week and maxes out at 36 miles per week, with four days of running per week. If you're a complete newbie runner who has never run before or you haven't run a step since high school gym class 20 years ago, give yourself more than 20 weeks to prepare. How much time you need to prepare for a marathon depends on many factors, including the point from which you're starting and how many days per week you can devote to training. You may need an entire year to train if you run three days per week and you want to run the whole marathon.

The program is divided into four 4-week cycles and two 2-week cycles, with a seamless transition from one cycle to the next. The final week of each cycle serves as a recovery week, during which you absorb and respond to the training you completed during the preceding weeks. If you need more than 20 weeks to prepare for your marathon, repeat the weeks of each cycle and insert a recovery week every 3 to 5 weeks. For example, do week 1 in the program twice, then do week 2 twice, and then take a recovery week before moving on to week 3.

The recovery weeks are just as important as the harder training weeks, so take them just as seriously. Don't try to run more or faster during the recovery weeks. By the end of the recovery weeks, you should feel physically and mentally ready to take on more work during the next training cycle.

Note: On the rest days in training cycles 1 through 5, you can cross-train with other types of cardiovascular exercise (elliptical, bike, swim, and so on) to improve your cardiovascular fitness (see Chapter 12) or try strength training to build your muscle strength and power (flip to Chapter 11). But eliminate all cross-training activities during the taper (cycle 6).

This program is your blueprint for success. I've laid it out for you in an easy-to-follow, calendar-style format that includes each day's specific training. Feel free to add dates to the calendar, working back from the date of your marathon.

Training cycle 1

The emphasis of this first four-week cycle is on building endurance by increasing your weekly running mileage and your long runs. The mileage increases for the first three weeks before backing off for one recovery week (see Table 8-1). You also improve your running technique with form drills three times per week (see Chapter 4 for an explanation of how to do different form drills).

Table 8-1

Training Cycle 1

Week	Mon.	Tues.	Wed.	Thurs.	Fri.	Sat.	Sun.	Total Miles
1	Rest	Form drills + 2 miles	Form drills + 3 miles	Rest	Form drills + 4 miles	Rest	6 miles	15 miles
2	Rest	Form drills + 2 miles	Form drills + 3 miles	Rest	Form drills + 4 miles	Rest	7 miles	16 miles
3	Rest	Form drills + 3 miles	Form drills + 4 miles	Rest	Form drills + 5 miles	Rest	8 miles	20 miles
4	Rest	Form drills + 2 miles	Form drills + 3 miles	Rest	Form drills + 3 miles	Rest	5 miles	13 miles

Training cycle 2

This four-week cycle continues to build endurance by increasing your weekly running mileage and long runs (see Table 8-2). You also continue the form drills three times per week.

Table 8-2   **Training Cycle 2**

Week	Mon.	Tues.	Wed.	Thurs.	Fri.	Sat.	Sun.	Total Miles
5	Rest	Form drills + 2 miles	Form drills + 4 miles	Rest	Form drills + 5 miles	Rest	9 miles	20 miles
6	Rest	Form drills + 2 miles	Form drills + 4 miles	Rest	Form drills + 5 miles	Rest	10 miles	21 miles
7	Rest	Form drills + 3 miles	Form drills + 5 miles	Rest	Form drills + 6 miles	Rest	11 miles	25 miles
8	Rest	Form drills + 2 miles	Form drills + 3 miles	Rest	Form drills + 4 miles	Rest	7 miles	16 miles

Training cycle 3

This four-week cycle gets you up to 25 to 30 miles per week, and you reach half the marathon distance (13.1 miles) in your long runs (see Table 8-3). You also continue the form drills three times per week to ingrain proper running technique. The cycle ends with a 10K race to test your fitness.

Table 8-3   **Training Cycle 3**

Week	Mon.	Tues.	Wed.	Thurs.	Fri.	Sat.	Sun.	Total Miles
9	Rest	Form drills + 3 miles	Form drills + 4 miles	Rest	Form drills + 6 miles	Rest	12 miles	25 miles
10	Rest	Form drills + 3 miles	Form drills + 4 miles	Rest	Form drills + 6 miles	Rest	13 miles	26 miles
11	Rest	Form drills + 4 miles	Form drills + 5 miles	Rest	Form drills + 7 miles	Rest	14 miles	30 miles
12	Rest	Form drills + 2 miles	Form drills + 4 miles	Rest	Form drills + 5 miles	Rest	1–2 miles warm-up – 10K Race – 1 mile cool-down	19–20 miles

Training cycle 4

This four-week cycle continues to increase mileage slightly with long runs that start to get pretty long (see Table 8-4). It also introduces some quality aerobic running with a tempo workout once per week to increase your acidosis threshold (AT) and improve your ability to hold a faster pace (turn to Chapter 5 for the skinny on AT pace). The cycle ends with a half-marathon to test your fitness and to help you project what pace you can hold for the marathon.

Table 8-4

Training Cycle 4

Week	Mon.	Tues.	Wed.	Thurs.	Fri.	Sat.	Sun.	Total Miles
13	Rest	Form drills + 4 miles	Tempo Intervals – 1 mile warm-up – 4 × 800 meters (½-mile) at AT pace with 1 min. rest between each rep – 1 mile cool-down	Rest	Form drills + 7 miles	Rest	15 miles	30 miles
14	Rest	Form drills + 4 miles	Tempo Intervals – 1 mile warm-up – 5 × 800 meters (½-mile) at AT pace with 1 min. rest between each rep – 1 mile cool-down	Rest	Form drills + 7 miles	Rest	16 miles	32 miles
15	Rest	Form drills + 4 miles	Tempo Intervals – 1 mile warm-up – 6 × 800 meters (½-mile) at AT pace with 1 min. rest between each rep – 1 mile cool-down	Rest	Form drills + 8 miles	Rest	17 miles	34 miles
16	Rest	Form drills + 2 miles	Tempo Intervals – 1 mile warm-up – 4 × 800 meters (½-mile) at AT pace with 1 min. rest between each rep – 1 mile cool-down	Rest	Form drills + 5 miles	Rest	Half-Marathon	24 miles

Training cycle 5

This two-week cycle holds the mileage steady from training cycle 4 but continues to lengthen the long runs (see Table 8-5). This cycle places a greater emphasis on quality aerobic running, with a tempo workout twice per week to increase your acidosis threshold and improve your ability to hold a faster pace.

Table 8-5   **Training Cycle 5**

Week	Mon.	Tues.	Wed.	Thurs.	Fri.	Sat.	Sun.	Total Miles
17	Rest	<u>Tempo Intervals</u> – 1 mile warm-up – 6 × 800 meters (½-mile) at AT pace with 1 min. rest between each rep – 1 mile cool-down	Rest	Form drills + 7.5 miles	<u>Tempo Run</u> – 1 mile warm-up – 1.5 miles at AT pace – 1 mile cool-down	Rest	18 miles	34 miles
18	Rest	<u>Tempo Intervals</u> – 1 mile warm-up – 4 × 1,200 meters (¾-mile) at AT pace with 1 min. rest between each rep – 1 mile cool-down	Rest	Form drills + 7 miles	<u>Tempo Run</u> – 1 mile warm-up – 2 miles at AT pace – 1 mile cool-down	Rest	20 miles	36 miles

Training cycle 6

Your training program finishes with a two-week taper in mileage leading into the marathon (see Table 8-6). Some intensity remains in week 19 with two tempo workouts before the training drops in both mileage and intensity in week 20. (Check out Chapter 14 for more details about tapering.)

Table 8-6		Training Cycle 6						
Week	Mon.	Tues.	Wed.	Thurs.	Fri.	Sat.	Sun.	Total Miles
19	Rest	Tempo Intervals – 1 mile warm-up – 5 × 1,200 meters (¾-mile) at AT pace with 1 min. rest between each rep – 1 mile cool-down	Rest	5 miles	Tempo Run – 1 mile warm-up – 2.5 miles at AT pace – 1 mile cool-down	Rest	10 miles	25 miles
20	Rest	Tempo Intervals – 1 mile warm-up – 4 × 1,200 meters (¾-mile) at AT pace with 1 min. rest between each rep – 1 mile cool-down	Rest	5 miles	3 miles	Rest or 1 to 2 miles very easy	**Marathon — Good Luck!**	13–15 miles (+ marathon)

Chapter 9

Prepping for Your Next Race as an Intermediate Runner

. . . .

In This Chapter

▶ Explaining the intermediate runner's marathon training plan

▶ Combing through the components of your workouts

▶ Following the cycles of your training plan

. . . .

*I*ntermediate runners are like the middle child: experienced enough to handle more work than a beginner, but not experienced enough to handle the responsibility of high-level training. As an intermediate runner, your marathon training program focuses on improving your aerobic capacity with more mileage, quality aerobic workouts, and some emphasis on interval training. If you've run a couple of marathons and a modest amount of mileage, this chapter is for you. Here, I give you a plan to run a better marathon.

Understanding and Using the Intermediate Runner's Program

The emphasis of the intermediate program is on improving your aerobic endurance with a steady increase in weekly mileage and long runs. The 20-week program slowly increases mileage as you include quality aerobic running with tempo workouts (introduced in Chapter 5), followed by more intense interval workouts (see Chapter 7). The program emphasizes tempo training given the importance of your acidosis threshold (AT) for the marathon. (Turn to Chapter 5 for info on AT.) The program finishes with a three-week taper in mileage; the intensity is kept high in week 18 before the program drops in both mileage and intensity in weeks 19 and 20. (Flip to Chapter 14 for info on tapering.)

I also include races at the end of selected cycles, which you can use to test your progress and to readjust your training paces. If your race is on Saturday instead of Sunday, adjust the days of the week accordingly by moving everything up a day.

From a physiological perspective, I spend more time training runners with tempo workouts at AT pace than at marathon pace. Although running at marathon pace can give you confidence, you don't derive much benefit from it other than to practice that pace, because marathon pace doesn't correspond to any physiological variable that influences marathon performance. If you improve your AT speed, your marathon pace will get faster. For even the best marathon runners, AT pace is faster than marathon pace. So I usually come down on the side of targeting the physiology. If you want to practice marathon pace for the confidence it gives you for race day, you can substitute some of the longer tempo runs and tempo/LSD combo runs in the program with marathon pace runs.

Try to find a half-marathon about four weeks before the marathon (at the end of training cycle 4). Running a half-marathon gives you confidence and a good idea of the pace you can expect to run in the marathon.

As you follow the program, make your training *polarized* — that is, run hard on your hard days to provide stress and run easy on your easy days so you can truly recover. Note that hard running doesn't always mean fast running, though. In marathon running, endurance always predominates, so hard running usually means increasing the volume of work you do at a specific pace (or decreasing the recovery interval). When designed this way, with both stress and recovery given equal attention and diligence, your training plan is an elegant system that works.

To meet the purpose of polarized training, the program is flexible. Always do the workouts the way I describe them, but you can make a workout harder by adding more reps or decreasing the recovery intervals. There's no magic in the number of reps listed for each workout (there *is* magic, however, in how the number of reps increase over time). The point of the workouts is to become fatigued. So, for example, if an interval workout of four reps of 1,000 meters at VO_2max pace doesn't sufficiently fatigue you, feel free to add another rep or two. (Chapter 3 has info on VO_2max and other aspects of running physiology.) However, never end a workout completely spent; you should always feel in control of the pace and finish the workout feeling like you could've done another rep. If you add more volume to a workout, cut the mileage from another day so the weekly mileage adheres to what's listed.

If you miss a long run or any other type of workout, don't do the next long run or workout without first completing the long run or workout you missed. Always keep your training systematic; never make big jumps in mileage, length of long run, or workout difficulty.

Breaking Down the Components of the Intermediate Program

To optimize your training so you get the largest return on your investment, follow the workout descriptions in this section. (You can find more detailed descriptions and instructions elsewhere in this book.)

You don't need to warm up or stretch before easy runs. The runs are at an easy enough pace that the first few minutes serve as your warm-up. Stretch after your runs. Before more intense workouts like tempo runs and intervals, warm up and do some dynamic stretching. (For specific stretching exercises, stride on over to Chapter 12.) After your workouts, be sure to cool down.

Easy runs

Easy runs make up most of your marathon training. They increase your aerobic fitness by meeting specific weekly mileage totals. They're significantly shorter than your long runs, typically two-thirds of the distance or less.

Unless otherwise noted in the program, do all your runs at an easy, gentle pace. The speed of your easy runs isn't as important as their duration because the goal is to build endurance. The easier you take your runs, the more mileage you can handle each week.

If any of the weeks is especially challenging or you feel like the mileage is fatiguing you, repeat a week in the program before moving on to the next week. The program includes recovery weeks every few weeks, but listening to your body is important, so repeat a week if you think it's necessary. If you do your long runs with a group, don't feel obligated to always do what the group does. Be smart about your training and do what's right for you.

For more details about easy runs, recovery, and building your weekly mileage safely, flip to Chapter 5.

Strides

Strides are quick, short bursts of running that recruit some of your fast-twitch muscle fibers and prepare you for the program's upcoming, faster-paced interval training. When you run *strides,* you run fast but controlled with good form for 10 to 25 seconds (50 to 150 meters) at about mile race-pace effort (about 35 to 40 seconds per mile faster than your current 5K race pace). Aim for a fast, smooth feeling and focus on correct running form. Don't sprint all-out. Do strides on flat ground with good footing. Take full recovery between each. For more details on running form and strides, stride over (couldn't help that one!) to Chapter 4.

Long runs

Unless otherwise noted in the program, run all your long runs slowly enough that you can complete the distance. As the runs get very long (17 or 18 miles or more), you should feel very tired by the end. Use the long runs as dress rehearsals for the marathon — wear the same clothes you plan to wear in the marathon, practice consuming carbohydrate gels, and drink the same drinks that they'll have on the marathon racecourse. (Chapter 2 has details on running gear; Chapter 6 has more on long runs, hydrating, and fueling.)

Long runs are scheduled on Sundays, with a rest day on Saturday. If you'd rather have a rest day the day after your long run, switch Monday and Saturday so that your rest day is on Monday with a shorter run on Saturday. Or, if you prefer to do the long run on Saturday, switch Saturday and Sunday so that your long run is on Saturday and your rest day is on Sunday. For the weeks during which you have a second formal workout scheduled on Friday (tempo run or interval workout), move that workout to Thursday so you don't have a hard workout the day before the long run.

Tempo intervals

For *tempo intervals,* run at AT pace for the distance listed, with short rest intervals. Run the same pace for tempo intervals as for tempo runs. Run each repetition at exactly the same pace, completing all reps within as close a time to one another as possible. Stand or walk around a bit between each rep.

Tempo runs

For *tempo runs,* run continuously at your AT pace for the mileage listed. The pace should feel comfortably hard and at the upper end of being purely aerobic, a 7 to 8 on a scale of 1 to 10. Keep the pace of tempo runs as steady as possible, with little to no fluctuation.

Don't try to run each tempo run faster than the one before it; the goal is to lengthen the amount of time you can hold the pace. Don't increase the pace of your tempo runs unless your races show that your fitness has reached a higher level or the workouts begin feeling too easy.

For details on all types of tempo workouts and pointers on how to calculate your AT pace, stride on over to Chapter 5.

Tempo+ intervals

For *tempo+ intervals,* run slightly (10 to 15 seconds per mile) faster than AT pace, with very short rest intervals.

Tempo/LSD combo runs

For *tempo/long slow distance (LSD) combo runs* (a marathon prep workout), mix easy running with segments of running at AT pace. If you want to practice running at marathon pace, substitute marathon pace for AT pace.

Aerobic power intervals

For *aerobic power intervals,* run at your VO_2max pace for the distance listed, with recovery intervals equal to or slightly less than the time you spend running. (To learn how to perform these intervals and calculate your VO_2max pace, stride over to Chapter 7.) Jog easily during the recovery intervals.

Long tempo runs

Run slightly (15 to 20 seconds per mile) slower than AT pace for *long tempo runs.* In this program, 7 miles and longer are long tempo runs, while 6 miles and shorter are tempo runs. You may have to adjust that distance based on your individual AT pace. If your tempo runs take longer than about 35 to 40 minutes, do them as long tempo runs at slightly slower than AT pace to accommodate the longer distance.

Moving through the Intermediate 20-Week Program

The 20-week intermediate marathon program outlined in this section begins with 30 miles per week and maxes out at 50 miles per week, with five to six days of running per week. If you haven't run a marathon in a few years or haven't been running at least 25 miles per week, give yourself more than 20 weeks to prepare or start with the beginner's program in Chapter 8.

The program is divided into four 4-week cycles and two 2-week cycles, with a seamless transition from one cycle to the next. The final week of each cycle serves as a recovery week, during which you absorb and respond to the training you completed during the preceding weeks.

The recovery weeks are just as important as the harder training weeks, so take them just as seriously. Don't try to run more or faster during the recovery weeks. By the end of the recovery weeks, you should feel physically and mentally ready to take on more work during the next training cycle.

If you have fewer than 20 weeks to prepare for your marathon, eliminate the third week from the 4-week cycles — don't get rid of the recovery weeks. For example, if you have 18 weeks, eliminate the third week from the first two 4-week cycles. If you have 16 weeks, eliminate the third week from each of the 4-week cycles.

If you need more than 20 weeks to prepare for your marathon, repeat the weeks of each cycle and insert a recovery week every three to five weeks. For example, do week 1 in the program twice, then week 2 twice, and then take a recovery week before moving on to week 3.

This program is your blueprint for success. I've laid it out for you in an easy-to-follow, calendar-style format that includes each day's specific training. Feel free to add dates to the calendar, working back from the date of your marathon.

Training cycle 1

The emphasis of this first four-week cycle is on building endurance by increasing your weekly running mileage and your long runs (see Table 9-1). The weekly mileage and the long runs increase for the first three weeks before backing off for one recovery week (this pattern is repeated in the following cycles). This cycle also introduces some quality aerobic running with a tempo workout once per week to increase your acidosis threshold (AT) and to improve your ability to hold a faster pace. (You alternate between tempo intervals and tempo runs, both of which I discuss in Chapter 5.) I also include strides in this cycle and throughout the program as a sharpening tool to get you ready for the upcoming interval training. Given their different purpose, they're not part of the weekly mileage totals.

Table 9-1   Training Cycle 1

Week	Mon.	Tues.	Wed.	Thurs.	Fri.	Sat.	Sun.	Total Miles
1	3 miles + 4 × 150-meter strides	5 miles	Tempo Intervals – 2 miles warm-up – 3 × 1 mile at AT pace with 1 min. rest between each rep – 1 mile cool-down	Rest	6 miles + 4 × 150-meter strides	Rest	10 miles	30 miles
2	3 miles + 4 × 150-meter strides	5 miles	Tempo Run – 2 miles warm-up – 3 miles at AT pace – 1 mile cool-down	Rest	6 miles + 4 × 150-meter strides	Rest	11 miles	31 miles
3	3 miles + 4 × 150-meter strides	6 miles	Tempo Intervals – 2 miles warm-up – 4 × 1 mile at AT pace with 1 min. rest between each rep – 1 mile cool-down	Rest	7 miles + 4 × 150-meter strides	Rest	12 miles	35 miles
4	2 miles + 4 × 150-meter strides	4 miles	Tempo Run – 2 miles warm-up – 3 miles at AT pace – 1 mile cool-down	Rest	3 miles + 4 × 150-meter strides	Rest	8 miles	23 miles

Training cycle 2

This four-week cycle continues to build endurance by increasing your weekly running mileage through easy runs and long runs (see Table 9-2). This cycle places a greater emphasis on quality aerobic running, with two tempo workouts per week (intervals and a continuous run) to increase your acidosis threshold and to improve your ability to hold a faster pace. Choose a 5K or 10K race at the end of the cycle that you run as an all-out race to test your fitness.

Table 9-2

Training Cycle 2

Week	Mon.	Tues.	Wed.	Thurs.	Fri.	Sat.	Sun.	Total Miles
5	4 miles + 5 × 150-meter strides	Tempo Intervals – 2 miles warm-up – 4 × 1 mile at AT pace with 1 min. rest between each rep – 1 mile cool-down	Rest	5 miles + 5 × 150-meter strides	Tempo Run – 2 miles warm-up – 3 miles at AT pace – 1 mile cool-down	Rest	13 miles	35 miles
6	3 miles + 5 × 150-meter strides	Tempo Intervals – 2 miles warm-up – 5 × 1 mile at AT pace with 1 min. rest between each rep – 1 mile cool-down	Rest	4 miles + 5 × 150-meter strides	Tempo Run – 2 miles warm-up – 4 miles at AT pace – 1 mile cool-down	Rest	14 miles	36 miles

(continued)

Table 9-2 (continued)

Week	Mon.	Tues.	Wed.	Thurs.	Fri.	Sat.	Sun.	Total Miles
7	4 miles + 5 × 150-meter strides	<u>Tempo Intervals</u> – 2 miles warm-up – 6 × 1 mile at AT pace with 1 min. rest between each rep – 1 mile cool-down	Rest	5 miles + 5 × 150-meter strides	<u>Tempo Run</u> – 2 miles warm-up – 4 miles at AT pace – 1 mile cool-down	Rest	15 miles	40 miles
8	4 miles + 6 × 150-meter strides	Rest	<u>Tempo</u> – 2 miles warm-up <u>Intervals</u> – 3 × 1 mile at AT pace with 1 min. rest between each rep – 1 mile cool-down	6 miles	4 miles + 4 × 150-meter strides	Rest	– 1–2 miles warm-up **5K or 10K Race** – 1 mile cool-down	26–29 miles

Training cycle 3

This four-week cycle continues the pattern of the preceding cycle and builds endurance by increasing your weekly running mileage slightly (see Table 9-3). However, the tempo intervals of the preceding cycle have been changed to tempo+ intervals to make the workouts slightly more difficult, and one of the long runs is replaced by a tempo/LSD combo run. The cycle ends with a 10K race that you run as an all-out race to test your fitness.

Table 9-3

Training Cycle 3

Week	Mon.	Tues.	Wed.	Thurs.	Fri.	Sat.	Sun.	Total Miles
9	4 miles + 5 × 150-meter strides	Tempo+ Interval – 2 miles warm-up – 2 sets of 3 × 1,000 meters at 5–10 secs./mile faster than AT pace with 45 secs. rest between reps and 2 min. between sets – 1 mile cool-down	Rest	6 miles + 5 × 150-meter strides	Tempo Run – 2 miles warm-up – 5 miles at AT pace – 1 mile cool-down	Rest	15 miles	40 miles
10	5 miles + 5 × 150-meter strides	Tempo+ Interval – 2 miles warm-up – 2 sets of 3 × 1,000 meters at 5–10 secs./mile faster than AT pace with 45 secs. rest between reps and 2 min. between sets – 1 mile cool-down	Rest	7 miles + 5 × 150-meter strides	Tempo Run – 2 miles warm-up – 5 miles at AT pace – 1 mile cool-down	Rest	Tempo/ LSD Combo 11 miles + 2 miles at AT pace	40 miles

Week	Mon.	Tues.	Wed.	Thurs.	Fri.	Sat.	Sun.	Total Miles
11	5 miles + 5 × 150-meter strides	<u>Tempo+ Interval</u> – 2 miles warm-up – 2 sets of 4 × 1,000 meters at 5–10 secs./mile faster than AT pace with 45 secs. rest between reps and 2 min. between sets – 1 mile cool-down	Rest	7 miles + 5 × 150-meter strides	<u>Tempo Run</u> – 2 miles warm-up – 6 miles at AT pace – 1 mile cool-down	Rest	16 miles	45 miles
12	5 miles + 4 × 150-meter strides – 2 miles warm-up – 4 × 1 mile at AT pace with 1 min. rest	Rest	<u>Tempo Intervals</u> – 1 mile cool-down	5 miles + 4 × 150-meter strides	4 miles	Rest	– 1–2 miles warm-up **10K Race** – 1 mile cool-down	30 miles

Training cycle 4

This four-week cycle continues to build endurance by increasing your weekly running mileage (see Table 9-4). The tempo+ intervals of the preceding cycle have been changed to aerobic power intervals to train your VO_2max (see Chapter 7 for details), and the tempo runs are replaced by long tempo runs to train for longer distances and prepare for the marathon. The cycle ends with a half-marathon to test your fitness and to project your marathon pace.

Table 9-4

Training Cycle 4

Week	Mon.	Tues.	Wed.	Thurs.	Fri.	Sat.	Sun.	Total Miles
13	4 miles + 6 × 150-meter strides	Aerobic Power Intervals – 2 miles warm-up – 4 × 800 meters at VO_2max pace with 2:30 recovery between each rep – 1 mile cool-down	6 miles	3 miles + 6 × 150-meter strides	Long Tempo Run – 2 miles warm-up – 7 miles at 15 secs./mile slower than AT pace – 1 mile cool-down	Rest	17 miles	45 miles
14	5 miles + 6 × 150-meter strides	Aerobic Power Intervals – 2 miles warm-up – 5 × 800 meters at VO_2max pace with 2:30 recovery between each rep – 1 mile cool-down	7 miles	3.5 miles + 6 × 150-meter strides	Long Tempo Run – 2 miles warm-up – 7 miles at 15 secs./mile slower than AT pace – 1 mile cool-down	Rest	Tempo/LSD Combo 11 miles + 3 miles at AT pace	45 miles
15	5 miles + 6 × 150-meter strides	Aerobic Power Intervals – 2 miles warm-up – 4 × 1,000 meters at VO_2max pace with 3 min. recovery between each rep – 1 mile cool-down	7 miles	3.5 miles + 6 × 150-meter strides	Long Tempo Run – 2 miles warm-up – 8 miles at 15 secs./mile slower than AT pace – 1 mile cool-down	Rest	18 miles	50 miles

(continued)

Table 9-4 (continued)

Week	Mon.	Tues.	Wed.	Thurs.	Fri.	Sat.	Sun.	Total Miles
16	3 miles +4 × 150-meter strides	Rest	Tempo+ Intervals – 2 miles warm-up – 4 × 1,000 meters at 5–10 secs./mile faster than AT pace with 45 secs. rest between each rep – 1 mile cool-down	5 miles +4 × 150-meter strides	4 miles	Rest	– 1 mile warm-up – 1 mile cool-down	33 miles

Training cycle 5

This two-week cycle holds the mileage steady from the preceding cycle for one week before starting a three-week taper in mileage (see Table 9-5). It also includes a 20-mile run. This cycle emphasizes aerobic power with two interval workouts per week to increase your VO_2max.

Table 9-5

Training Cycle 5

Week	Mon.	Tues.	Wed.	Thurs.	Fri.	Sat.	Sun.	Total Miles
17	4.5 miles + 6 × 150-meter strides	<u>Aerobic Power Intervals</u> – 2 miles warm-up – 4 × 1,000 meters at VO$_2$max pace with 3 min. recovery between each rep – 1 mile cool-down	6 miles	8 miles + 6 × 150-meter strides	<u>Aerobic Power Intervals</u> – 2 miles warm-up – 6 × 800 meters at VO$_2$max pace with 3 min. recovery between each rep – 1 mile cool-down	Rest	20 miles	50 miles
18	3 miles + 6 × 150-meter strides	<u>Aerobic Power Intervals</u> – 2 miles warm-up – 3 × 1,200 meters at VO$_2$max pace with 3 min. recovery between each rep – 1 mile cool-down	Rest	5 miles + 6 × 150-meter strides	<u>Tempo+ Intervals</u> – 2 miles warm-up – 3 × 2,000 meters at 10K race pace with 2:30 recovery between each rep – 1 mile cool-down	Rest	<u>Tempo/ LSD Combo</u> 12 miles + 3 miles at AT pace	35 miles

Training cycle 6

Your training program finishes with a continued taper in mileage leading into the marathon (see Table 9-6). Week 19 includes two workouts at your projected marathon pace, and week 20 includes one brief tempo workout.

Table 9-6

Training Cycle 6

Week	Mon.	Tues.	Wed.	Thurs.	Fri.	Sat.	Sun.	Total Miles
19	3 miles + 6 × 150-meter strides	Rest	1 mile easy + 7 miles at marathon pace	3 miles + 6 × 150-meter strides	6 miles	Rest	5 miles easy + 5 miles at marathon pace	25 miles
20	4 miles + 3 × 150-meter strides	Tempo+ Intervals – 2 miles warm-up – 4 × 1,000 meters at 5–10 secs./mile faster than AT pace with 45 secs. rest between each rep – 1 mile cool-down	Rest	5.5 miles + 3 × 150-meter strides	2 miles	Rest *or* 1–2 miles very easy	**Marathon — Good Luck!**	17–19 miles (+ marathon)

Chapter 10

Pushing Yourself as an Advanced Runner

In This Chapter

▶ Describing the advanced runner's marathon training plan

▶ Putting together the pieces of your workouts

▶ Making your way through the cycles of your training plan

*I*f you're an advanced runner who has been running competitively for years and has finished a number of marathons, your marathon training program is all about pushing the envelope to get faster. To achieve something you've never had, you must do something you've never done. In this chapter, I give you a program to push your limits so you can run your fastest marathon.

Understanding and Using the Advanced Runner's Program

Overall, the mileage in this plan is higher and the workouts are more difficult than those in the intermediate runner's plan in Chapter 9. The program's initial emphasis is on improving aerobic endurance with a steady increase in mileage, long runs, and quality medium-long runs. The 20-week program slowly increases mileage as you include quality aerobic running with tempo workouts (introduced in Chapter 5), followed by more intense interval workouts (introduced in Chapter 7). The program emphasizes tempo training given the importance of your acidosis threshold (AT) for the marathon (see Chapter 5 for more about AT). The program finishes with a three-week taper in mileage; the intensity is kept high in week 18 before the program drops in both mileage and intensity in weeks 19 and 20. (Chapter 14 has full details on tapering.)

From a physiological perspective, I spend more time training runners with tempo workouts at AT pace than at marathon pace. Although running at marathon pace can give you confidence, you don't derive much benefit from it other than to practice that pace, because marathon pace doesn't correspond to any physiological variable that influences marathon performance. If you improve your AT speed, your marathon pace will get faster. For even the best marathon runners, AT pace is faster than marathon pace. So I usually come down on the side of targeting the physiology. If you want to practice marathon pace for the confidence it gives you for race day, you can substitute some of the longer tempo runs and tempo/LSD combo runs in the program with marathon pace runs.

I also include races at the end of selected cycles, which you can use to test your progress and to readjust your training paces. If your race is on Saturday instead of Sunday, adjust the days of the week accordingly by moving everything up a day.

Try to find a half-marathon about four weeks before the marathon (at the end of training cycle 4). Running a half-marathon gives you confidence and a good idea of the pace you can expect to run in the marathon.

As you follow the program, make your training *polarized* — that is, run hard on your hard days to provide stress and run easy on your easy days so you can truly recover. Hard running doesn't always mean fast running, though. In marathon running, endurance always predominates, so hard running usually means increasing the volume of work you do at a specific pace (or decreasing the recovery interval). When designed this way, with both stress and recovery given equal attention and diligence, your training plan is an elegant system that works.

To meet the purpose of polarized training, the program is flexible. Always do the workouts the way I describe them, but you can make a workout harder by adding more reps or decreasing the recovery intervals. There's no magic in the number of reps listed for each workout (there *is* magic, however, in how the number of reps increase over time). The point of the workouts is to become fatigued. So, for example, if an interval workout of four reps of 1,000 meters at VO_2max pace doesn't sufficiently fatigue you, feel free to add another rep or two (see Chapter 7 for more about VO_2max pace). However, never end a workout completely spent; you should always feel in control of the pace and finish the workout feeling like you could've done another rep. If you add more volume to a workout, cut the mileage from another day so the weekly mileage adheres to what's listed.

If you miss a long run or any other type of workout, don't do the next long run or workout without first completing the long run or workout you missed. Always keep your training systematic; never make big jumps in weekly mileage, length of long run, or workout difficulty.

Breaking Down the Components of the Advanced Program

To optimize your training so you get the largest return on your investment, stick to the workout descriptions in this section. (You can find more detailed descriptions and instructions elsewhere in this book.)

You don't need to warm up or stretch before easy runs. The runs are at an easy enough pace that the first few minutes serve as your warm-up. Stretch after your runs. Before more intense workouts like tempo runs and intervals, warm up and do some dynamic stretching. (For specific stretching exercises, stride on over to Chapter 12.) After your workouts, be sure to cool down.

Easy runs

Even as an advanced runner, easy runs make up most of your marathon training. They increase your aerobic fitness by meeting specific weekly mileage totals. They're significantly shorter than your long runs, typically two-thirds of the distance or less.

Unless otherwise noted in the program, do all your runs at an easy, gentle pace. The speed of your easy runs isn't as important as their duration because the goal is to build endurance. The easier you take your runs, the more mileage you can handle each week.

As the mileage gets high, I divide the mileage for some days into two runs. Although you may be tempted to combine the two runs into one run to save time, doing them as two runs is better to decrease the overall training stress. If work or family prevents you from doing two runs in a day, you have two choices: Combine the two runs into one run or don't do one of the runs, which means not hitting the total miles for the week. Listen to your body to determine which option is right for you.

If any of the weeks is especially challenging or you feel like the mileage is fatiguing you, repeat a week in the program before moving on to the next week. The program includes recovery weeks every few weeks, but listening to your body is important, so repeat a week if you think it's necessary.

For more details about easy runs, recovery, and building your weekly mileage safely, turn to Chapter 5.

Strides

Strides are quick, short bursts of running that recruit some of your fast-twitch muscle fibers and prepare you for the program's upcoming, faster-paced interval training. They help maintain your speed so all the slow running doesn't make you a slow runner. When you run *strides,* you run fast but controlled for 10 to 25 seconds (50 to 150 meters) at about mile race-pace effort (about 35 to 40 seconds per mile faster than your current 5K race pace). Aim for a fast, smooth feeling. Do strides on flat ground with good footing. Take full recovery between each. For more details on strides, stride over (couldn't help that one!) to Chapter 4.

Long runs

Unless otherwise noted in the program, run all your long runs slowly enough that you can complete the distance. As the runs get very long (17 or 18 miles or more), you should feel very tired by the end. Use the long runs as dress rehearsals for the marathon — wear the same clothes you plan to wear in the marathon and drink the same drinks that they'll have on the marathon racecourse. (Chapter 2 has more on running gear; Chapter 6 has details on long runs and hydrating.)

As an advanced strategy, try doing some of your long runs without consuming carbohydrates so you deplete your carbohydrate fuel tank and cause your body to make even greater adaptations. However, be sure to consume carbohydrates and protein and rehydrate immediately after your long runs to recover as quickly as possible so you're ready to run the next day. Check out Chapter 6 to find out more about this long run training secret.

Long runs are scheduled on Sundays, with a rest day on Saturday. If you'd rather have a rest day the day after your long run, switch Monday and Saturday so that your rest day is on Monday with a shorter run on Saturday. Or, if you prefer to do the long run on Saturday, switch Saturday and Sunday so that your long run is on Saturday and your rest day is on Sunday. For the weeks during which you have a second formal workout scheduled on Friday (tempo run or interval workout), move that workout to Thursday so you don't have a hard workout the day before the long run.

Tempo intervals

For *tempo intervals,* run at AT pace for the distance listed, with short rest intervals. Run the same pace for tempo intervals as for tempo runs. Run each repetition at exactly the same pace, completing all reps within as close a time to one another as possible. Stand or walk around a bit between each rep.

Tempo runs

For *tempo runs,* run continuously at your AT pace for the mileage listed. The pace should feel comfortably hard and at the upper end of being purely aerobic, a 7 to 8 on a scale of 1 to 10. Keep the pace of tempo runs as steady as possible, with little to no fluctuation.

Don't try to run each tempo run faster than the one before it; the goal is to lengthen the amount of time you can hold the pace. Don't increase the pace of your tempo runs unless your races show that your fitness has reached a higher level or the workouts begin feeling too easy.

Flip to Chapter 5 for details on all types of tempo workouts and pointers on how to calculate your AT pace.

Tempo+ intervals

For *tempo+ intervals,* run slightly (10 to 15 seconds per mile) faster than AT pace, with very short rest intervals.

Tempo/LSD combo runs

A *tempo/long slow distance (LSD) combo run* is a type of marathon prep workout (see Chapter 5); to do it, mix easy running with segments of running at AT pace. If you want to practice running at marathon pace, substitute marathon pace for AT pace.

Aerobic power intervals

For *aerobic power intervals*, run at your VO_2max pace for the distance listed, with recovery intervals equal to or slightly less than the time you spend running. (To check out different kinds of aerobic power intervals and calculate your VO_2max pace, stride over to Chapter 7.) Jog easily during the recovery intervals.

Long tempo runs

Run slightly (15 to 20 seconds per mile) slower than AT pace for *long tempo runs.* In this program, 8 miles and longer are long tempo runs, and 6 miles and shorter are tempo runs. You may have to adjust that distance based on your individual AT pace. If your tempo runs take longer than about 35 to 40 minutes, do them as long tempo runs at slightly slower than AT pace to accommodate the longer distance.

Moving through the Advanced 20-Week Program

The 20-week advanced marathon program outlined in this section begins with 50 miles per week and maxes out at 70 miles per week, with six days of running per week. The program is divided into four 4-week cycles and two 2-week cycles, with a seamless transition from one cycle to the next. The final week of each cycle serves as a recovery week, during which you absorb and respond to the training you completed during the preceding weeks.

The recovery weeks are just as important as the harder training weeks, so take them just as seriously. Don't try to run more or faster during the recovery weeks. By the end of the recovery weeks, you should feel physically and mentally ready to take on more work during the next training cycle.

Because the weekly mileage is high, recovery is very important. So everything else in your life — nutrition, sleep, other physical activity, stress, hydration — must support your ability to recover as quickly as possible so you can handle and thrive off of the training. For more on optimal recovery strategies, flip to Chapter 12.

If you have fewer than 20 weeks to prepare for your marathon, eliminate the third week from the 4-week cycles — don't skip the recovery weeks. For example, if you have only 19 weeks to train, eliminate the third week from the first 4-week cycle. If you have 17 weeks, get rid of the third week from the first three 4-week cycles.

This program is your blueprint for success. I've laid it out for you in an easy-to-follow, calendar-style format that includes each day's specific training. Feel free to add dates to the calendar, working back from the date of your marathon.

Training cycle 1

The emphasis of this first four-week cycle is on building endurance by increasing your weekly running mileage and your long runs (see Table 10-1). The weekly mileage and the long runs increase for the first three weeks before backing off for one recovery week (this pattern is repeated in the following cycles). This cycle also introduces some quality aerobic running with a tempo workout once per week to increase your acidosis threshold (AT) and to improve your ability to hold a faster pace. (These workouts alternate between tempo intervals and tempo runs, both of which I cover in Chapter 5.) I also include strides in this cycle and throughout the program as a sharpening tool to get you ready for the upcoming interval training and maintain your leg speed. Given their different purpose, they're not part of the weekly mileage totals.

Table 10-1 **Training Cycle 1**

Week	Mon.	Tues.	Wed.	Thurs.	Fri.	Sat.	Sun.	Total Miles
1	6 miles + 5 × 150-meter strides	8 miles	Tempo Intervals – 2 miles warm-up – 4 × 1 mile at AT pace with 1 min. rest between each rep – 2 miles cool-down	7 miles + 5 × 150-meter strides	9 miles	Rest	12 miles	50 miles
2	6 miles + 5 × 150-meter strides	8 miles	Tempo Run – 2 miles warm-up – 4 miles at AT pace – 2 miles cool-down	6 miles + 5 × 150-meter strides	9 miles	Rest	13 miles	50 miles
3	7 miles + 5 × 150-meter strides	9 miles	Tempo Intervals – 2 miles warm-up – 5 × 1 mile at AT pace with 1 min. rest between each rep – 2 miles cool-down	7 miles + 5 × 150-meter strides	9 miles	Rest	14 miles	55 miles
4	4 miles + 5 × 150-meter strides	6 miles	Tempo Run – 2 miles warm-up – 3 miles at AT pace – 2 miles cool-down	4 miles + 5 × 150-meter strides	6 miles	Rest	9 miles	36 miles

Training cycle 2

This four-week cycle continues to build endurance by increasing your weekly running mileage through easy runs and long runs (see Table 10-2). This cycle places a greater emphasis on quality aerobic running, with two tempo workouts per week (intervals and a continuous run) to increase your acidosis threshold and to improve your ability to hold a faster pace. Choose a 5K or 10K race at the end of the cycle that you run as an all-out race to test your fitness.

Table 10-2

Training Cycle 2

Week	Mon.	Tues.	Wed.	Thurs.	Fri.	Sat.	Sun.	Total Miles
5	8 miles + 6 × 150-meter strides	<u>Tempo Intervals</u> – 2 miles warm-up – 5 × 1 mile at AT pace with 1 min. rest between each rep – 2 miles cool-down	7 miles + 6 × 150-meter strides	8 miles	<u>Tempo Run</u> – 2 miles warm-up – 4 miles at AT pace – 2 miles cool-down	Rest	15 miles	55 miles
6	7 miles + 6 × 150-meter strides	<u>Tempo Intervals</u> – 2 miles warm-up – 6 × 1 mile at AT pace with 1 min. rest between each rep – 2 miles cool-down	5 miles + 6 × 150-meter strides	8 miles	<u>Tempo Run</u> – 2 miles warm-up – 5 miles at AT pace – 2 miles cool-down	Rest	16 miles	55 miles
7	8 miles + 6 × 150-meter strides	<u>Tempo Intervals</u> – 2 miles warm-up – 7 × 1 mile at AT pace with 1 min. rest between each rep – 2 miles cool-down	6 miles + 6 × 150-meter strides	8 miles	<u>Tempo Run</u> – 2 miles warm-up – 6 miles at AT pace – 2 miles cool-down	Rest	17 miles	60 miles

Week	Mon.	Tues.	Wed.	Thurs.	Fri.	Sat.	Sun.	Total Miles
8	4 miles + 6 × 150-meter strides	6 miles	Tempo Intervals – 2 miles warm-up – 4 × 1 mile at AT pace with 1 min. rest between each rep – 2 miles cool-down	7 miles	5 miles + 4 × 150-meter strides	Rest	– 2 miles warm-up **5K or 10K Race** – 1 mile cool-down	36–39 miles

Training cycle 3

This four-week cycle continues the pattern of the preceding cycle and builds endurance by increasing your weekly running mileage slightly (see Table 10-3). I've broken up some of the daily runs into two runs to lessen the stress. The tempo intervals of the preceding cycle are changed to tempo+ intervals to make the workouts slightly more difficult, and a couple of long runs are replaced with tempo/LSD combo runs. The cycle ends with a 10K race to test your fitness.

Table 10-3 — Training Cycle 3

Week	Mon.	Tues.	Wed.	Thurs.	Fri.	Sat.	Sun.	Total Miles
9	– A.M.: 4 miles – P.M.: 5 miles + 6 × 150-meter strides	Tempo Run – 2 miles warm-up – 6 miles at AT pace – 2 miles cool-down	– A.M.: 4 miles – P.M.: 7 miles	10 miles	7 miles + 6 × 150-meter strides	Rest	Tempo/LSD Combo 2 miles + 2 miles at AT pace + 6 miles + 3 miles at AT pace	60 miles
10	6 miles + 6 × 150-meter strides	Tempo+ Intervals – 2 miles warm-up – 2 sets of 4 × 1,000 meters at 5–10 secs./mile faster than AT pace with 45 secs. rest between reps and 2 min. between sets – 2 miles cool-down	– A.M.: 4 miles – P.M.: 6 miles	7 miles +6 × 150-meter strides	Tempo Run – 2 miles warm-up – 6 miles at AT pace – 2 miles cool-down	Rest	18 miles	60 miles

(continued)

Table 10-3 (continued)

Week	Mon.	Tues.	Wed.	Thurs.	Fri.	Sat.	Sun.	Total Miles
11	– A.M.: 4 miles – P.M.: 6 miles + 6 × 150-meter strides	Tempo+ Intervals – 2 miles warm-up – 2 sets of 4 × 1,000 meters at 5–10 secs./mile faster than AT pace with 45 secs. rest between reps and 2 min. between sets – 2 miles cool-down	– A.M.: 5 miles – P.M.: 7 miles	– A.M.: 5 miles – P.M.: 6 miles + 6 × 150-meter strides	Tempo Run – 2 miles warm-up – 6 miles at AT pace – 2 miles cool-down	Rest	Tempo/LSD Combo 10 miles + 3 miles at AT pace	65 miles
12	5 miles + 4 × 150-meter strides	7 miles	Tempo Intervals – 2 miles warm-up – 4 × 1 mile at AT pace with 1 min. rest between reps – 2 miles cool-down	7 miles + 4 × 150-meter strides	6 miles	Rest	– 2 miles warm-up **10K Race** – 1 mile cool-down	42 miles

Training cycle 4

This four-week cycle continues to build endurance by increasing your weekly running mileage (see Table 10-4). The tempo+ intervals of the preceding cycle are changed to aerobic power intervals to train your VO_2max (see Chapter 7 for details), and the tempo runs are replaced by long tempo runs to train for longer distances and prepare for the marathon. The cycle ends with a half-marathon to test your fitness and to project your marathon pace.

Table 10-4

Training Cycle 4

Week	Mon.	Tues.	Wed.	Thurs.	Fri.	Sat.	Sun.	Total Miles
13	– A.M.: 3.5 miles – P.M.: 5 miles + 6 × 150-meter strides	Aerobic Power Intervals – 2 miles warm-up – 4 × 1,000 meters at VO_2max pace with 2:30 recovery between reps – 2 miles cool-down	– A.M.: 4 miles – P.M.: 6 miles	– A.M.: 4 miles – P.M.: 6 miles + 6 × 150-meter strides	Long Tempo Run – 2 miles warm-up – 8 miles at 15 secs./mile slower than AT pace – 1 mile cool-down	Rest	19 miles	65 miles
14	– A.M.: 5 miles – P.M.: 6 miles + 6 × 150-meter strides	Aerobic Power Intervals – 2 miles warm-up – 5 × 1,000 meters at VO_2max pace with 2:30 recovery between reps – 2 miles cool-down	– A.M.: 5 miles – P.M.: 6 miles	– A.M.: 4 miles – P.M.: 7 miles + 6 × 150-meter strides	Long Tempo Run – 2 miles warm-up – 8 miles at 15 secs./mile slower than AT pace – 1 mile cool-down	Rest	Tempo/LSD Combo 10 miles + 4 miles at AT pace	65 miles

Week	Mon.	Tues.	Wed.	Thurs.	Fri.	Sat.	Sun.	Total Miles
15	– A.M.: 4 miles – P.M.: 6 miles + 6 × 150-meter strides	Aerobic Power Intervals – 2 miles warm-up – 6 × 1,000 meters at VO_2max pace with 3 min. recovery between reps – 2 miles cool-down	– A.M.: 4 miles – P.M.: 6 miles	– A.M.: 4 miles – P.M.: 6 miles + 6 × 150-meter strides	Long Tempo Run – 2 miles warm-up – 9 miles at 15 secs./mile slower than AT pace – 1 mile cool-down	Rest	20 miles	70 miles
16	5 miles + 4 × 150-meter strides	7 miles	Tempo+ Intervals – 2 miles warm-up – 4 × 1,000 meters at 5–10 secs./mile faster than AT pace with 45 secs. rest between each rep – 2 miles cool-down	7 miles + 4 × 150-meter strides	5 miles	Rest	– 1–2 miles warm-up **Half-Marathon** – 1 mile cool-down	46 miles

Training cycle 5

This two-week cycle holds the weekly mileage steady from the preceding cycle for one week before starting a three-week taper in mileage (see Table 10-5). It also includes a 22-mile run. This cycle emphasizes aerobic power with two interval workouts per week to increase your VO_2max.

Table 10-5 — Training Cycle 5

Week	Mon.	Tues.	Wed.	Thurs.	Fri.	Sat.	Sun.	Total Miles
17	– A.M.: 4 miles – P.M.: 5 miles + 6 × 150-meter strides	Aerobic Power Intervals – 2 miles warm-up – 4 × 1,200 meters at VO_2max pace with 3 min. recovery between each rep – 2 miles cool-down	– A.M.: 5 miles – P.M.: 7 miles	– A.M.: 5 miles – P.M.: 7 miles + 6 × 150-meter strides	Aerobic Power Intervals – 2 miles warm-up – 8 × 800 meters at VO_2max pace with 3 min. recovery between each rep – 2 miles cool-down	Rest	22 miles	70 miles
18	6 miles + 6 × 150-meter strides	Aerobic Power Intervals – 2 miles warm-up – 4 × 1,200 meters at VO_2max pace with 3 min. recovery between each rep – 2 miles cool-down	6 miles	7 miles + 6 × 150-meter strides	Tempo+ Intervals – 2 miles warm-up – 4 × 2,000 meters at 10K race pace with 2:30 min. recovery between each rep – 2 miles cool-down	Rest	AT/LSD Combo 9 miles + 4 miles at AT pace + 1 mile faster than AT pace	49 miles

Training cycle 6

Your training program finishes with a continued taper in mileage leading into the marathon (see Table 10-6). Week 19 includes two workouts at your projected marathon pace, and week 20 includes one brief tempo workout.

Table 10-6   **Training Cycle 6**

Week	Mon.	Tues.	Wed.	Thurs.	Fri.	Sat.	Sun.	Total Miles
19	3 miles + 6 × 150-meter strides	5 miles	1 mile easy + 7 miles at marathon pace	3 miles + 6 × 150-meter strides	6 miles	Rest	5 miles easy + 5 miles at marathon pace	35 miles
20	5 miles + 3 × 150-meter strides	Tempo+ Intervals – 2 miles warm-up – 4 × 1,000 meters at 5–10 secs./mile faster than AT pace with 45 secs. rest between each rep – 1 mile cool-down	6.5 miles	4 miles + 3 × 150-meter strides	3 miles	Rest or 1–2 miles very easy	**Marathon— Good Luck!**	24–26 miles (+ marathon)

Part III

Going Above and Beyond to Stay Strong and Healthy

The 5th Wave   By Rich Tennant

In this part...

Although running is the most important part of your marathon training, preparing for a marathon isn't only about running. This part is about everything non-running to keep you strong and healthy — strength training, cross-training, stretching, and recovery. I also give you a detailed guide to common running-related injuries, including the secrets of preventing them!

Chapter 11

Producing Powerful Muscles with Strength Training

. . . .

In This Chapter

▶ Understanding the benefits and limitations of strength training

▶ Conditioning with circuits

▶ Lifting weights to improve your muscle strength

▶ Using plyometrics to increase your muscle power

. . . .

*H*ave you ever walked through a gym and been intimidated by all the dumbbells, barbells, and machines that put you in awkward positions that are best reserved for the bedroom? You're not alone. If you've never lifted weights before, it can be daunting. And when you consider the many different types of exercises, the amount of weight to lift, the number of repetitions and sets, and the amount of rest between sets, you practically need a PhD to understand it all. But don't worry — muscles don't have PhDs and don't even know the difference between a dumbbell and a gallon of milk. They only know how to contract to overcome resistance. Lifting weights in a gym isn't much different from lifting your 4-year-old to reach the monkey bars. It's just a more formal way to reach your specific goals.

At first glance, marathon running doesn't seem to have much to do with lifting weights to get big, strong muscles. Indeed, the best runners in the world are quite small, with slim legs and arms that would make some Hollywood actresses drool. But as I tell the runners I coach, what your muscles look like isn't important; what they do is what matters. And if you train them properly, you can teach your muscles to do some amazing things. Just ask the Kenyan and Ethiopian marathoners with the skinny legs.

As your weekly running mileage and length of your long runs climb, your leg muscles and core strength become more important. Weak muscles lower your chance of withstanding the stress of marathon training. And if you get injured, you'll be watching the marathon from the sidewalk. This chapter shows you how to make your muscles stronger and more powerful without bulking up so you can run better and avoid injuries.

Using Strength Training as a Supplement to Running

When I was in eighth grade, I broke the school record for chin-ups. I still have the certificate of achievement from the school's principal proudly displayed on my wall. I still brag about the accomplishment to others. It doesn't matter that it was so many years ago or that some tough kid has probably come along since to break my record. At the time, I had the strongest biceps and forearms in junior high. I used chin-ups to show off to the girls in class. My mother even bought a chin-up bar and attached it to my bedroom door frame so I could train at home. I did chin-ups every day. What I learned from doing chin-ups is that there's power in strength.

The best way to strength train to become a better runner is ironically similar to what football players do — train with heavy weights and explosive movements to improve muscle *power*. Power is the product of muscle strength and speed. For your muscles to be powerful, they must be strong and they must be fast.

Although strength training should never take the place of running when training for a marathon (and I can't say that strongly enough), developing strong, powerful muscles can help you run better and reduce your risk of injuries. Think of strength training as supplemental exercises that prepare you for more formal running training and help you handle greater training loads. In other words, supplemental training trains you to train.

In the following sections, I describe the advantages of strength training, explain what strength training can't do for you as a marathon runner, and note when you should add strength training to your program.

Assessing the advantages of strength training

Although many people lift weights to improve their physical appearance and self-image, strength training has many functional benefits as well, including

✔ **Increased muscle strength:** Increasing your muscle strength reduces the percentage of your maximal strength required for each muscle contraction when you run, which delays fatigue.

✔ **Increased muscle power:** Because your feet are in contact with the ground for only a fraction of a second with each step, your muscles don't have enough time to generate maximal force; producing as much force as you can against the ground as quickly as possible is far more important. By increasing your muscle power, your muscles become better at producing force quickly, so you have stronger muscle contractions in a shorter time.

✔ **Improved communication between your brain and your muscles:** Strength training does just as much for your brain as it does for your muscles. Lifting weights trains your central nervous system to recruit your muscle fibers quicker. It's like changing from a dial-up modem to broadband for your Internet connection. The faster your brain recruits your muscle fibers, the faster your muscles work and the faster you run.

✔ **Reduced risk of muscle and joint injuries:** Some muscle injuries occur because of an imbalance in strength between opposing muscle groups. For example, you can injure your hamstrings if they're much weaker than your quadriceps. Because muscles stabilize joints, joint injuries can occur if the muscles surrounding them are weak. Increasing the strength of muscles that support your joints can prevent injuries to those joints.

✔ **Improved posture and coordination:** Stronger muscles help you move better and maintain correct running posture when you fatigue, which helps you run better.

✔ **Prevention of loss of muscle tissue that accompanies aging:** One of the defining changes to your body as you age is a loss of muscle mass, which reduces your muscle strength and power. Strength training can prevent that loss of muscle mass and even replace muscle you've already lost so you can regain your strength and power.

✔ **Increased bone density:** Bones become weaker as you age, increasing your risk of *osteoporosis,* a common degenerative bone condition. Strength training has a potent effect on bones, making them denser, which reduces your risk of running-related bone injuries like stress fractures.

✔ **Improved running economy:** *Running economy* is the amount of oxygen you use to maintain a specific submaximal pace and is one of the three major factors that affect your marathon performance. When you lift heavy weights or perform quick, explosive movements, you recruit nearly all your muscle fibers, which trains your central nervous system. As a result, your muscles increase the rate at which they produce force, getting stronger, quicker, and more powerful, without the negative side effect of increasing muscle size. More effective muscle force production translates into better running economy. For more information on running economy, stride over to Chapter 3.

Understanding what strength training can't improve

Although strength training can play a supportive role in increasing muscle strength and power and reducing your risk of injuries (see the preceding section for details), it can't improve the most important factors that enable you to run a marathon, including the following (see Chapter 3 for more info):

- ✔ Your cardiac output, which determines how much blood your heart pumps per minute.

- ✔ The amount of hemoglobin in your blood, which determines how much oxygen is transported in your blood to your muscles.

- ✔ Your muscles' capillary density, which determines how much oxygen is delivered to your muscles.

- ✔ The amount of mitochondria in your muscles, which determines how much oxygen your muscles use to produce energy.

- ✔ Your ability to dissipate heat when running for a long period, which affects cardiovascular function and your ability to maintain your marathon pace.

- ✔ Your muscles' ability to use fat as fuel, which occurs only when you've been running long enough that your muscles start running out of carbohydrates.

Strength training can't improve your aerobic ability, and the marathon is, after all, an aerobic task. So strength training can't directly make you a better marathon runner. The most direct way to become a better runner is to run. Surprise!

Strength training may even hinder you, especially if you do it at the expense of more marathon-specific training. The physiological changes that result from strength and endurance training are contradictory.

✔ For example, when you strength train with heavy weights, you stimulate your muscles to get larger. Larger muscles increase body weight, which reduces your running economy because you need more oxygen to transport a heavier weight. In contrast, endurance training decreases body weight, optimizing your use of oxygen.

✔ Larger muscles also have a smaller density of capillaries and mitochondria, which is detrimental to endurance. As a marathon runner, you want as many capillaries and mitochondria per area of muscle as possible to facilitate the delivery and use of oxygen. Endurance training causes muscles to respond in an opposite way, increasing the number of capillaries and mitochondria in your muscles. You don't want bigger muscles to run a marathon.

Despite its limitations, strength training can help make you stronger and minimize or eliminate any muscle strength imbalances you may have, which helps prevent injuries. You can avoid an increase in muscle size while still getting stronger by lifting very heavy weights only a few times.

Knowing when to try strength training

You have only so much energy and time for training, so you want to get the greatest return on your investment. If you're running 30 miles per week and you have a choice between staying at 30 miles and adding strength training or running 10 more miles per week, the latter strategy has a greater impact on your performance. Most runners, especially beginning and intermediate runners, are better served by improving the cardiovascular and metabolic factors associated with the marathon than by strength training. (Check out Chapter 3 for more info on those cardiovascular and metabolic factors.) Therefore, provided you have enough weeks to train before the marathon to slowly and carefully increase your weekly mileage, running more miles is a better strategy.

Unless you have a documented muscle imbalance that may cause injury if not addressed, you don't *need* to strength train to train for a marathon. If you're training for a short distance race, like a 5K or shorter, strength training is more important because you need more strength and power for short races, which have a large *anaerobic,* or oxygen-independent, component to them. The longer the race, the more *aerobic,* or oxygen-dependent, it is. However, in some cases you can benefit from strength training when training for a marathon, including the following:

✔ **You've already maximized your running training by increasing both mileage and intensity.** If you're an advanced runner already running more than 80 miles per week and including tempo and interval workouts, and you can't do any more — or higher quality — running, you may want to give strength training a try if you still have more time and energy to train.

✔ **You can't handle the physical stress of running more miles and would get injured if you ran more.** If you're running as much as your body can handle without getting injured and still want to do something else to potentially become a better runner, try strength training.

✔ **You're a new runner training for your first marathon.** If you're training for your first marathon only five or six months away, you probably aren't going to be able to increase your running mileage above 30 to 35 miles per week without drastically increasing the risk of injury. In this case, you may benefit from strength training because it can increase your overall fitness without the physical stress of more running.

✔ **You've reached your genetic limit for adaptation to your running training.** Not everyone can keep running more and more miles and keep adapting. Some runners, like Olympians, may continue to adapt with 100 miles per week, while others may stop adapting at 30 miles per week. Your DNA controls how responsive to training you are. If you've tried running more and it hasn't worked for you, strength training can be another option to improve your performance.

Building Muscle Endurance and Strength with Circuits

Before you start lifting heavy weights and training with plyometric movements (I explain plyometrics later in the chapter), both of which can be dangerous given their intensity, you should have an underlying base of muscle strength and conditioning, which you can acquire over a couple of months with lower-intensity strength training. The circuit workouts in the following sections develop total body muscle endurance and strength using your own body weight. (And they're a lot of fun!) I prefer body weight exercises to dumbbells because, as a runner, you want to increase your strength relative to your body weight so you can master the weight of your own body.

Do each circuit a couple of times per week for a month or two before moving on to the heavier weights and plyometric training that I describe later in this chapter. Do the running circuit as a stand-alone workout at a separate time of the day from your easy runs. You can do the core circuit either immediately after your easy runs or at a separate time of the day.

Running circuit

The running circuit mixes periods of fast running with body weight exercises. The running periods should be challenging, but the exact pace isn't that important because this workout is more for general conditioning. You can do the running portions of the circuit on a track and the other exercises on the grass infield or you can do the entire circuit on a grass field in a park. If you live in a cold-weather location where it's snowing, you can do the running segments on a treadmill and the other exercises in the gym. Run through the circuit two to three times a couple of times per week. Do 20 reps of each non-running exercise. Warm up for 10 to 15 minutes with a light jog before the circuit and cool down for about 10 minutes afterward.

400-meter run

Run 400 meters (¼ mile) at about 5K-pace effort. You should be breathing hard but not completely out of breath. If you do the circuit on a grass field in a park rather than on a measured track, run hard for 1 to 2 minutes.

Squat jumps

Squat jumps improve the power of your *quadriceps* (thigh muscles) and *glutes* (butt muscles). To perform a squat jump, follow these steps:

1. **Stand with your hands on your hips and squat down until your thighs are parallel to the ground (see Figure 11-1a).**

2. **Jump straight up as high as you can (see Figure 11-1b).**

3. **Landing with soft knees by bending your legs, squat back down in one smooth motion and immediately jump up again.**

a   b

Photographs by Maurice Roy Photography

Figure 11-1: Explode off the ground with squat jumps.

Crunches

Crunches work your abdominal muscles to create a stronger core.
Follow these steps to perform a crunch:

1. **Lie on your back on the ground, lift your legs, bend your
   knees, cross your feet at the ankles, and place your hands
   across your chest or behind your head (see Figure 11-2a).**

2. **Contract your abs, lifting your shoulder blades and upper
   back off the ground (see Figure 11-2b), and then return to
   the position in Step 1.**

You can add resistance by holding a medicine ball against your
chest or by lying on a decline bench and raising your torso against
gravity.

a

b

Photographs by Maurice Roy Photography

Figure 11-2: Lift your shoulder blades off the ground during crunches.

Push-ups

Push-ups are one of the best upper-body exercises because they involve a lot of muscles, including your *pectorals* (chest muscles), *triceps* (muscles on the back of your upper arm), and *deltoids* (shoulder muscles). Do a push-up safely by following these steps:

1. **Position yourself on the ground with your hands slightly greater than shoulder-width apart, your palms on the ground, your legs lifted off the ground, and your back straight and parallel to the ground (see Figure 11-3a).**

2. **Lower yourself down until your face and chest come close to touching the ground (see Figure 11-3b); keep your elbows close to your body.**

3. **Push yourself back up until your arms are straight.**

a

b

Photographs by Maurice Roy Photography

Figure 11-3: Make sure your chest comes close to the ground for push-ups.

For a greater challenge and to work your abs while doing push-ups, place your hands on a stability ball instead of on the ground.

If you don't have enough upper-body strength for push-ups, you can modify this standard push-up position by placing your knees on the ground, flexed to 90 degrees with your ankles crossed (see Figure 11-4).

400-meter run

Run 400 meters (¼ mile) at about 5K-pace effort. If you do the circuit on a grass field in a park rather than on a measured track, run hard for 1 to 2 minutes.

a

Photographs by Maurice Roy Photography

b

Figure 11-4: Modify push-ups by leaning on your knees.

Split-jump lunges

This exercise increases the power of your thighs and glutes and also trains your balance. Follow these steps to perform a split-jump lunge:

1. **Stand with your feet together and step forward with one leg, bending your front knee until your thigh is almost parallel to the ground, like you're doing a forward lunge (see Figure 11-5a).**

2. **From this forward lunge position, jump up and switch leg position in mid-air (see Figure 11-5b).**

3. **Land with soft knees, lowering back down into a lunge position with the other leg in front (see Figure 11-5c).**

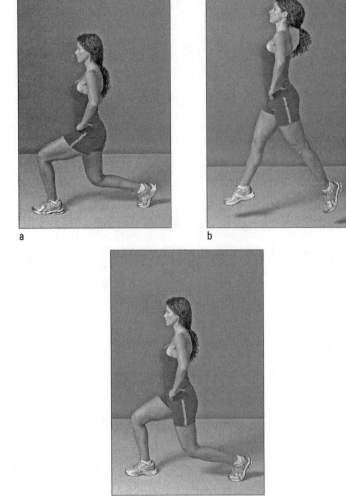

a   b   c

Photographs by Maurice Roy Photography

Figure 11-5: Keep your weight centered over your legs for split-jump lunges.

V-sits

V-sits target your abdominal muscles and *hip flexors* (muscles in front of your hip). Perform a V-sit with these steps:

1. **Sit on the ground with your legs straight and off the ground and your hips flexed at about 45 degrees.**

   Keep your arms to your sides and the palms of your hands on the ground (see Figure 11-6a).

2. **Contract your abs and curl your upper body while simultaneously bringing your knees toward your chest to create a V-shape.**

   Your hips should be the point of the V as you balance on your buttocks in the V-position (see Figure 11-6b). Return to the position in Step 1.

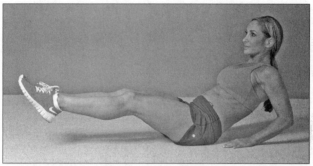

a

b

Photographs by Maurice Roy Photography

Figure 11-6: Move your torso and your legs at the same time for V-sits.

400-meter run

Run 400 meters (¼ mile) at about 5K-pace effort. If you do the circuit on a grass field in a park rather than on a measured track, run hard for 1 to 2 minutes.

Overhead press

The overhead press targets your *deltoids* (shoulder muscles). Do an overhead press by following these steps:

1. **Stand with your feet shoulder-width apart and hold a dumbbell (or the handles of a resistance band) in each hand with your elbows bent and pointing down and your palms facing forward (see Figure 11-7a).**

2. Press the dumbbells (or resistance band handles) up and in together over your head until they meet (see Figure 11-7b).

3. Lower the dumbbells (or resistance band handles), keeping the resistance balanced over your elbows until your elbows are just below shoulder level.

a   b

Photographs by Maurice Roy Photography

Figure 11-7: Keep your arms in line with your shoulders throughout the overhead press.

Twist crunches

This variation of crunches trains your *obliques*, the muscles on the side of your abdomen. Follow these steps:

1. Sit on the ground with your knees bent at about 90 degrees and your feet on the ground.

2. Lean back about 45 degrees and squeeze your abs to keep your back straight.

3. Clasp your hands together out in front of you and twist to your right side (see Figure 11-8a), tapping the ground beside your body.

4. Rotate to your left side (see Figure 11-8b) and tap the ground.

a

b

Photographs by Maurice Roy Photography

Figure 11-8: Work your whole core during twist crunches.

For a greater challenge, hold a medicine ball in your hands and touch the ball to the ground as you twist from side to side (as shown in Figure 11-8).

Traveling push-ups

This exercise takes the classic push-up and makes you work even harder by adding a side movement to it. Follow these steps:

1. **Position yourself on the ground with your hands slightly greater than shoulder-width apart, your palms on the ground, your legs lifted off the ground, and your back straight and parallel to the ground (see Figure 11-9a).**

2. **Lower yourself down until your face and chest come close to touching the ground.**

3. **Push yourself back up until your arms are straight.**

4. **Before repeating another push-up, travel across the ground by moving your hands and legs a few inches to your left side (see Figures 11-9b and 11-9c).**

   After doing a few push-ups moving to the left, change direction.

If you don't have enough upper-body strength for push-ups, you can do this exercise with your knees on the ground.

a

b

c

Photographs by Maurice Roy Photography

Figure 11-9: Keep your abs tight and move side to side with traveling push-ups.

Core circuit

The core circuit improves the strength and endurance of your core muscles — the muscles of your abdomen and lower back. Do the circuit two to three times and do each exercise for 30 seconds, moving from one exercise to the next with no rest in between.

Crunches

Follow these steps to perform crunches (refer to Figure 11-2):

1. **Lie on your back on the ground, lift your legs, bend your knees, cross your feet at the ankles, and place your hands across your chest or behind your head.**

2. **Contract your abs, lifting your shoulder blades and upper back off the ground, and then return to the position in Step 1.**

Push-ups

Follow these steps to perform push-ups (refer to Figure 11-3):

1. **Position yourself on the ground with your hands slightly less than shoulder-width apart, your palms on the ground, your legs lifted off the ground, and your back straight and parallel to the ground.**

2. **Lower yourself down until your face and chest come close to touching the ground; keep your elbows close to your body.**

3. **Push yourself back up until your arms are straight.**

Superman

Pretend to be Superman with these steps (just don't try to fly out of a window):

1. **Lie face down on the ground, with your legs together and straight and your arms straight and extended above your head.**

   Keep your head and neck in a neutral position, looking down at the ground (see Figure 11-10a).

2. **Keeping your torso stationary, lift your right arm and left leg about 5 to 6 inches off the ground (see Figure 11-10b).**

3. **Lower your right arm and left leg while raising your left arm and right leg.**

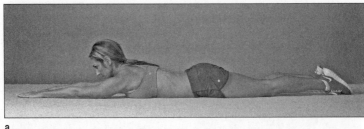

a

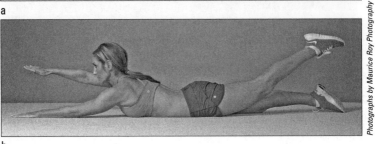

b

Photographs by Maurice Roy Photography

Figure 11-10: Lift your opposing arm and leg during this superman exercise.

Medicine ball crunches

Do a medicine ball crunch by following these steps:

1. **Lie on your back on the ground, bend your knees, and place your feet flat on the ground.**

2. **With your partner standing in front of you, have him throw you a medicine ball in different directions — straight at you, to your left, and to your right (see Figure 11-11a).**

3. **Catch the ball by moving only your torso and arms, do a crunch with the medicine ball by lowering yourself to the ground (see Figure 11-11b), and throw the medicine ball back to your partner while lifting your torso (see Figure 11-11c).**

You can add resistance by increasing the weight of the medicine ball.

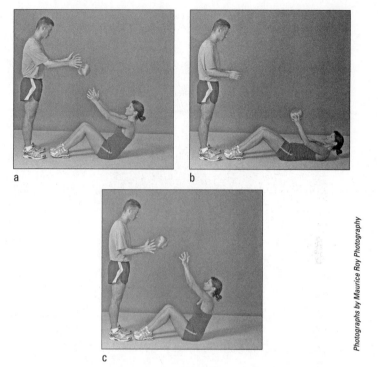

Figure 11-11: Train all your abdominal muscles with medicine ball crunches.

Photographs by Maurice Roy Photography

Side planks

Try a side plank by following these steps:

1. **Lie on your side with your right hand or elbow and fore-arm on the ground (see Figure 11-12a).**

2. **Lift yourself up to form a plank, with your right arm straight (or bent at the elbow) and your left hand on your hip (see Figure 11-12b).**

    Keep your body in a straight line.

3. **Hold the plank position for 30 seconds, and then repeat on the other side.**

V-sits

Perform a V-sit with these steps (refer to Figure 11-6):

1. **Sit on the ground, with your legs straight and off the ground and your hips flexed at about 45 degrees.**

Keep your arms to your sides and the palms of your hands on the ground.

a

b

Figure 11-12: Hold still and contract your abs for side planks.

Photographs by Maurice Roy Photography

2. **Contract your abs and curl your upper body while simultaneously bringing your knees toward your chest to create a V-shape.**

Your hips should be the point of the V as you balance on your buttocks in the V-position. Return to the position in Step 1.

Increasing Muscle Strength with Weights

You should aim any strength training you do to supplement your running at improving muscle strength without increasing muscle size. As I explain earlier in this chapter, adding muscle mass reduces running economy because you have to use more oxygen to transport a heavier body weight. And that's not a good thing for a marathon runner. (Imagine carrying a bowling ball while you run a marathon!)

A clever way to increase your muscle strength without making your muscles bigger is to lift very heavy weights for only a few repetitions. When you do this, you target your central nervous system's ability to recruit muscle fibers rather than add muscle mass. And as a runner, that's exactly what you want.

Given the intensity and stress of this type of strength training, I recommend spending a few weeks preparing your muscles first using circuits (which I describe earlier in this chapter), followed by formal weight training twice per week using lighter weights and more repetitions to give your muscles a chance to adapt. Before the strength-training workout, warm up by doing some light cardio-vascular activity for 5 to 10 minutes, and precede each exercise in the following sections with one or two warm-up sets using a light weight. Then perform two to three sets of 15 to 20 reps at 70 percent of your *1-rep max,* which is the maximum amount of weight you can lift just once (I explain how to figure out this number in the next section). Take 30 to 60 seconds rest between sets.

If you run six days per week, do the strength training workout after an easy run; if you run fewer than six days per week, you can do the workout on a rest day.

After you've completed a few weeks of these muscular endurance workouts, you can start training with heavier weights once or twice per week to increase your muscle strength. Precede the workout with a warm-up as described earlier. For each exercise, do three to four sets of three to five reps at 90 percent of your 1-rep max. Take 3 to 5 minutes rest between sets.

Before you begin: Finding your 1-rep max

Heavy weight training focuses on the strength component of power. For the exercises in the following sections, you need to use equipment in a gym. Testing your 1-rep max can be a little tricky. Unless you have a lot of experience in a gym, you need someone to help you. If you can't test your 1-rep max for each exercise, just choose a weight that fatigues your muscles within the prescribed rep range so that the last one or two reps of each set is very diffi-cult. To train the muscle, you have to fatigue the muscle.

To find your 1-rep max, first warm up with five to ten repetitions using a moderate weight (40 to 60 percent of your perceived maxi-mum). Then do another three to five reps with a slightly greater weight (60 to 80 percent of your perceived maximum). Make a con-servative increase in the amount of weight and try to lift the weight just once. If you successfully lift the weight, rest for 3 to 5 minutes before making another slight increase in weight and trying to lift the weight again. Repeat these steps until you reach a weight that you can't lift. When you reach that weight, decrease the weight slightly (but still more than what you successfully lifted in the prior attempt) and try to lift the weight. The goal is to isolate the exact amount of weight you can lift just once.

Make sure you take enough time between lifts to adequately recover. Because of the strenuous nature of 1-rep max tests, work with a spotter or friend or ask a personal trainer at the gym to help you. Because you have a different 1-rep max for each muscle group, do a 1-rep max test for each of the following exercises.

If you can't do 1-rep max tests, you can estimate your 1-rep max by lifting a submaximal weight until your muscles fatigue. Men should use the following equation:

1-RM = weight lifted in pounds ÷ [1.0278 − (number of reps × 0.0278)]

For this equation, you can use any combination of weight and reps as long as the number of reps to fatigue is ten or fewer.

Women should use the following equation:

1-RM = (0.482 × weight lifted in pounds) + (0.58 × number of reps) − (0.20 × age in years) − 3.41

For this equation, women should lift a weight that's 45 percent of their body weight.

Squats

Squats are one of the best strength training exercises for your lower body. This exercise targets the quadriceps muscles on the front of your thighs and your gluteal muscles. Follow these steps:

1. **With your feet shoulder-width or slightly greater than shoulder-width apart, stand in front of a barbell that's sitting on a rack.**

2. **Place the barbell across the back of your shoulders, below your neck, and grab the barbell from behind with a grip slightly greater than shoulder-width.**

3. **Lift the barbell off the rack so it rests on your shoulders and upper back (see Figure 11-13a).**

4. **Keeping your back straight, bend your knees and squat down until your thighs are parallel to the floor.**

Move your hips back as if you're attempting to sit in a chair (see Figure 11-13b).

a   b

Figure 11-13: Focus on sitting back with your butt during squats.

> 5. **Straighten your legs and stand up to return to the starting position in Step 1.**

Power cleans

This advanced exercise targets most of the muscles of your lower body. Attempt this exercise only after you feel comfortable with the leg press and squats.

Do a power clean by following these steps:

> 1. **Stand with your feet hip- to shoulder-width apart, bend your legs, and grab a barbell with an overhand grip at slightly wider than shoulder width.**
>
> Your thighs should be parallel to the floor, and your shoulders should be square and directly over the bar (see Figure 11-14a).
>
> 2. **To lift the barbell, push with your legs, keeping your back straight.**
>
> When the bar passes your knees, bend your legs again to lower your upper body so your chest passes underneath the bar (see Figure 11-14b).
>
> 3. **Push your legs to a standing position, with the bar resting in front of your shoulders (see Figure 11-14c).**

4. **From the standing position, bend your legs again and drop your arms to lower the bar back to the starting position in Step 1.**

Hamstring curls

Hamstring curls target the muscles of the back of your thighs, which bend your knees after you push off the ground when you run.

Follow these steps to perform hamstring curls:

1. **Lie on your stomach on the bench of a hamstring curl machine, with the pad just below your calves and your hips flat against the bench.**

   Grab the side handles and adjust your position so that your knees are in line with the machine's pivot point (see Figure 11-15a).

2. **Lift the weight by curling your legs toward your butt (see Figure 11-15b).**

   To address any strength imbalances between legs, use one leg at a time.

3. **Lower your legs to the starting position in Step 1.**

If you don't have easy access to a hamstring curl machine, you can lie on your stomach on the floor with a resistance band looped around your ankle and tethered to an immovable object. Curl your left leg toward your butt and lower; repeat with your right leg.

a

b

c

Photographs by Maurice Roy Photography

Figure 11-14: Keep your thighs parallel to each other during power cleans.

a

b

Photographs by Maurice Roy Photography

Figure 11-15: Bring your heels to your butt for hamstring curls.

Calf raises

Calf raises target your calf muscles, which are among the final muscles to contract as you push off the ground when you run. Here's how you do a calf raise (this exercise uses your body weight and doesn't require a 1-rep max test):

1. **Stand with your feet together, with one foot off the ground (see Figure 11-16a).**

   You can lean against a wall for support.

2. **Push against the ground with the ball of your other foot to raise yourself up (see Figure 11-16b).**

To make the exercise harder, hold a dumbbell in each hand or rest a barbell or weighted bar across the back of your shoulders and neck. Use a weight that makes it challenging to complete the desired reps in each set.

You can also do calf raises on the edge of a stair or platform by hanging your heel over the edge (see Figures 11-16c and 11-16d).

Bench press

The bench press is one of the best upper body exercises because it involves many of your upper body muscles, including your pectorals (chest), shoulders, and triceps. Here's how you do a bench press (for safety, ask a trainer or someone in the gym who's working out near you to be a spotter):

1. **Lie on your back on a flat bench, with your feet flat on the floor and your chest directly underneath a barbell on a rack.**

2. **Grip the barbell with an overhand grip and your hands greater than shoulder-width apart (see Figure 11-17a).**

3. **Lift the barbell from the rack and lower the weight to your chest (see Figure 11-17b).**

4. **Push the barbell back up to the starting position until your arms are fully extended.**

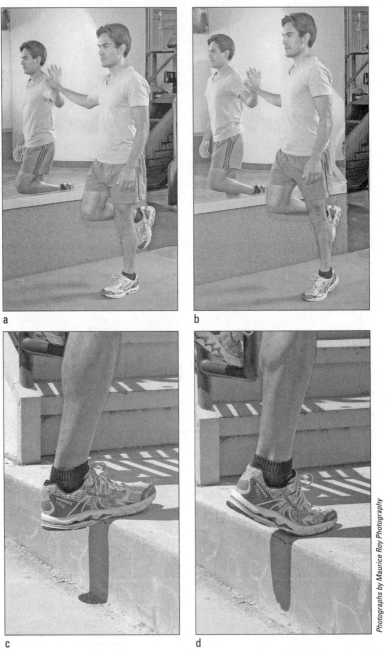

a   b

c   d

Figure 11-16: Push strongly from the ball of your foot to target the calves.

a

b

Photographs by Maurice Roy Photography

Figure 11-17: Touch the barbell to your chest during a bench press.

Cable cross-overs

This exercise targets the back of your shoulders, helping you maintain posture when you run. Check out these steps:

1. With the pulley and handles set down by your feet, stand with your feet shoulder-width apart next to the pulley.

2. Bend down to grab the pulley across your body with an overhand grip, and then stand up while holding the pulley.

   Your hand should be in front of your opposite hip (see Figure 11-18a).

3. Use your upper back muscles to lift your arm up and away from your body until your arm is fully extended (see Figure 11-18b).

4. Lower your arm back down across your body to lower the weight to the starting position in Step 2.

a   b

Photographs by Maurice Roy Photography

Figure 11-18: Keep your arm straight as it moves across your body during cable cross-overs.

Amplifying Muscle Power with Plyometrics

Plyometrics focus on the speed component of power. They include hopping, jumping, and bounding exercises that quickly stretch the muscles before they contract so they contract more forcefully.

Muscles produce more force during the *concentric* (shortening) contraction if the contraction is immediately preceded by an *eccentric* (lengthening) contraction. This happens because muscles store elastic energy during the eccentric contraction, which is then used during the subsequent concentric contraction. Plyometric exercises exploit this elastic property, making the muscles more explosive and powerful.

After you've completed a month or two of the conditioning circuits I describe earlier in this chapter and another month or two of strength training with weights, you can progress to plyometrics. Begin with two sets of ten reps of each exercise in the following sections twice per week, progressing to four sets, with full recovery between sets. Do the plyometrics as a stand-alone workout at a separate time of the day from your easy runs.

Keep these things in mind when doing plyometrics:

✔ Do plyometric exercises on soft surfaces with good footing, such as grass, artificial turf, or a rubber mat. Plyometrics are very stressful on your muscles, bones, and joints, so you don't want to be jumping around on hard surfaces.

✔ Warm up with 10 to 15 minutes of jogging before doing plyometrics. Warming up prepares your muscles and joints for explosive activity. Cool down for another 5 to 10 minutes after doing plyometrics.

✔ Spend as little time on the ground as possible between hops, bounds, and jumps. The quick change in direction between landing and jumping up — and the different muscle contractions associated with those opposing movements — trains your muscles to become more powerful.

✔ Progress from the lower-intensity plyometric exercises (single leg hops) to the moderate-intensity exercises (bleacher hops, bounds, and squat jumps) and finally to the high-intensity exercises (depth jumps and box jumps). Don't attempt the high-intensity exercises until you master the lower- and moderate-intensity exercises.

Single leg hops

The focus of these hops is the ankle joint, with the power coming from your calf muscles. Do three hopping exercises on one leg at a time:

✔ **Hop up and down (see Figures 11-19a and 11-19b)**

✔ **Forward and back (see Figure 11-19c)**

✔ **Side to side (see Figure 11-19d)**

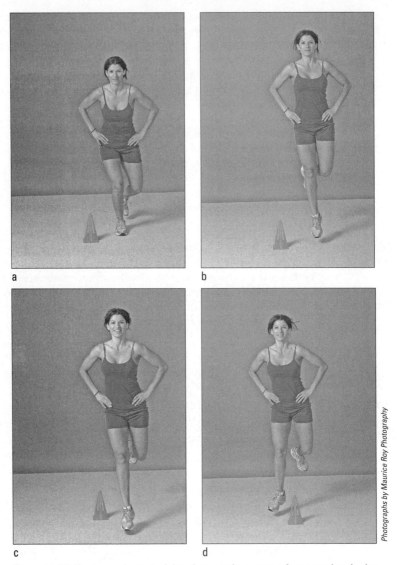

a
b
c
d

Photographs by Maurice Roy Photography

Figure 11-20: Keep your legs straight when you hop so you focus on developing power in your calves and ankles.

Bleacher hops

This exercise is similar to the single leg up-and-down hops in the preceding section, but you progress to jumping up stairs. It uses all your leg muscles and trains each leg separately.

Choose a set of bleachers that have small steps. Standing at the bottom of the bleacher steps on one leg, hop up the steps (see Figure 11-20). If the steps aren't small enough to jump up by just using your calf and ankle, bend your knees and use your quads to jump up the steps. Walk back down the steps and hop up on the other leg.

Photograph by Maurice Roy Photography

Figure 11-20: Pop off the steps like a kangaroo during bleacher hops.

Bounds

Bounds are great for teaching your legs to "pop" off the ground. Bounds look like a combination of running and jumping. Using an exaggerated running motion, bound forward from one leg to the other, pushing strongly off your back leg (see Figure 11-21).

Squat jumps

Squat jumps target the quadriceps muscles of your thighs and the gluteal muscles of your butt. Here's how you do one (refer to Figure 11-1):

1. **Stand with your hands on your hips and squat down until your thighs are parallel to the ground.**

2. Jump straight up as high as you can.

3. Landing with soft knees by bending your legs, squat back down in one smooth motion and immediately jump up again.

Depth jumps

This exercise is similar to the preceding squat jump exercise, but you progress to jumping onto the ground from a height. Here's how you do a depth jump:

1. Stand on a 2-foot-tall box (see Figure 11-22a).

2. Jump onto the ground and land in a squat position (see Figure 11-22b).

3. From this squat position, jump straight up as high as you can (see Figure 11-22c).

Photograph courtesy of Jason R. Karp, PhD

Figure 11-21: No tiptoeing through the tulips here! Bound aggressively against the ground.

Photographs by Maurice Roy Photography

Figure 11-22: Jump up immediately after landing on the ground for depth jumps.

Box jumps

This exercise is a progression from the preceding depth jump exercise because you jump up onto a box before jumping off and onto the ground. Here's how you do a box jump:

1. **Stand with your feet shoulder-width apart and your knees bent in a squat position behind a box about 2 feet high (see Figure 11-23a).**

2. **Jump with two feet onto the box (see Figure 11-23b).**

3. Immediately jump into the air and back down to the ground on the other side of the box, landing in a squat position (see Figure 11-23c).

As you get experienced with the exercise, try jumping with one foot at a time to focus on strengthening each leg separately.

a

b

c

Figure 11-23: Pop off the box immediately after landing on it.

Photographs by Maurice Roy Photography

Chapter 12

Stretching, Cross-Training, and Recovery during Training

· ·

In This Chapter

▶ Getting the lowdown on stretching

▶ Doing different kinds of stretching exercises

▶ Adding cross-training to your fitness mix

▶ Recovering quickly to train better

· ·

My friend jokes that I'm the laziest person she's ever met. All she sees me do is lie on the couch with my feet up, stuffing my face with carbohydrates. I convince her, in a reassuring voice, "I'm recovering."

Although running is the main activity when you train for a marathon, you need to address many non-running issues to stay healthy and run your best, including stretching, cross-training, and recovery. This chapter is all about those topics.

The Basics of Stretching Your Body

Have you ever run with a dog or watched a horse race? If you have, you probably noticed something interesting — none of these animals stretch before or after they run. Stretching seems to be something that only we humans do. If you've ever run before, you've likely been told that you should stretch before or after running to prevent injuries and to improve the quality of your workouts. But is what you've heard true? In the following sections, I debunk some myths about stretching and describe the benefits of stretching.

Clarifying the facts about stretching

Stretching attracts a lot of controversy. Although most people have been stretching since their middle school gym class days to prevent injuries, improve exercise performance, and reduce muscle soreness, the research on stretching tells a different story.

Whether stretching can prevent injuries depends on the type of activity you're doing and the type of injury you're trying to prevent:

- ✔ If the activity includes explosive or bouncing movements, like those in volleyball, basketball, and the plyometric exercises described in Chapter 11, stretching can reduce injuries by increasing the compliance of your tendons and improving their ability to absorb energy.

  However, for low-intensity activities that don't include bouncing movements, like running, cycling, and swimming, stretching doesn't prevent injuries because you don't need very compliant tendons for those activities.

- ✔ In regard to the type of injury, stretching can prevent muscle injuries, such as sprains and strains, but not bone or joint injuries. Bone and joint injuries, which are common among runners, are caused by increasing the training load too much too soon. (For information on how to prevent running-related injuries, stride on over to Chapter 13.)

Despite what your high school gym teacher may have told you, stretching doesn't improve exercise performance. Unfortunately, you won't run faster or longer just because you bend down to touch your toes before you run. If you stretch a lot before doing the strength training exercises described in Chapter 11, you may actually limit how much weight you can lift because stretching before the activity has the potential to affect the ability of muscles to contract effectively.

Stretching before or after you run also has a minimal effect on how sore you feel after your workout. When you exercise harder or longer than you're used to, whether running or strength training, microscopic damage occurs to your muscle fibers, which is a normal part of training. In response to the muscle fiber damage, you get inflammation, as more blood travels to the site, bringing with it white blood cells to start the healing process. You feel sore a day or two after a hard workout because of the damage-induced inflammation, which is called *delayed-onset muscle soreness* (DOMS). Stretching doesn't make your muscle fibers heal any quicker, so stretching won't make you feel less sore.

Seeing the benefits of stretching

If stretching doesn't reduce the risk of many running-related injuries, improve your running performance, or reduce muscle soreness in the days after a workout, what's the purpose of stretching? Great question! I'm glad you asked.

 The major benefit of stretching is to increase mobility and *flexibility* — a joint's range of motion — thereby priming your muscles to move dynamically through their full ranges of motion, which is important for runners. When stretching to increase flexibility, doing it apart from your workout makes it even more effective because running, especially long runs, can shorten and tighten your muscles, which reduces your flexibility.

A number of characteristics influence flexibility, including

- ✔ **Age:** With age, your muscles shorten from a lack of physical activity and a loss in elasticity in the connective tissues surrounding them. As a result, people tend to become less flexible with age.

- ✔ **Exercise:** Exercising on a regular basis increases flexibility, especially when that exercise involves moving your limbs through a full range of motion. A sedentary lifestyle decreases flexibility.

- ✔ **Joint structure:** The type of joint determines the range of motion. For example, a ball-and-socket joint, like the shoulder, has a greater range of motion than a hinge joint, like the elbow.

- ✔ **Pregnancy:** During pregnancy, your pelvic joints and ligaments are relaxed and capable of a greater range of motion.

- ✔ **Sex:** Females tend to be more flexible than males of similar age throughout life, generally because of anatomical variations in joint structures. (Sex, as an activity, also increases flexibility if done creatively, just in case you were wondering.)

- ✔ **Temperature:** An increase in either body temperature (as a result of exercise) or environmental temperature increases your range of motion. That's why it's better to stretch after you've warmed up your muscles.

Stretching Exercises to Improve Your Flexibility

Stretching exercises that specifically target each muscle group help improve your flexibility. The following sections describe three of the most common methods of stretching, with exercises for each one.

Always warm up before stretching by jogging or doing some other form of cardiovascular exercise for about five to ten minutes.

Do dynamic stretching exercises before you run to increase mobility and save the static and PNF stretching for after your run.

Static stretching

Static stretching is the most common way to stretch your muscles. It includes those bend-down-and-touch-your-toes hamstring stretches you did in high school gym class. As their name implies, static stretches don't move; you stretch a muscle passively and hold the position for a certain amount of time. Hold each of the following static stretches for 30 seconds, which is the most effective length of time to hold a stretch. The following stretches target the muscles that easily become tight while training for a marathon. Do your static stretching after you run.

Glutes

Follow these steps to stretch your glutes, or buttocks muscles:

1. **Sit with your legs out in front of you.**

   Bend your left leg and cross it over your right leg, placing your left foot on the ground to the right side of your right knee.

2. **Turn your shoulders so that you're facing to the left.**

   Press your right arm against your left knee to help you twist to the side. Put your left arm on the ground for support (see Figure 12-1). Feel the stretch in your glutes and along the length of your spine.

3. **Repeat with your other leg.**

Hamstrings

Follow these steps to stretch your hamstrings, the big muscles in the back of your thighs:

1. **Sit on the ground with both legs straight out in front of you.**

   Bend your left leg and place the sole of your left foot along the inside of your right leg.

2. **Bend forward toward your right toes, keeping your back straight (see Figure 12-2).**

   Feel the stretch in the hamstrings of your right leg.

3. **Repeat with your other leg.**

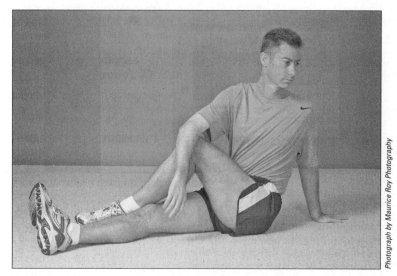

Figure 12-1: You may look like a pretzel with this glute stretch.

Figure 12-2: Keep your legs straight to stretch your hamstrings.

Quadriceps

Follow these steps to stretch your quadriceps, the big muscles in the front of your thighs:

1. **Standing next to a wall or chair for balance, bend your left knee and bring your left foot toward your butt.**

   Grab your left foot with your left hand. Keep your back straight and don't bend forward at the hips (see Figure 12-3). Feel the stretch in your left quadriceps.

2. **Repeat with your other leg.**

Calves

Follow these steps to stretch your calves, the muscles on the back of your lower legs:

1. **Stand with your left leg in front of your right leg, hands flat and at shoulder height against a wall.**

   Keep your right leg straight and press your right heel firmly into the ground. Keep your hips facing the wall and your right leg and spine in a straight line (see Figure 12-4). Feel the stretch in the calf of your right leg.

2. **Repeat with your other leg.**

Photograph by Maurice Roy Photography

Figure 12-3: Bring your heel to your butt to stretch your quads.

Photograph by Maurice Roy Photography

Figure 12-4: Push against the wall to stretch your calves.

Dynamic stretching

In contrast to static stretching (see the preceding section), dynamic stretching includes repetitive movements, using momentum from a moving limb to increase your range of motion. In many dynamic stretches, you contract the muscle group opposing the one that you're stretching, causing the stretched muscle group to relax so you can obtain a greater stretch as you move your limb through its complete range of motion.

The dynamic stretches in the following sections focus on the runner's important body parts — hips (including glutes and hip flexors), hamstrings, quads, adductors, and calves. Do these dynamic stretches before you run. You can also do them after.

Move actively through the range of motion, contracting the muscle group opposing the one you're stretching. Use a rope for light assistance at the end of the range of motion to increase how far you can move your limb.

Leg swings (side to side)

Stand a couple of feet in front of a wall, chair, or fence with your hands on the wall. Swing your right leg side to side from your hip through its entire range of motion, passing your right leg in front of your left leg (see Figure 12-5). Repeat the side-to-side motion five to ten times before switching to the other leg.

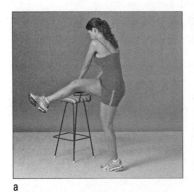

a   b

Figure 12-5: Swing your legs from one side to the other.

Leg swings (forward and back)

Stand with the right side of your body facing a wall, chair, or fence with your right hand on the wall. Swing your left leg forward and back from your hip through its entire range of motion (see Figure 12-6). Repeat the forward-and-back motion five to ten times before switching to the other leg.

Figure 12-6: Swing your legs forward and back.

Hamstrings

Follow these steps to stretch your hamstrings:

   1. **Lie on your back with your right knee bent and your right foot flat on the ground.**

2. **Make a loop with the rope and place your left foot into the loop, locking your knee so your left leg is extended straight out (see Figure 12-7a).**

3. **From your hip and using your quadriceps, lift your left leg toward your chest, aiming your left foot toward the ceiling.**

   Grasp the ends of the rope with both hands and slightly pull the rope toward you to assist at the end of the stretch (see Figure 12-7b).

4. **Hold the stretch for one to two seconds, return to the position in Step 2, and repeat five to ten times before switching to the other leg.**

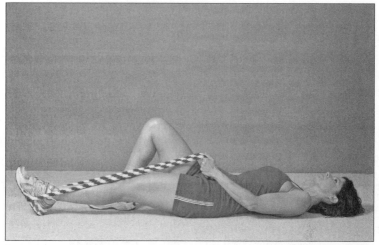

a

b

Figure 12-7: Use a rope to pull your leg to stretch your hamstrings.

Photographs by Maurice Roy Photography

Quadriceps

Follow these steps to stretch your quadriceps:

1. **Lie on your right side with your knees bent (in a fetal position).**

   Slide your right arm under your right thigh (see Figure 12-8a).

2. **Reach down with your left hand and grasp the shin, ankle, or forefoot of your left leg.**

   Keep your knees bent and your legs parallel to the ground.

3. **Contract your hamstrings and glutes and move your left leg back as far as you can, using your hand or a rope to give a gentle assist at the end of the stretch (see Figure 12-8b).**

4. **Hold the stretch for one to two seconds, return to the starting position in Step 1, and repeat five to ten times before switching to the other leg.**

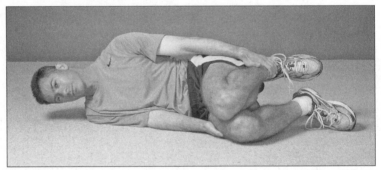

a

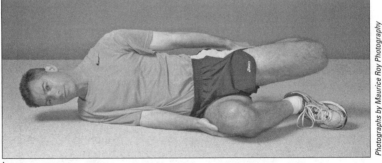

b

Photographs by Maurice Roy Photography

Figure 12-8: Assume the fetal position to stretch your quads.

Calves

Follow these steps to stretch your calves:

1. **Sit with both legs straight out in front of you and loop a rope around your left foot (see Figure 12-9a).**

2. **Flex your foot back toward your ankle, using the rope for a gentle assist at the end of the movement (see Figure 12-9b).**

3. **Hold the stretch for one to two seconds, return to the starting position in Step 1, and repeat five to ten times before switching to the other leg.**

Proprioceptive neuromuscular facilitation (PNF) stretching

Proprioceptive neuromuscular facilitation (PNF) is an advanced technique that increases your range of motion by focusing on specific properties of a muscle and how it responds to signals from your central nervous system. Despite its intimidating name (what a mouthful!), it's actually a cool way to increase flexibility. With PNF stretching, you alternate contracting and relaxing your muscles, as a partner assists in providing resistance and moving your limbs. The two kinds of PNF stretching are

✔ **Contract-relax:** First, your partner moves your limb to the far end of its range of motion until you feel a stretch. Then, your partner tells you to contract your muscles, and she provides resistance as you forcefully push your limb against her for a few seconds. Finally, you relax the contracted muscle group and your partner stretches those muscles by again moving your limb to the far end of its range of motion, which is now a bit farther than it was previously. You and your partner repeat this sequence of contracting and relaxing the muscle group a few times.

✔ **Contract-relax agonist contract:** With this method, you contract the *opposing* muscle group after the contraction and stretch of the muscle group you're stretching. Because muscle groups work in opposing pairs, contracting one muscle group makes the opposing muscle group relax so you can stretch it more.

The following sections walk you through several types of PNF stretches (be sure to do them after you run).

a

b

Figure 12-9: Pull your toes toward you to stretch your calves.

Glutes and hamstrings

To stretch your glutes and hamstrings using the first PNF method, follow these steps:

1. **Lie with your back on the floor, legs straight, and arms to your sides.**

   Have a partner kneel beside you and lift your left leg up toward your head, keeping your left leg straight so you feel a stretch in your hamstrings. Your partner can rest your leg on his shoulder (see Figure 12-10a). Keep your right leg flat against the ground.

2. **Stretch your hamstrings to the point of limitation, and then contract your hamstrings for a few seconds by pushing your left leg against your partner's resistance, trying to lower your leg.**

3. **Have your partner restretch your left hamstrings to the point of limitation, which should be slightly farther than the initial stretch (see Figure 12-10b).**

4. **Repeat four to five times before switching to the other leg.**

For the second PNF method that contracts the opposing muscle group, after you've contracted and restretched your hamstrings, have your partner provide resistance against your quadriceps, and contract your quadriceps by pushing against your partner for a few seconds (follow the steps in the next section). Relax your quadriceps and then have your partner lift your leg toward your head to restretch your hamstrings again to a new point of limitation.

Quadriceps

To stretch your quadriceps using the first PNF method, follow these steps:

1. **Lie face down on the floor with your legs straight and your hands above your head.**

   Have your partner kneel on your right side and bend your right leg, until you feel a stretch in your quadriceps. Your partner should have one hand on your quadriceps under your thigh and the other hand on your ankle (see Figure 12-11a).

2. **Contract your quadriceps for a few seconds by pushing your foot against your partner's resistance, trying to extend your leg.**

3. **Have your partner restretch your quadriceps to the point of limitation, which should be slightly farther than the initial stretch (see Figure 12-11b).**

4. **Repeat four to five times before switching to the other leg.**

For the second PNF method that contracts the opposing muscle group, after you've contracted and restretched your quadriceps, have your partner provide resistance against your hamstrings, and contract your hamstrings by pushing against your partner for a few seconds (refer to the steps in the preceding section). Relax your hamstrings and then have your partner restretch your quadriceps to a new point of limitation.

a

b

Figure 12-10: Contract your hamstrings to increase flexibility in the back of your legs.

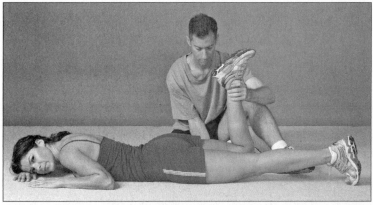

a

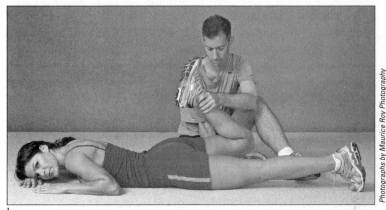

b

Photographs by Maurice Roy Photography

Figure 12-11: Contract your quads to increase flexibility in the front of your legs.

Cross-Training to Improve Your Fitness

I probably get asked about cross-training at least once a week. *Cross-training* is any activity or exercise that supplements your main activity. Although cross-training won't directly help you run a marathon and should never replace your running, it has certain benefits:

 ✔ **It increases your aerobic fitness apart from running.** If you're a beginning runner, you can't expect to run 50 miles or more per week to train for a marathon. Getting your mileage that high takes time. In this case, you can supplement your running with cross-training on the days you don't run to boost your aerobic fitness without the physical stress (and injury risk) of running more.

✔ **It helps you lose weight.** In addition to increasing aerobic fitness if you're a beginner runner, cross-training also gives you the opportunity to burn more calories, which can help you lose weight. Losing weight helps you run better.

✔ **It maintains your cardiovascular fitness while you're injured.** An injury often prevents you from running, but cross-training with a different activity that doesn't directly put stress on the injured body part enables you to stay fit while your injury heals so that you're not completely out of shape when you start running again.

✔ **It works different muscles.** Cross-training helps strengthen your non-running muscles and rests your running muscles. You can focus on specific muscles that don't get trained as much from running and may be weaker than your running muscles.

✔ **It reduces the risk of overuse injuries.** Cross-training varies the training load and spreads the stress across different muscles.

✔ **It boosts recovery after tough workouts.** Cross-training the day after an interval workout or long run brings blood full of oxygen and nutrients to your muscles without the extra stress to your running muscles and joints.

✔ **It makes you more flexible.** Running a lot can decrease your range of motion, causing certain muscles, like hamstrings and calves, to tighten. Cross-training with activities different from running can increase flexibility by moving your limbs through larger ranges of motion.

The following sections list a number of cross-training options for marathon runners.

Working your running muscles

Don't know what cross-training you should do? As a runner, you might choose activities that use the same muscles as running. The top three are

✔ **Cross-country skiing machine:** Only one activity improves your aerobic fitness more than running: cross-country skiing. If you don't have access to snow or ski equipment, try a cross-country skiing machine in the gym, such as a NordicTrack. Although it takes some time to learn the skill, it's a great cross-training activity that burns tons of calories and raises your heart rate.

How does stretching work?

Two sensory organs inside your skeletal muscles function as protective mechanisms against injury during passive and active stretching.

✔ The most abundant of these sensory organs, or *proprioceptors* (structures that sense movement), are the muscle *spindles,* which are located in the middle of the belly of your muscles. When you stretch, the muscle spindle sends a message to your central nervous system. If the muscle is overstretched or stretched too fast, the central nervous system activates the motor neurons of the stretched muscle through a feedback loop, causing the muscle to contract. This feedback loop is called the *stretch reflex.* Therefore, the muscle spindle protects your muscles from being stretched too far or too fast.

✔ Your other proprioceptor is the *Golgi tendon organ,* which sits at the junction between your muscle and your tendon. When you generate excessive force in your muscle, the Golgi tendon organ triggers a reflex opposite that of the muscle spindle to inhibit muscle contraction, causing your muscle to relax. The Golgi tendon organ helps prevent muscle injuries by preventing your muscle from developing too much force or tension during active stretching. It also causes your contracted muscles to relax more, which enables you to increase flexibility by moving the limb through a greater range of motion.

✔ **Elliptical trainer:** The elliptical trainer, which is one of the most popular pieces of cardio equipment in the gym, most closely resembles the movement of running without the impact, and it's still weight-bearing.

✔ **Water running:** Running in deep water is a great opportunity to run without impact. The resistance from the water gives you a great workout. You can run in the water with or without a flotation vest (such as an AquaJogger) to keep you buoyant. Although this is a great cross-training activity for your legs, your heart rate doesn't get as high when you're in the water.

Giving your running muscles a break

If you want to use cross-training as a way to take a physical and psychological break from running-related activities or you need to give your running muscles and joints a rest while you're rehabbing an injury, try these other cross-training options:

✔ **Cycling:** Cycling is a no-impact activity that gives you a break from running while still giving you a great workout for your legs. It's a great way to develop leg power, although the range of motion is less compared to running. Use a stationary bike in the gym or take a high-intensity spinning class.

✔ **Rowing machine:** Rowing is a great whole-body, no-impact cross-training activity. It makes your cardiovascular system fit, and it works your upper and lower body at the same time, although the power of the stroke comes mainly from the legs. To get the most out of rowing, you first have to learn proper technique, which includes pushing with your legs before pulling with your arms.

✔ **Strength training:** Strength training can help eliminate muscle strength imbalances to prevent running-related injuries, improves posture and coordination, reverses the loss of muscle that accompanies aging, and increases bone density. And if you do it right, focusing on complex movements rather than isolating specific muscles, it can also increase muscle power, which can turn you from marathoner slowpoke to marathoner speedster. For specific strength training exercises, stride over to Chapter 11.

✔ **Swimming:** Swimming is a great activity to train your upper body muscles, which are often neglected in runners. Swimming also gives your legs a break from the pounding. If you have poor posture and a weak upper body, cross-train with swimming to work on your upper body postural muscles and increase your upper body strength.

✔ **Yoga:** If you're like me, you hate yoga. Or at least dislike it. Or don't understand it. On the surface, yoga and running don't mix. One is very active, with the effort spread over many muscles; the other, very stationary, with the effort concentrated to specific muscles. Most runners don't like stationary activities. But I'm slowly becoming a convert. (Perhaps it's because I live in Southern California, where yoga is just as popular as sushi.) Although it may be hard to say to yourself at mile 22 of a marathon, "I'm prepared for this; I did yoga," it can be a valuable cross-training complement to your running. Yoga works on your flexibility, balance, and strength, and its meditative component enhances your breathing and focus (and you'll need a lot of focus at mile 22 of the marathon). If you do yoga, choose the athletic ashtanga or vinyasa versions or a class that's specifically designed for runners.

Optimal Recovery Strategies to Help You Train Better

Most runners tend to focus on miles and paces. Improvements in fitness, however, occur during the recovery period between runs, not during the runs themselves. The physiological adaptations to training described in Chapter 3 occur with a correctly timed alternation between stress and recovery. You must give equal attention to both to run your best or sometimes to even run at all.

When you finish a long run or a race, you're weaker, not stronger. How much weaker depends on how hard or how long the workout or race is. If the physical stress of the workout is high and you don't recover before your next workout or race, your training suffers, and your ability to adapt to subsequent workouts declines. Sometimes, you may even get sick or injured. For example, bone and tendon injuries often happen because the stress of running is too much or is introduced at too quick of a rate for the bone or tendon to adapt. That's why you have to train smartly and not increase the volume or intensity of training too quickly.

When you train a lot, your immune system can also become compromised, leaving you vulnerable to getting sick. Very long runs especially have a way of weakening your immune system.

Therefore, what you do the rest of the day when you're not running is just as important as your running. You have a lot of options to help you recover quickly, as you find out in the following sections.

Nutrition

Refueling nutrient-depleted muscles is possibly the single most important aspect of optimal recovery from hard or long workouts. And the most important nutrient to replenish is carbohydrate because it's your muscles' preferred fuel. (The carbohydrate you ingest after your runs also helps prevent you from getting sick when training for your marathon because carbohydrate strengthens your immune system.)

How well and how far you run is influenced by the amount of *glycogen* — the stored form of carbohydrate — in your skeletal muscles and liver. When you run a lot, you decrease your glycogen stores. Muscles are picky when it comes to the time for synthesizing and storing carbohydrate. Although glycogen will continue to be synthesized from the carbohydrate you eat or drink until storage in your muscles is complete, the process is most rapid if you consume carbohydrate within the first 30 to 60 minutes after you run. If you don't ingest carbohydrate until a couple of hours after you run, you significantly reduce the rate that you synthesize and store new glycogen, which slows your recovery and makes your next run more difficult.

 To maximize the synthesis and storage of glycogen and be ready for your next run, consume 0.7 gram of carbohydrate (simple sugar, preferably glucose) per pound of body weight within 30 minutes after you run, and continue to consume 0.7 gram per pound every two hours for four to six hours afterward. Because you absorb nutrients from fluids more quickly than from solid foods, consume carbohydrate and protein from fluids when you first finish your run, before eating a meal later. Despite the popularity of commercial sports drinks, any drink that contains carbohydrate and protein is great for recovery. Chocolate milk, which is high in both carbo-hydrate and protein, is a great post-run recovery drink!

Protein is another important nutrient to consume after hard and long workouts because protein helps repair muscle fibers that have been damaged during training. It's also used to synthesize new structures like hemoglobin, mitochondria, enzymes, and capillaries, all of which facilitate the transportation and use of oxygen and make you a better runner (as I explain in Chapter 3).

 Consume 20 to 30 grams of complete protein (which contains all essential amino acids) after you run. Initially, consume the protein in a drink. Continue to consume protein in the hours after your run to contribute to further tissue repair. Good sources of protein are eggs, tuna, cheese, and lean meats.

Sleep

 Sleep is very important when you're training for a marathon because all the adaptations you're trying to make with your training happen during recovery. And you're never recovering more than when you're sleeping. The more you train, the more sleep you need. Many of the world's best marathon runners don't do much else besides run, eat, and sleep. Even if you're not trying to win the Boston Marathon, not getting enough sleep for just one or two nights can cause your workouts to suffer. Try to get at least seven to eight hours of sleep every night while training for your marathon. If you can't get seven to eight hours of sleep every night, try to take short naps during the day.

Hydration

Despite the occasional compliment you may get about your well-defined muscles, water, not muscle, is the major component of your body. So when you lose water, you face consequences. Water is vital for many chemical reactions that occur inside your cells, including the production of energy so your muscles can contract. Hydration is critical to your success as a runner because of its role in regulation of body temperature and maintenance of blood volume. Maintaining proper fluid balance ensures peak performance, while failing to adequately rehydrate during and after running leads to dehydration. When dehydration occurs, your body temperature increases, your performance suffers, and serious medical problems can occur.

When you sweat, you lose body water, which decreases your muscles' ability to produce energy. Your blood volume also decreases and becomes thicker if you don't replace fluids, which causes decreases in your stroke volume, cardiac output, and oxygen delivery to your muscles (see Chapter 3 for more about these concepts). Your running performance starts to decline with only a 2 to 3 percent loss of body mass due to fluid loss.

To rehydrate after you run, drink fluids with sodium, which stimulates your kidneys to retain water. If you run at an easy pace for less than one hour, you can rehydrate with plain water and a balanced diet.

To adequately hydrate, follow these guidelines:

- ✓ **Before running:** Drink 16 ounces (two glasses) two hours before you run.

- ✓ **During running:** Drink about 8 ounces every 15 to 20 minutes. If you sweat a lot, drink more.

- ✓ **After running:** Drink 16 ounces per pound of body weight lost during your run. To find out how much weight you lose, weigh yourself before and after your run.

If your run lasts more than an hour or if you have a sodium deficiency, then before, during, and after running consume 0.5 to 0.7 gram (about one tenth of a teaspoon) of salt per liter of fluid. Most commercial sports drinks already contain adequate sodium. If you don't have a sodium deficiency, you should already get a sufficient amount of sodium in your diet.

Drink often to stay hydrated. A good indicator of your hydration level is the color of your urine. When your urine is a light color, like lemonade, you're adequately hydrated. If your urine looks like apple juice, keep drinking. Carry a water bottle with you throughout the day.

Stress relief

Have you ever had a bad workout immediately after a stressful event in your life? Stress has a way of affecting everything you do. So if you're in the middle of some life-changing event, that's not the best time to train for a marathon. Although you can't often control what happens to you, you *can* control how you react and respond to what happens to you. And that makes a lot of difference when training for a marathon. Here are some stress-reducing strategies:

- **Get a pet.** Unless you get a pit bull that constantly attacks your neighbors, pets have a calming effect on humans and can reduce stress. Nothing like a cute cat purring in your lap to make you feel calm! If it weren't for my cat, Boomerang, I'd probably have a Type A++ personality!

- **Go for a run.** That's right — the very activity that you're training for can reduce stress. In fact, running is actually very effective for doing that. Leave your watch and heart rate monitor at home and don't worry about distance or pace or time. Just run in a scenic place based on how you feel.

- **Meditate.** You can meditate as part of a yoga class or on your own before you go to bed.

- **Subscribe to a stress-free philosophy.** Here's a great philosophy I once learned from a sports psychologist: It ain't worth worrying if it's in your control, because if it's in your control, it ain't worth worrying. And it ain't worth worrying if it's out of your control, because if it's out of your control, it ain't worth worrying. Besides sounding catchy, it can work if you really believe it.

Inflammation reduction

With marathon training comes muscle damage and inflammation, which leads to muscle soreness and reduced muscle force production. The quicker you can get rid of that inflammation and soreness, the sooner you can do another quality run.

Nutrition plays a big part in reducing inflammation. Foods that contain antioxidants like vitamins A, C, and E act as anti-inflammatories and help your muscles recover quicker. Some of the best antioxidant foods for runners include

- **Almonds:** Nuts, especially almonds, are an excellent source of vitamin E. Eat a small handful of almonds at least three to five times per week.

- **Dark chocolate:** Of course I had to include this one! Chocolate, especially the dark variety, is rich in antioxidants called *flavonols.*

- **Mixed berries:** Blueberries, cherries, blackberries, and raspberries contain a powerful group of antioxidants called *anthocyanins,* which give the berries their rich colors.

- **Oranges:** One orange gives you 100 percent of the recommended daily value of the popular antioxidant vitamin C.

- **Salmon:** Salmon is one of the best food sources of omega-3 fatty acids, which help balance the body's inflammation.

- **Stir-fry vegetables:** With their mix of red and yellow peppers, onions, bok choy, and soybeans, stir-fry veggies offer a potent mix of antioxidants.

- **Sweet potatoes:** One average-sized sweet potato gives you over 250 percent of the recommended daily value for vitamin A in the form of beta carotene, a powerful antioxidant. They're also a good source of vitamin C.

Other strategies to reduce inflammation include ice massages, cold water immersion, and *contrast baths* (submersion of a limb in alternating hot and cold water). Cold water baths have become common among runners, especially after long runs. Fill up your bathtub with cold water (about 50 degrees) and sit in it for a few minutes after your long runs. Or, if you run near the ocean, take a dip in the water after your run. It may feel cold at first, but it feels refreshing!

 When taking a cold water bath, wear a hat to prevent hypothermia and limit your stay in the water to about ten minutes to prevent frostbite.

 Taking over-the-counter, non-steroidal, anti-inflammatory drugs like aspirin and ibuprofen is a popular method to reduce inflammation and soreness, but they may actually retard healing. If possible, I suggest that you avoid drugs to mask any symptoms of soreness. Popping an aspirin every time you feel sore sends a message that a cure for soreness and a quicker recovery can be swallowed, while what's really important is that you listen to what your body is telling you. Only that way can you avoid injury and train better. Use anti-inflammatory drugs as a last resort.

Chapter 13

Recognizing (And Avoiding) Common Running Injuries

....

In This Chapter

▶ Understanding why running injuries happen

▶ Discovering how to train smarter to avoid injuries

▶ Reviewing the causes, symptoms, and treatments of common running injuries

▶ Assessing the female athlete triad

....

I'm proud to say that in all my years of running, I've never had a running-related injury. However, for the majority of runners, the statistics tell a different story: The longer you're a runner, the more likely you are to get injured. At least half of all runners deal with at least one injury per year, and 25 percent of runners are injured at any given time. Although you're less likely to become one of those injured runners if you follow the advice in this book, sometimes you can get injured without any apparent reason and no matter how careful you are. In this chapter, I give you a detailed guide to the most common running-related injuries, including the secrets of how to get darn close to completely preventing them.

Focusing on Factors That Affect Your Chance of Injury

The main reason why injuries happen is because the physical stress from running is too much for your body to handle at that time. The human body is great at adapting to stress, but only when you apply that stress in small doses. When you apply the stress too quickly for your body to adapt, something breaks down. This is especially true with running because running is the most stressful sport on the skeleton. Every time your foot lands on the ground, your leg absorbs two to three times your body weight. Multiply that by the number of steps you take to run ten miles — and multiply *that* by how many times you run each week — and you can see how much stress your legs have to deal with to train for a marathon.

The causes of running injuries can be divided into *intrinsic factors* (which are personal) and extrinsic factors (which are related to your training and environment).

Intrinsic factors

Intrinsic factors are characteristics specific to you and include

- **Age:** Older runners are more susceptible to injuries because they take longer to recover from workouts and adapt to the training.

- **Bone density:** Low bone density increases the risk of stress fractures (which I describe later in this chapter). As a marathon runner, dense bones help you withstand the stress of pounding the pavement week after week.

- **Foot type:** Flat feet that pronate excessively when you run can cause injuries because overpronation is a big cause of many running-related injuries. (Flip to Chapter 2 for more about pronation.)

- **Lack of running experience:** If you're a new runner, you have a greater risk for injuries because you're not yet used to the stress of running.

- **Previous injury:** If you've had an injury in the past, you're at an increased risk for another one. Already having an injury shows that that body part is vulnerable.

- **Sex:** Female runners often have a greater risk of injury than male runners. Certain conditions, like irregular menstrual cycles and menopause, cause a drop in or an absence of estrogen, which protects women's bones. Females' bones are less dense than males' bones to begin with, so their bones are more susceptible to injury. (For more on female-specific conditions that can cause injury, see the later section, "Recognizing the Female Athlete Triad.")

Extrinsic factors

Extrinsic factors are characteristics of your training and environment and include

- **Intensity:** Running at a faster pace, like you do during interval workouts (see Chapter 7), places a greater stress on your legs.

- ✔ **Mileage:** How many miles you run per week is the greatest predictor of injury risk. It's hard to say exactly how many miles per week increases the risk of injury because that's an individual matter. You may be able to handle 50 miles per week, and your running partner may get injured with 30. Some runners (called Olympians) can run more than 100 miles per week and not get injured! On average, the risk of getting injured is two to three times greater when running at least 40 miles per week.

- ✔ **Shoes:** Running shoes have specific combinations of support and stability designed for different running gaits. Running in the wrong shoes can adversely affect lower extremity alignment, making you more susceptible to injury. A cushioning shoe isn't a good choice for an overpronator, who needs a shoe that offers more stability. Anytime you get a running-related injury, that's a good sign to change your shoes, usually to a different type. To find out the right shoe for you, stride on over to Chapter 2.

Training Smarter to Avoid Injury

There's really no good reason why so many people training for a marathon should get injured. Yet it happens all the time, mostly because people don't train smartly, or they follow programs that are faulty in design. If you train smarter, I can almost guarantee that you won't get injured. When training for your marathon, follow these smart training guidelines:

- ✔ **Increase your weekly running mileage and the distance of your long runs very slowly.** From a training standpoint, how quickly you increase your weekly mileage probably has the greatest impact on whether you get injured. The slower you increase your weekly mileage and the distance of your long runs, the less chance you'll get injured. When you increase your mileage, add only about a mile per day of running so that you spread the stress around. (Check out the programs in Chapters 8, 9, and 10 for good examples of how to increase your weekly mileage.)

    Don't increase the distance of your long run every week, especially if you're training for your first marathon. This is a big mistake among recreational marathon runners, and it often leads to injury.

- ✔ **Run the same mileage for two to four weeks before increasing it.** This goes for your long run, too. Give your legs a chance to fully adapt to the workload before increasing it. Most marathon training groups make this mistake because their training programs are only five to six months long, so they increase the distance of the long run (and often the weekly mileage along with it) every week throughout their programs until it's time to taper two to three weeks before the marathon. That's a good way for new or recreational runners to get injured. If you're running your first marathon and you're starting from a very low level of mileage and a short long run, you need to give yourself much longer than five or six months to prepare without risk of injury.

✔ **Every few weeks, decrease your weekly mileage by about a third for one recovery week to give your legs a chance to absorb and respond to the training you've done.** For example, if you've run 35 miles per week for the last three weeks, back off to about 23 miles for a week. You'll notice the difference it makes in how your legs feel.

✔ **Don't increase your weekly mileage and the intensity of your workouts at the same time.** When you begin to include interval training in your program, either drop your overall mileage for the week or maintain the mileage from where it was prior to adding interval training. Your legs can handle only so much stress at once. Trying to increase your running while also increasing the intensity of your workouts is too much for most runners to handle.

✔ **Alternate hard and easy days.** Every day you run hard, follow it with at least one day of easy running. And make sure your easy days really are easy. Don't run hard more than two to three days per week.

✔ **Get adequate recovery.** If you recover between runs, your muscles, bones, tendons, and ligaments won't break down. The older you are, the more time you need to recover from training, so the longer you need before increasing your weekly running mileage and intensity. Young runners can get away with training mistakes; older runners can't. To find out how to recover quicker, turn to Chapter 12.

✔ **Reduce pronation.** Because overpronation is a common cause of many running-related injuries (most injuries start with the feet!), try to reduce any pronation that's more than normal. Try these strategies to reduce overpronation:

• Wear the correct shoes for you (see Chapter 2 for guidance).

• Stay away from cambered roads (especially in the gutter near the curb), which increase ankle pronation of the outside foot.

• Strengthen your calf muscles, which helps stabilize your lower leg when it lands on the ground. (Check out Chapter 11 for tips on strengthening your calves.)

Looking at Some Common Running Injuries

If I had a dollar for every time someone asked me if I've ever had knee problems from running, I'd have a lot of dollars. Although running isn't bad for your knees, the knee is the most common site of running-related injuries, with patellofemoral pain syndrome accounting for 25 percent and iliotibial band friction syndrome accounting for 12 percent of all running-related injuries. I discuss these injuries in this section, along with others that affect the lower half of the body.

For all running-related injuries, focus your treatment on the underlying cause rather than on the symptoms.

With all running-related injuries that require you to back off from running, cross-train with other activities that don't aggravate the condition to maintain cardiovascular fitness. See Chapter 12 for more about cross-training.

Patellofemoral pain syndrome

Patellofemoral pain syndrome is the fancy medical term for knee pain. When you extend and bend your knee to straighten and flex your leg, your *patella* (knee bone) glides back and forth within a groove in the end of your *femur* (thigh bone). The patella and groove in the femur comprise the *patellofemoral joint*.

The patellofemoral joint is stabilized by soft-tissue structures that control movement of the patella within the groove, a function called *patellar tracking.* Any alterations in normal patellar tracking can cause patellofemoral pain syndrome, including

- ✔ Anatomical factors such as hip width and angle of femur meeting the patella
- ✔ Excessive or insufficient pronation
- ✔ Hip muscle weakness
- ✔ Increased stress across the patellofemoral joint
- ✔ Strength imbalance in stabilizing muscles
- ✔ Suboptimal lower-leg running mechanics

Interestingly, female runners experience patellofemoral pain syndrome more than men do. Women, especially ones with wide hips, have a greater angle at which the femur bone meets the tibia bone (called the *Q-angle;* see Figure 13-1). A larger Q-angle increases the forces the quadriceps muscle exerts on the patella, which may predispose the patella to abnormal tracking, causing knee pain.

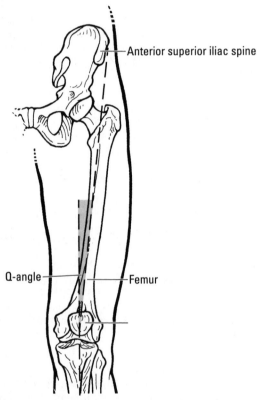

Anterior superior iliac spine

Q-angle

Femur

Illustration by Kathryn Born, MA

Figure 13-1: A large Q-angle due to wide hips can cause patellofemoral pain syndrome.

Symptoms

With patellofemoral pain syndrome, you feel pain behind, below, or around your patella (see Figure 13-2). The pain usually comes on gradually and gets worse when you run or when you walk up or down stairs.

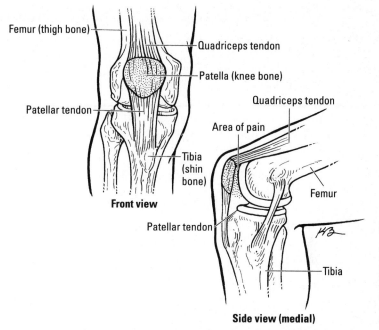

Front view

Side view (medial)

Illustration by Kathryn Born, MA

Figure 13-2: Patellofemoral pain syndrome can affect any part of your knee.

Treatment

To treat patellofemoral pain syndrome, follow these guidelines:

- ✔ **Discontinuation of hill running:** Because hill running, especially downhill running, puts extra stress on your knees, stay away from hills until the pain subsides.

- ✔ **Knee braces, knee sleeves, and patellar straps:** Putting something around your knee to stabilize it while you run may give you some relief of the symptoms.

- ✔ **Muscle strengthening:** Strengthen the muscles that support your knee to reduce patella tracking, including quadriceps, hamstrings, hips, and glutes. (See Chapter 11 for help.)

- ✔ **Orthotics:** Orthotics help stabilize the foot when running and reduce impact. They're helpful for runners who severely overpronate (their foot rolls inward excessively upon landing) or underpronate (their foot doesn't roll inward enough upon landing to adequately absorb shock). For more information on orthotics, stride on over to Chapter 2.

- ✔ **Reduction of running volume:** You may need to back off on your running until the pain subsides.

Iliotibial band friction syndrome

Iliotibial band friction syndrome is the most common cause of pain on the lateral (outside) of the knee among runners. The *iliotibial band* is a sheath of connective tissue that runs down your thigh from your hip to just below your knee. The iliotibial band assists with outward movement of your thigh and stabilizes the lateral part of your knee. With iliotibial band friction syndrome, the iliotibial band repeatedly rubs up against the outside of the knee, causing friction and pain.

Causes of iliotibial band friction syndrome include

- ✔ Excessive or abrupt increases in running mileage
- ✔ High-arched feet that don't adequately pronate, which transfers the shock of landing to other parts of the leg
- ✔ Hip and gluteal muscle weakness
- ✔ Preexisting iliotibial band tightness
- ✔ Stiff shoes that limit pronation
- ✔ Too much downhill running
- ✔ Too much running on cambered roads, which causes overpronation
- ✔ Too much unidirectional running around a track

Symptoms

Symptoms often begin with a sensation of tightness on the outside of your knee (see Figure 13-3). With time and continued activity, the tightness progresses to a localized pain or burning sensation, especially when you bend your knee, run downhill, or walk down stairs. Pressing on the outside of the knee while flexing the knee usually reproduces the pain. Some runners experience a clicking sensation that results from the iliotibial band tightening and snapping across the joint when their knees flex and extend.

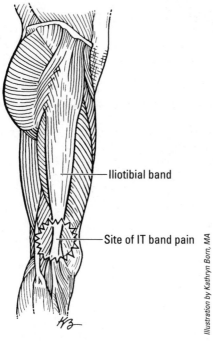

Iliotibial band

Site of IT band pain

Illustration by Kathryn Born, MA

Figure 13-3: The classic sign you have iliotibial band friction syndrome is pain on the outside of the knee.

Treatment

To treat iliotibial band friction syndrome, follow these guidelines:

- ✔ **Foam rolling:** Lie on the side of your injured leg with a foam roller directly underneath your iliotibial band. Roll yourself up and down on the foam roller to massage the area (see Figure 13-4). Foam rolling helps loosen the iliotibial band and the surrounding tissues.

- ✔ **Ice:** Fill a Styrofoam cup with water and freeze it. Tear away some of the foam from the top so the ice protrudes. Massage the ice over the injured area using a circular motion for ten minutes. Repeat three to four times per day.

Photograph by Maurice Roy Photography

Figure 13-4: Use a foam roller to treat iliotibial band friction syndrome.

✔ **Muscle strengthening:** Strengthen the muscles that control your leg when it first lands on the ground, including your hips and glutes. (Check out Chapter 11 for exercises.)

✔ **Rest:** If the pain is severe, you may have to cut back or stop running until the pain subsides.

✔ **Stretching:** Lie on your back with both legs out straight. Put the foot of the injured leg in the loop of a rope, positioning the rope between your heel and the ball of your foot. Wrap the rope around the outside of your ankle so that its ends are on the inside. Contract your *adductors* (inner thigh muscles) and sweep the leg across your body, passing just above your other leg. Keep your knee locked. When you feel tension in your leg, gently pull on the rope to extend the range of the stretch. Hold the stretch for one to two seconds, return to the starting position, and repeat five to ten times.

To stretch your iliotibial band while standing, lean against a wall with your injured leg away from the wall. Put your non-injured leg behind the opposite leg. Lean into the wall, away from the injured leg, until you feel a stretch along your iliotibial band (see Figure 13-5).

Photograph by Maurice Roy Photography

Figure 13-5: Lean in the direction opposite the injury to stretch the iliotibial band.

Achilles tendonitis and tendinosis

Achilles tendonitis and *tendinosis* are very common injuries in runners. The Achilles tendon attaches your two calf muscles *(gastrocnemius* and *soleus)* to your heel and is the thickest and strongest tendon in your body. Because of its location and the stress it bears from running, runners have 30 times the risk of developing Achilles tendonitis and tendinosis compared to people who don't run. An injury to the Achilles tendon occurs when the amount of stress on the tendon exceeds the ability of the tendon to adapt to the load.

Causes of Achilles tendonitis and tendinosis include

- ✔ Calf weakness
- ✔ Hill running
- ✔ Inadequate recovery time between workouts
- ✔ Inappropriate increases in mileage
- ✔ Overpronation
- ✔ Poor calf muscle flexibility
- ✔ Too much interval training

Symptoms

For the first few days of this injury, you may have inflammation (tendonitis — *itis* means inflammation), but any pain you feel is the result of a degenerative process (tendinosis) in the collagen fibers that make up the tendon. Over time, the fibers may weaken, leading to a partial tearing of the tendon.

Achilles tendonitis and tendinosis are very easy to diagnose. The only symptom is a gradual onset of pain on the Achilles tendon (see Figure 13-6). In mild cases, you may experience pain only when you run. As it becomes more severe, you may experience pain with your normal daily activities or even at rest. In worse cases, the tendon becomes tender to the touch and visibly swollen. Pinching the tendon between your thumb and forefinger usually reproduces the pain.

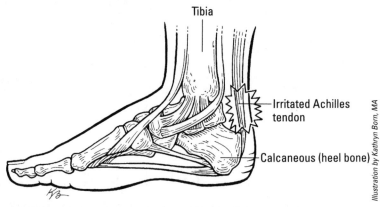

Tibia

Irritated Achilles tendon

Calcaneous (heel bone)

Illustration by Kathryn Born, MA

Figure 13-6: The symptom of Achilles tendonitis and tendinosis is unmistakable — pain on your Achilles tendon that is tender to the touch.

Treatment

To treat Achilles tendonitis and tendinosis, follow these guidelines:

✔ **Get different shoes:** If overpronation is the cause of your Achilles tendonitis and tendinosis, you may need to change your shoes to ones that offer more medial support to prevent your foot from pronating. For more on how to choose running shoes, turn to Chapter 2.

✔ **Ice:** Fill a Styrofoam cup with water and freeze it. Tear away some of the foam from the top so the ice protrudes. Massage the ice over the injured area using a circular motion for ten minutes. Repeat three to four times per day.

✔ **Muscle strengthening:** Strengthen your calf muscles, especially with eccentric training, during which your muscle fibers lengthen while they contract. Eccentric strength training promotes the formation of *collagen,* the main component of your tendon, which strengthens the tendon. For calf strengthening exercises, stride carefully to Chapter 11.

✔ **Reduce your training:** Back off on the types of workouts that put extra stress on the Achilles tendon, such as interval training and hill running. Faster-paced workouts, during which you push your foot harder against the ground, and the flexed position of your foot when running uphill activate your calves more, putting extra stress on your Achilles tendon.

Plantar fasciitis

The *plantar fascia* is a band of connective tissue on the bottom of your foot that runs from your heel to your toes. It acts like a ligament that helps support the arch of your foot when you run. Similar to Achilles tendinosis (see the preceding section), plantar fasciitis is a degenerative condition in which the fascia on the bottom of your foot has become irritated. As a result of this degeneration, microscopic tears occur when the plantar fascia is overloaded, and it loses its ability to support your arch.

Causes of plantar fasciitis include

✔ Calf muscle weakness

✔ Flat or high-arched feet

✔ Increasing mileage or speed training too quickly

✔ Weakness in the muscles of the sole of the foot

Symptoms

With plantar fasciitis, you can feel pain on your heel or arch, but the pain usually occurs where the fascia meets your heel bone (see Figure 13-7). The pain is often worse during the first few steps in the morning when you get out of bed or when you get up to walk after you've been sitting for a long time. It usually decreases slightly when you run and aches after you run. As the condition becomes more severe, the pain may be present all the time when you walk or run.

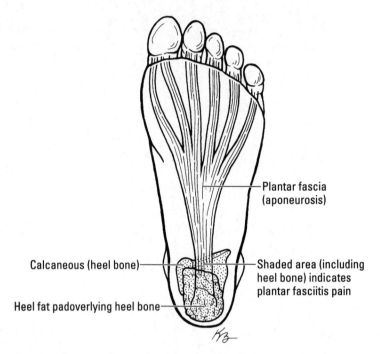

Plantar fascia
(aponeurosis)

Calcaneous (heel bone)

Shaded area (including
heel bone) indicates
plantar fasciitis pain

Heel fat padoverlying heel bone

Illustration by Kathryn Born, MA

Figure 13-7: You feel plantar fasciitis as pain on the bottom of your foot.

Treatment

Plantar fasciitis can be a stubborn injury. To treat it, follow these guidelines:

- ✔ **Exercises for the sole of your foot:** Roll your foot over a small foam roller or golf or tennis ball for a few minutes at a time for a few times each day (see Figure 13-8).

- ✔ **Rest:** As with most overuse injuries, back off on the volume and intensity of running.

- ✔ **Strengthening and stretching your calf muscles:** Your calf muscles, along with your Achilles tendons, support the opposite side of the hinge joint from your plantar fascia. For strengthening exercises, see Chapter 11; for stretching exercises, see Chapter 12.

- ✔ **Tension splint:** Wear a splint overnight to hold your foot in a flexed position while you sleep. This stretches the fascia on the bottom of your foot.

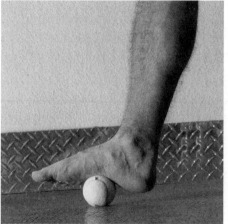

Figure 13-8: Roll your foot on a ball to treat plantar fasciitis.

Shin splints

Shin splints are a common injury in new and inexperienced runners whose bones aren't yet used to the impact of running. Shin splints (officially called *medial tibial stress syndrome*) occur because the *tibia* (the larger of the two lower leg bones that bear your weight) is exposed to excessive shock to which it's initially unable to adapt. Although shin splints aren't a serious injury, if they're not properly treated, they may progress to the more serious injury of a stress fracture (see the next section).

Causes of shin splints include:

- ✔ Excessive ankle pronation
- ✔ Excessively tight calf muscles, which can cause excessive pronation
- ✔ Increasing running mileage or intensity too quickly
- ✔ Running on hard surfaces, like concrete and asphalt

Symptoms

As its medical name implies, you feel pain along the medial (inner) border of the tibia (see Figure 13-9). The pain is usually dull and poorly localized and feels like someone has kicked you repeatedly.

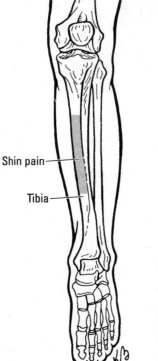

Shin pain
Tibia

Illustration by Kathryn Born, MA

Figure 13-9: Shin splints most commonly occur on the medial side of the tibia.

Treatment

Shin splints often heal on their own as your lower leg adapts to the stress of running. To be proactive in treating shin splints, follow these guidelines:

- ✔ **Get different shoes:** Shoes with sufficient shock-absorbing characteristics can reduce forces on your lower legs and prevent repeat episodes of shin splints. For more on running shoes, stride on over to Chapter 2.

- ✔ **Ice:** Fill a Styrofoam cup with water and freeze it. Tear away some of the foam from the top so the ice protrudes. Massage the ice over the injured area using a circular motion for ten minutes. Repeat three to four times per day.

- ✔ **Muscle strengthening:** Strengthen the muscles of your lower leg, including calves and shin muscles. (Check out Chapter 11 for some exercises.)

Stress fractures

A more serious progression from shin splints (see the preceding section), a *stress fracture* is a hairline fracture in a bone caused by the bone being exposed to repeated stress. It occurs when either an abnormal stress is applied to a healthy bone or when a normal stress is applied to a weakened bone.

Healthy bone adapts to both the stress of bearing weight and the stress of muscle forces. External stress is so important to bone health that the absence of stress by immobilization causes your bone density to decrease by 1 percent per week! So your bones need stress; just not too much of it applied too quickly.

Running provides a great stress to your bones. When you run, your bones get stronger through a process called *bone remodeling.* Like a fickle homeowner who can't decide whether to remodel the kitchen in English country or art deco, bones are constantly remodeling themselves. Bone cells called *osteoclasts* remove small areas of old bone, a process called *resorption,* and other cells called *osteoblasts* synthesize new bone in its place, a process called *formation.* This cyclic process of bone resorption and formation occurs throughout your life. A stress fracture occurs when there's an imbalance in the bone remodeling process and the bone is unable to adequately adapt to the repetitive stress of running.

Causes of stress fractures include

- ✔ Increasing running mileage too quickly
- ✔ Insufficient recovery between runs
- ✔ Low bone mineral density, which can be caused by osteoporosis or a calcium or vitamin D deficiency

Under certain conditions, female runners have a greater risk of stress fractures than male runners. Causes of stress fractures in female runners include

- ✔ **Lack of muscle mass in the lower leg:** A major role of muscles is to absorb energy. With a small lower leg muscle mass, energy absorption is compromised and your bones absorb more of the stress when you run.

- ✔ **Low estrogen level:** Estrogen protects bone and therefore plays a big part in women's bone health. Any condition that lowers estrogen level, such as irregular or absent menstrual cycles or menopause, increases the risk of a stress fracture. If you're a woman with an irregular menstrual cycle, you have a two to four times greater risk of a stress fracture than women with regular menstrual cycles, and you have an increased risk of having another stress fracture. (For more on the effects of low estrogen, see the later section, "Recognizing the Female Athlete Triad.")

✔ **Not consuming enough calories:** Women, even more so than men, need to consume enough calories to balance their caloric expenditure from running. When you don't consume enough calories, you can have problems with your menstrual cycle, which causes bones to become weaker.

Symptoms

Stress fractures are classified as low-risk and high-risk based on the fracture site and their risk of complications. Most stress fractures in runners are low-risk. The most common stress fracture site in runners is the medial (inside) or posterior (back) portion of the tibia bone (see Figure 13-10). The next most common site is the metatarsal bones in your foot, especially the second, third, and fourth metatarsals. Stress fractures in the neck of the femur and pelvis are more common in female runners and carry a risk of serious complications if they're not properly treated.

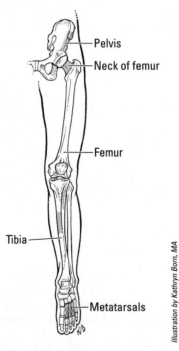

Pelvis

Neck of femur

Femur

Tibia

Metatarsals

Illustration by Kathryn Born, MA

Figure 13-10: The most common sites for a stress fracture.

With a stress fracture, you feel a gradual onset of pain that develops toward the end of a run. Stress fractures are characterized by a sharp pain at a specific point on the bone that can be felt when pressing on it. Sometimes, swelling over the fracture site occurs. With continued running, the pain increases and starts earlier in the run. If left untreated, pain occurs with walking and even at rest. In the case of a femoral neck stress fracture, the pain is usually felt in the groin and is often confused with a groin strain.

Treatment

Most runners hate getting a stress fracture because it means they can't run. But bones actually heal faster than other tissues, like tendons and ligaments. If you take care of your stress fracture, it won't linger like other injuries can.

To treat a stress fracture, follow these guidelines:

- ✔ **Ice:** Fill a Styrofoam cup with water and freeze it. Tear away some of the foam from the top so the ice protrudes. Massage the ice over the injured area using a circular motion for ten minutes. Repeat three to four times per day.

- ✔ **Muscle strengthening:** Strengthen the muscle groups surrounding the joints above and below the fracture site. (Chapter 11 has some strengthening exercises you can try.)

- ✔ **Stop running:** Most stress fractures require four to eight weeks of no running.

 In addition to training smarter and not increasing your weekly running mileage or the distance of your long runs too quickly, maintaining your bone health is the greatest defense against stress fractures. Training for a marathon puts a lot of stress on your bones, so you need to make sure you consume adequate amounts of calcium and vitamin D. Both men and women need 1,000 milligrams of calcium and 400 International Units (IU) of vitamin D per day. If you're a woman over 50 or are post-menopausal, you need a little more: 1,200 milligrams of calcium and 600 to 800 IU of vitamin D per day.

Chronic muscle strain

A *chronic muscle strain* is the most common muscle injury in runners. A partial tearing of the muscle occurs from excessive tension due to too much repetition or high forces. Running long distances and having weak muscles can cause muscle strains as the muscles fatigue.

Symptoms

With a chronic muscle strain, there's a gradual onset of pain coming from deep within the muscle that usually comes on after you run and then starts to become bothersome during running. The pain almost always occurs in a large muscle group, including the buttocks, hamstrings, groin, or calves (see Figure 13-11). The severity of the pain depends on how much of the muscle has been torn. When you press firmly into the affected area of the muscle, it feels like a hard knot and reproduces the pain.

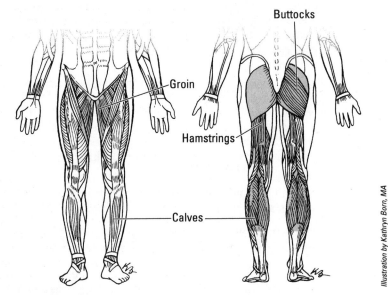

Figure 13-11: Muscle tears occur in big muscle groups.

Illustration by Kathryn Born, MA

Treatment

Besides rest, only one treatment is effective for a chronic muscle strain — *deep tissue massage,* sometimes called *cross-friction massage,* applied to the painful area. If you can handle the pain of cross-friction massage yourself, press very firmly with your thumbs into the muscle and rub your thumbs in opposing directions. Because this maneuver hurts, I suggest you ask someone else to apply cross-friction massage to your muscle or go to a physical therapist. Most chronic muscle strains respond rapidly to a few sessions of cross-friction massage.

Recognizing the Female Athlete Triad

I've known for a long time that women are more complicated than men. When it comes to running-related injuries, female runners have specific issues to look out for that men never have to deal with.

The *female athlete triad* refers to a collection of associated characteristics that, when present, dramatically increases the risk for stress fractures in female runners. The female athlete triad includes

- ✔ **Disordered eating:** Disordered eating, common among female runners because of external or self-imposed pressure to lose weight, refers to eating an unbalanced diet that lacks nutrients and calories. It's not the same as an eating disorder like anorexia or bulimia. When training for a marathon, don't restrict calories, as doing so can lead to irregular menstruation and low bone density.

- ✔ **Menstrual irregularities:** Running a lot can cause irregular or even absent menstrual cycles (called *amenorrhea*), which increases the risk for osteoporosis and stress fractures. When your cycle becomes irregular or doesn't occur at all, your estrogen level drops, which puts your bones at risk. Female runners with irregular menstruation or amenorrhea have a lower bone density than female runners with normal menstruation.

- ✔ **Osteoporosis:** *Osteoporosis,* which literally means *porous bones,* is a severe reduction in bone density. Estrogen deficiency is the most significant risk factor for osteoporosis in active women.

If you have any of the characteristics of the female athlete triad, get your bone density assessed to determine whether you're at risk for injury. If you have low bone density, you need to take extra care to protect your bones from injury while you train for your marathon. Strategies to increase bone density include

- ✔ Birth-control pills, which provide bone-protecting estrogen
- ✔ Calcium and vitamin D supplements
- ✔ Strength training

When your estrogen level is normal, bone resorption and formation are in balance and your skeletal strength and integrity are maintained. However, when your estrogen level is low, as occurs with menstrual irregularities or after you've gone through menopause, you lose bone. The loss of estrogen reduces bone mass in two ways:

✔ First, calcium excretion is increased, resulting in disruption in calcium balance and a need for more calcium.

✔ Second, bone resorption is accelerated without an increase in bone formation to compensate.

Part IV

Gearing Up for Race Day (And Beyond)

The 5th Wave   By Rich Tennant

"You've got to start tapering back. This is the third time you've fallen out of the wheel this week."

In this part...

You're almost there! After all that training, it's time to put the finishing touches on your preparation and attend to all the little details for the big day — including calming those nerves!

This part covers the final preparations for the marathon, including details about what to do during your marathon taper, insightful pre-race and during-race strategies to run your best race, and, when it's all over, how to recover after you cross the finish line — and get ready for your next marathon!

Chapter 14

Backing Off Before You Give Your All: The Marathon Taper

. . . .

In This Chapter

▶ Seeing why tapering helps you run a better marathon

▶ Designing your own taper plan

▶ Consuming extra carbohydrates during your taper

. . . .

For months, you've poured all your energy and concentration into training. You've increased your mileage, built your intensity, and maybe even quickened your pace. And as the day you've worked so hard for approaches, of course you want to . . . slow down? Actually, yes. You want to taper.

Tapering, or reducing your training load, enables you to recover from the training you've completed so that you're fresh and ready to go on race day. The marathon taper is a time to get excited. You've done all the hard training and can begin to relax and look forward to your upcoming marathon.

Because most marathoners are a driven bunch by nature or by training, you may think that cutting your weekly running mileage to a fraction of your peak training just before the race is unnatural. Marathoners tend to think they should always do more. But that's one of the most interesting things about fitness — the adaptations to training occur during the *recovery* from training, not during the training itself. In this chapter, I give you all the details you need to know about the marathon taper, including how much and how long to taper your training.

Understanding the Marathon Taper

A *taper* is a decrease in mileage leading into your marathon. You taper for a couple of reasons:

✔ **To adapt to the training you've completed:** Adapting to training is all about stress and recovery. During training, you experience stress. During recovery, you adapt to that stress. When you taper your training, you provide your body the opportunity to recover, adapt, and overcompensate to the training you've done so that you're prepared to run your best race.

✔ **To reduce the fatigue from the training you've completed:** Because it gives your body a rest, tapering is one of the main factors that enables you to have fresh legs to run your best race.

As with any type of training, the way your body responds to tapering depends on a lot of factors unique to you. You'll probably respond to a taper differently from your running partner. In the following sections, I explain how the taper helps gear up your body for your marathon.

Checking out the benefits of tapering

Tapering has a number of effects that enable you to run a better race. They include the following (see Chapter 3 for more details about the physiology of running):

✔ **Better aerobic fitness:** Tapering increases or maintains VO_2max. *VO_2max* is the maximum volume of oxygen your muscles can consume per minute and is an important indicator of your aerobic fitness — your ability to succeed at endurance activities like the marathon.

✔ **Faster muscle contraction:** Tapering increases your aerobic enzyme activity. Because enzymes control the rate at which chemical reactions happen, having more aerobic enzymes in your muscles enables your muscles to regenerate energy for muscle contraction more quickly. The faster your muscles can do their job, the faster the pace you can sustain in the marathon.

✔ **Greater fuel storage in your muscles:** Tapering increases the amount of carbohydrates stored in your muscles, referred to as *glycogen.* More glycogen means more fuel, which helps you hold your marathon pace longer.

✔ **Healthy, healed muscle tissue:** *Creatine kinase,* an enzyme in muscles, appears in the blood only when you have muscle damage. You have less creatine kinase in your blood after a taper, which means the normal, microscopic muscle damage caused by training has healed, leaving you with muscles that can generate greater power and endurance.

✔ **Increased muscle strength and power:** Stronger, more powerful muscles take longer to fatigue, which is a good thing when you're running 26.2 miles!

✔ **More red blood cells to carry oxygen:** Greater red blood cell volume and healthier red blood cells mean that your blood can better carry oxygen to your working muscles. The muscles use the oxygen to produce energy so you can keep running for a long time. You also have greater blood volume, which means that your heart pumps out more oxygen-rich blood with each beat. All that adds up to better endurance.

The amount of marathon training you do is relative to the level of runner you are, and the more you run before the taper, the more you benefit from the taper. For example, if you run 60 miles per week before you taper, you reap a greater benefit from your taper than if you run 30 miles per week before tapering. It's hard to taper down something that hasn't been built up. Expect a much bigger difference in how your legs feel at the starting line when dropping weekly mileage from 60 to 20 compared to dropping mileage from 30 to 20. If you're a beginner, you may not run more than 30 miles per week to train for the marathon. That's fine, but you can't expect to reap as much from your taper as a more advanced runner who runs 60 miles per week (or more) before tapering.

Finding the sweet spot: The "why" behind your taper time

You taper so that your body has time to recover from the training you've done. However, you don't want to undo all your hard work. The idea is to decrease fatigue without losing fitness, and that's a delicate balance. You don't want to make your taper so long that you start to lose fitness, but you want it to be long enough that you're completely recovered from all the training and are as fresh as possible for the race.

For most runners, two weeks is usually adequate to taper before the marathon. However, the exact length of your taper depends on

✔ How much you ran in the weeks and months prior to the taper

✔ How quickly you lose fitness

✔ Your level of fatigue

If you tend to fall out of shape fast, you don't want a long taper. For most people, two weeks is the maximum taper — long enough that you get all the good, healing benefits but not so long that your fitness begins to decline. If you've been running more than about 50 miles per week, you may want to taper for up to three weeks.

Age and experience affect taper time. If you're 40 or older, you may need to taper for longer than two weeks because age increases the amount of time you need to recover from training. If you're a beginner, you may need to taper for less than two weeks because your weekly running mileage probably isn't very high in the first place, and you want to spend as much time as possible improving your endurance before the marathon.

Do the Math: Figuring Out Your Mileage during a Taper

You know tapering means running less mileage, but how much less, and how fast? A lot less: You can dramatically reduce how much you run per week during your taper, and you can do it quickly. The following sections help you crunch the numbers and build a specific taper plan.

Exactly what you do during your taper depends on what you did before the taper. You may feel a little guilty during the taper. That's okay; cutting back is hard for most runners. But don't worry — you really are doing wonders for your body and your mind by decreasing the workload and recovering before the big day.

Crunching the numbers for different taper lengths

The trick to maintaining fitness during the taper is to maintain the intensity of your workouts with tempo and interval training while reducing the number of miles you run per week.

If you're tapering for two weeks (which is best for beginner runners), reduce your peak weekly mileage by

- ✔ 30 percent the first week
- ✔ 60 percent the second week (not counting the marathon itself)

For a three-week taper (which is best for intermediate and advanced runners who've been running more than 50 miles each week), reduce your peak weekly mileage by

- ✔ 30 percent the first week
- ✔ 50 percent the second week
- ✔ 65 percent the third week (not counting the marathon itself)

For example, if you've been running 40 miles per week, you should taper for only two weeks. Drop your mileage over the final two weeks of your program by 30 percent (to 28 miles) and then by 60 percent (to 16 miles). In addition, decrease the length of your long run by the same percentage as the drop in your weekly mileage. So, if your weekly mileage drops 30 percent, decrease the length of your long run by 30 percent.

Reduce your mileage over the last few days leading into the marathon by using your weekly percentages so that the pattern of reduction is the same over the final few days as it is over the final few weeks. For a three-week taper, then, you'd cut back by 30 percent four days before the marathon, 50 percent three days before, 65 percent two days before, and not run the day before.

If you're a new runner training for your first marathon, I don't suggest tapering your mileage for three weeks and doing your last long run three weeks before the marathon. As a beginner, that's too much time to back off your training for a race that's so dependent on aerobic endurance. You'll end up losing fitness in those three weeks. You need to spend as much time as possible developing yourself aerobically, so taper for only two weeks at the most.

Building a taper plan

Although you want to keep up your intensity during tapering to maintain your fitness level, you need to reduce the number of intervals in each interval workout you do but continue running at the same pace. For example, if your normal interval workout is 5 reps of 800 meters, run only 3 or 4 intervals during your taper so that you maintain the intensity but decrease the running volume.

Table 14-1 shows you what a two-week pre-marathon taper might look like for a beginner runner who was running 36 miles per week at his or her peak during training (just like the plan in Chapter 8). Table 14-2 shows you what a three-week pre-marathon taper might look like for a runner who was running 50 miles per week at his or her peak during training (just like the plan in Chapter 9). Your actual mileage during a taper depends on your own weekly mileage.

Table 14-1   **Sample Two-Week Pre-Marathon Taper**

Week	Mon.	Tues.	Wed.	Thurs.	Fri.	Sat.	Sun.	Total Miles
1	Rest	Tempo Intervals – 1 mile warm-up – 5 × 1,200 meters (¾ mile) at acidosis threshold (AT) pace with 1 minute rest between each rep – 1 mile cool-down	Rest	5 miles	Tempo Run – 1 mile warm-up – 2.5 miles at AT pace – 1 mile cool-down	Rest	10 miles	25 miles
2	Rest	Tempo Intervals – 1 mile warm-up – 4 × 1,200 meters (¾ mile) at AT pace with 1 minute rest between each rep – 1 mile cool-down	Rest	5 miles	3 miles	Rest or 1–2 miles very easy	**Marathon**	13 to 15 miles (plus marathon)

Table 14-2 **Sample Three-Week Pre-Marathon Taper**

Week	Mon.	Tues.	Wed.	Thurs.	Fri.	Sat.	Sun.	Total Miles
1	4 miles	6 miles	Aerobic Power Intervals − 2 mile warm-up −4 × 1,000 meters (⅝ mile) at VO_2max pace with 2-minute jog recovery between each rep − 1 mile cool-down	5 miles	6 miles	Rest	AT/LSD Combo Run Continuous run of 6 miles easy + 2 miles at AT pace + 1 mile faster than AT pace	36 miles
2	2 miles	4 miles	Marathon Pace Run 5 miles at goal marathon pace	2 miles	4 miles	Rest	Marathon Pace Run Continuous run of 4 miles easy + 4 miles at goal marathon pace − 2 miles warm-up	25 miles
3	2.5 miles	Tempo Intervals −3 × 1,200 meters (¾ mile) at AT pace with 1 minute rest between each rep − 1 mile cool-down	5 miles	3 miles	1.5 miles	Rest	**Marathon**	17 miles (plus marathon)

Fueling Up while You Taper Down

Your muscles need carbohydrates to make it through a marathon. Carbs, in the form of glucose (sugar), are muscles' preferred fuel, so loading up on carbs *(carbo-load)* in the days leading up to the marathon pays off in your ability to run later.

Although a lot of attention has been given to dinner the night before the marathon, a pasta party in which you slurp up a big plate of spaghetti doesn't do the trick. Your muscles can store only a few hundred extra calories of carbohydrate per day, so eat a little more carbohydrate each day for a few days before the race while you taper.

To effectively carbo-load during your taper, gradually increase the percentage of carbohydrates you consume so that 70 percent of your daily calories come from carbohydrates. That's a lot of carbohydrates, but you're going to need them for the marathon. Think of the extra carbs as your jet fuel. You want to store as much as you can prior to the marathon and use up all the fuel as you run the race.

You need approximately 500 to 600 grams of carbohydrates per day to get your carbohydrate stores where you want them. Consume most of your carbohydrates as complex carbohydrates, such as bagels, pasta, potatoes, and other starches. Save the simple carbohydrates — such as fruit, chocolate milk, and nutrition bars and gels — for immediately after your runs to speed up glycogen storage.

But there's a caveat: Although men simply need to increase the percentage of their calories coming from carbohydrates in order to store more carbs in their muscles during the taper, women need to also increase the total number of calories in their diets to get the same effect. Increasing your total calories may make you gain some weight during the taper — especially because you're not training as much and therefore not burning as many calories — but don't worry about it. You'll lose it all during the marathon. If the thought of a few pounds really bothers you, decrease the amount of fat you consume during your taper.

Chapter 15

Getting a Boost with Practical and Motivational Pre-Race Strategies

● ●

In This Chapter

▶ Getting ready for the marathon

▶ Coming up with a race-day plan

● ●

*Y*ou've done all the training, you've tapered (with the help of Chapter 14), and now it's time to focus on the marathon. What separates successful marathon runners from unsuccessful ones is the attention to all the little things. Those little things add up to big things in the marathon. In this chapter, I give you many helpful strategies to put you at ease, increase your chances of running a good race, and minimize those crazy marathon jitters.

Gearing Up before the Big Day

The week before the marathon is all about attending to the little things, as you find out in the following sections. You need to take care of travel, pick up your race number at the expo, and prepare your marathon kit (among other tasks) so that on race day, all you have to do is run. Because you won't run much the last few days before the race, it's good that you have so many other things to think about! The week of the marathon, reduce outside stress in your life as much as possible. This isn't a good time to get married or divorced. And stay away from anything new: new speed work-outs, hot yoga, bungee jumping, or anything else that's not part of your normal routine.

Staying off your feet

I have a friend in California who ran the New York City Marathon. He traveled there with his wife and kids a couple of days before and toured the city. He was on his feet so much during those days that his legs felt lifeless in the marathon, and he ended up having a lousy race. Well, duh! You don't want lifeless legs in the marathon; you want fresh legs full of vitality. If you travel somewhere to run a marathon, especially if that place is a tourist destination like New York, San Francisco, or Boston, stay off your feet for the few days leading into the race and make sure you get adequate sleep. Run your marathon first and then go be a tourist.

The marathon race expo is the perfect opportunity to ruin your marathon. Everyone looks forward to the expo, where you get great deals on running shoes and clothes, hang out with your running buddies, check out all the vendors, and munch on free samples from various nutrition companies, all while walking around and standing on your feet! The expo isn't the time to go shopping for running clothes. Although you can get some good deals, don't sacrifice your race by being on your feet for a couple of hours at the expo the day before your marathon just so you can find a cute pair of running shorts. When you get inside the expo, pick up your race number and T-shirt and get out. I mean it. (See the later section "Picking up your race number" for more info.)

Preparing for the weather

The weather affects the marathon more than any other running race (except for ultra-marathons, but that's a whole different book!), so you better be prepared. Check the weather report a day or two before the race. If you're traveling to the race, check the weather before you travel so you know what to pack. Hot and cold marathons require different preparations. A hot marathon is worse than a cold one because of the consequences of dehydration and overheating.

Here's what to do if it's going to be hot:

- ✔ Wear loose-fitting, moisture-wicking, light-colored clothes that reflect the sunlight.
- ✔ Wear a moisture-wicking running hat to keep the sun off your face and eyes.
- ✔ Stay hydrated by drinking plenty of fluid in the days leading up to the race, and sip on a sports drink the morning of the race, up until a few minutes before the race starts.

✔ Wear sunscreen to protect yourself from getting sunburned.

✔ If you know in advance that it's going to be hot (like if you're running a marathon in Arizona or Hawaii), acclimatize to the heat beforehand by running some of your long runs in the heat. Chronically exposing yourself to a hot and humid environment stimulates adaptations that lessen the stress. Take two weeks to slowly introduce yourself to the heat to be fully acclimatized and prepared for the marathon. If you're traveling to a hot location from a colder one, try doing some of your runs on a treadmill indoors.

✔ The morning of the race, stay in a cool place for as long as possible before the marathon starts. If you have to be outside, find some shade or wear a hat.

✔ Run the first few miles of the marathon at a slower pace than you had originally planned.

Here's what to do if it's going to be cold:

✔ Wear something to keep you warm while you wait at the start line, like a garbage bag or old sweats that you can toss to the side at the last minute.

✔ Wear gloves to keep your hands warm.

✔ Wear a hat to cover your head and ears.

✔ Wear a long-sleeve polyester shirt.

✔ Wear an extra top that's polyester or a polyester-Lycra blend layer that you can peel off during the marathon if you get warm.

✔ If you know in advance that it's going to be cold (like if you're running a marathon in New York in November), acclimatize to the cold beforehand by running some of your long runs in the cold.

If it's raining, wear a hat with a brim to block the rain from getting into your eyes. Regardless of what you wear, dress for comfort and don't wear any cotton. If your legs get cold easily, you may want to wear running tights instead of shorts. Most runners are comfortable running in shorts until the temperature drops below 40 to 45 degrees, but you know your body better than anyone, so run in whatever makes you feel comfortable. Just keep in mind that you'll be out there for a while, so although you may be cold at the start, you may get warm a couple of miles into the race.

Putting together your marathon kit

Your marathon kit includes everything you need before, during, and after the race. After you put on the clothes you'll wear in the marathon (see the preceding section), check the bag with your extra items at the gear check so you have access to them after the race (I talk about the gear check later in this chapter). Pack your bag a night or two before the race so you don't forget anything. Your marathon kit should include

- ✔ Shoes
- ✔ Singlet or T-shirt (stay away from cotton!)
- ✔ Shorts, running pants, or running tights
- ✔ Socks
- ✔ Underwear (including a sports bra if you're a woman)
- ✔ Race number
- ✔ Timing chip (if the marathon uses one)
- ✔ Bodyglide or Vaseline to prevent chafing
- ✔ Safety pins to pin your number to your shirt
- ✔ Hat (optional)
- ✔ Gloves (if it's cold)
- ✔ Dry socks to put on after the race
- ✔ Extra shirt to put on after the race
- ✔ Extra pair of shoes or sandals to put on after the race
- ✔ Towel
- ✔ Sealed water bottle with water or sports drink

Your kit can also include any of the extra gear I list in Chapter 2, such as a running watch and sunglasses.

Picking up your race number

Picking up your race number at the expo a day or two before the race is a big marathon ritual. It's the day everyone looks forward to. It's the day that makes the marathon feel real. There's no turning back now.

The race expo can be a little crazy, but there's no reason to get overwhelmed, even if it's your first marathon. Find out where to go to pick up your race number; volunteers will be on hand to direct runners. Race numbers are either alphabetized by last name or organized by number. If they're organized by number, you have to look up your number at the expo (at some marathons, you can look up your number online before you go to the expo). Make sure you get four safety pins along with your number to pin your number to your shirt.

Minimizing your jitters

Every runner gets nervous before a marathon. That's perfectly normal. Being nervous means that you care. You've spent countless hours preparing for the race, and now the day is here. The important thing is not to let your nervousness get the better of you and prevent you from running a good race. Acknowledge that you're nervous, but use that nervousness as fuel.

The marathon is a chance for you to challenge yourself to be what you want to be, to literally and figuratively put yourself on the line. Few people get that chance. The following sections note some strategies to minimize nervousness before the race.

Follow a routine

Humans are a lot like cats; they love routine. Come up with your own pre-race routine that includes what you do and eat the night before, your warm-up and stretching exercises, your bathroom breaks, visualizing the race, putting on your shoes, and anything else you do before a race, leading right up to the starting line. Do everything in the same order. If you've never run a marathon before, this is your chance to establish a routine for your next one!

Visualize your race

I know an Olympic 400-meter runner who sat in his dark dorm room closet in the Olympic Village the night before his race so he could visualize it. Because he didn't know what lane on the track he would be assigned until shortly before the race, he visualized running the 400 meters from each lane, seeing himself run each curve, each straightaway, each of the other runners. He visualized the crowd and the cameras. The next day, he won the gold medal and set a new world record.

The mind is a powerful tool. Visualizing your marathon before you run it allows you to experience it beforehand, making the experience familiar and thus making you less nervous and more comfortable. For a race as long as the marathon, locking yourself in the closet and seeing the entire race isn't practical; you'd spend a few hours in the closet! So practice visualizing parts of your marathon each day for a few days before it, seeing the whole experience. Try to use all your senses in your visualization. See the race course, feel the contraction of your muscles, see yourself blowing past other runners, hear your feet touch the ground, smell the air, see your-self respond positively to the fatigue, feel your pace, see the time on the clock as you run toward the finish line, taste the entire experience. Then, when it's time for your race, you'll have already run it.

You can visualize from an internal perspective, seeing the race through your own eyes as you run it, or from an external perspec-tive, as a spectator observing yourself run the race. Either way, visualize the result you want to see as many times as possible to ingrain that result in your mind.

Engage in positive self-talk

Believe it or not, successful people talk to themselves. Often, they have ongoing conversations with themselves, verbalizing and solidifying in their own heads what they want to accomplish. Although you may not want to talk to yourself out loud in public for fear of being thought of as crazy, self-talk can be a very powerful strategy to run a successful race. Everybody needs to be encouraged, motivated, and inspired. Sometimes, that encouragement, motivation, and inspiration can come from other people, but those qualities can also come from you. After all, running is, at its essence, all about you. So give yourself a pep talk before your race.

 Remind yourself of all the work you've done to get to the starting line and that you're ready for a great performance. Try repeating a positive sentence or phrase like "I can do this!" or "I'm ready for a great performance!" Ignite the fire in you and pump yourself up. Look at yourself in the mirror if you want. Tell yourself to stand up to your hopes and fears and to run the best race you can.

Asking friends and family to watch your race

No one wants to do things in anonymity. You may have moments when you want to be alone, when the more private side of you comes out, but generally, people like to be social. When they accomplish things, they want to share those accomplishments with other people in their lives.

Having friends and family in attendance at your marathon helps you run faster than you normally would. Everybody wants to show off, even if only a little. When you have people you know cheering for you, the marathon becomes something more than just all about you; with friends and family present, you're doing it for them, too, and that helps improve your performance.

Making a Solid Race-Day Plan

This may come as a surprise, but I've never been pregnant. I've also never been married to anyone pregnant, so I've never had to make the infamous plan you have to make so you're not running ragged the moment your water breaks. If you or your spouse have ever been pregnant, you know how important that plan is. It makes the birth day a whole lot easier and less stressful.

The last thing you want before your marathon is anxiety. Anxiety does nothing to help you run a good race. Having a solid race-day plan prevents disasters from happening by removing some of the unknowns and giving you something to focus on besides the butterflies in your stomach. Plan for such things as

- ✔ **Traffic:** If you're driving to the race, account for traffic and leave yourself plenty of time.

- ✔ **Parking:** Big marathons can make parking a nightmare, especially because lots of roads will be blocked for the race. Plan ahead where you're going to park.

- ✔ **Warming up:** Although you don't need to warm up much before a marathon (unless you're going to be running 5-minute miles!), you may still want to jog around and stretch a little. Many big marathons, like New York and Boston, hold you in corrals before the start, so you don't have much room to move around. Expect this, and have a plan for any warm-up you want to do. If you don't have room at the start to warm up, you may want to warm up before taking your place in the starting line corral.

- ✔ **Gear check:** Most marathons have a gear check near the start. If you have gear you want to check, know where the gear check is and give yourself time to wait in line to check it.

- ✔ **Waiting in line for a portable toilet:** This can be the most time consuming part of the marathon race morning, as everyone's anxiety and excitement have a way of moving food down into their colons in a hurry. So make sure you give yourself enough time. (If you're a guy, you may have some other options if there are any bushes nearby.)

- ✔ **Finding the correct pace group:** Many marathons have pace groups with a designated runner responsible for running the pace to lead the group to its goal time. These pace groups line up at the start, and the pace leader holds a sign or a balloon with the goal time written on it. Big marathons are crowded at the start, so it may take some time to find your pace group.

- ✔ **Hydrating:** Bring a water bottle with you to the start so you can stay hydrated.

✔ **Pre-race rituals:** If you have any rituals you like to do before the marathon, like warming up, stretching, meditating, kissing your spouse, or even praying, give yourself enough time to carry out those rituals so you can begin the race relaxed and ready to give your best effort. And don't forget to apply Bodyglide before the start. When you run for long periods, you can get chafed in places you don't want to get chafed, which can make the marathon miserable. Rub Bodyglide on any body parts that you'll rub up against, including your inner thighs, nipples, and below your armpits.

The following sections cover some of the preceding tasks in more detail.

Fueling up with your pre-race meal

Most marathons begin very early in the morning. That means you have to get up very, very early in the morning to eat breakfast. When you first get up, your blood glucose and muscle and liver glycogen are low because you haven't eaten for many hours. The marathon requires carbohydrate for energy. When carbohydrate is unavailable, your muscles are forced to rely on fat, which slows down your pace because your muscles take longer to produce energy when they use fat than when they use carbohydrate. You want to have glucose ready to use in your blood so you can run a faster pace and make it to the finish line. So you need to fuel up before you run.

Your pre-race meal improves your energy level prior to the start of the marathon. Aim for 300 to 400 calories of easily digestible carbohydrate and protein, one to two hours before the start of the race, such as

✔ A banana

✔ An energy bar

✔ Juice or a sports drink

✔ A potato

✔ Rice- or corn-based cereal

✔ Scrambled eggs

✔ Toast with peanut butter

Every runner is different and can tolerate different types and amounts of food. Find out what works for you by practicing it first. Use your long runs during training (see Chapters 8 through 10) to practice your pre-race meal. Eat the same thing for your pre-race meal that you've eaten before your long runs.

Beware the following as you plan and partake of your pre-race meal:

✔ Don't run the marathon on an empty stomach, even if the race starts early in the morning. You're going to need as much fuel in the marathon as you can get.

✔ Don't eat anything in your pre-race meal that you haven't already tried before during training. The last thing you want is an upset stomach at the beginning of a marathon. Stick with what has worked in the past. If you picked up some new energy bars or gels at the expo the day before, put them away and don't look at them until after the race.

✔ Avoid fiber like the plague in your pre-race meal, unless you want to spend half the marathon in the portable toilets along the course.

If you're traveling to the marathon and staying in a hotel, you have to do some planning the day before so you have breakfast lined up the morning of the race. If you can, stay in a hotel with a refrigerator in the room. Go shopping the day before and stock up on food for your pre-race meal, as well as food for when you get back to the hotel after the race. The day and night before the marathon, don't eat anything different from what you normally eat. You'll be eating out at a restaurant instead of cooking at home, but still eat the same food you normally eat.

Hydrating before your race

Regardless of the weather, hydrating before the marathon is very important. Beginning the race fully hydrated delays dehydration, helps you maintain your pace, and, if it's hot outside, decreases the risk of heat-related illnesses. Drink 16 ounces of water or a sports drink two hours before the race, and include sodium to increase hydration. Keep sipping on a sports drink up until a few minutes before the start.

Going to the bathroom

I didn't think I'd write about going to the bathroom when I sat down to write this book, but the bathroom is actually a big part of the marathon. Most marathon runners have a bathroom story to tell (see mine in the nearby sidebar). Although the urge to go to the bathroom is often suppressed while running (especially during long races) to conserve water and prevent dehydration, nervousness and anxiety before the race often intensify that urge, so you better take care of business before the race. Try to run your race on as empty a colon as possible.

A bathroom story

When I was in high school, my cross-country teammates and I would often walk the racecourses before our races to familiarize ourselves with them. Before our freshmen district championships, we were out walking the course and got a bit lost just as the race was going to start. Our coach came looking for us and brought us back to the starting line area, where we had to rush to get ready. I didn't have time to complete a warm-up, go to the bathroom, or do any pre-race rituals. I was so full of anxiety, my coach had to pin my race number to my uniform because I couldn't keep my hands still enough to maneuver the safety pins. I was the favorite to win the race, and one of my teammates, who had never beaten me, was the favorite to place second. So I had some pressure on me.

I got to the starting line just in time for the race to start. The race started off well, with me and my teammate taking the early lead. We were running together for a while, but by the time I got to the one-mile mark, I could feel the anxiety in my stomach and my lunch in my colon. Without going into messy details, I ran the rest of that race trying to hold back the strong urge to go to the bathroom. My teammate picked up the pace, and I couldn't keep up with him, too distracted by the urge that was quickly starting to reveal itself. Somehow, I held on for second place, although I was very disappointed because I was expected to win. It was the first time my teammate had beaten me, and I knew that victory would give him confidence for the rest of the season. Immediately after the race, I ran to the bathroom, where I spent the next 15 minutes.

All marathons have many portable toilets near the start, and most have them along the racecourse as well. They have long lines, so get to the start as early as you can to give yourself enough time to go to the bathroom. If you travel to the race and stay at a hotel very close to the start, you may be able to avoid the portable toilets altogether if you use your hotel bathroom before leaving the hotel.

Checking your gear at the start

Most marathons allow you to check a bag at the start that's transported to the finish while you run so you can claim it at the end of the race. If you have a friend or relative with you who'll be at the finish, you can just leave your bag with him or her. The bag is your post-marathon kit, including all the items you want at the finish (I talk about preparing your marathon kit earlier in this chapter). Know exactly where the gear check is so you can find it quickly when you get to the starting area. Check the marathon website for specific information about the gear check.

Chapter 16

Running the Marathon: Race Strategies and Tips

. . . .

In This Chapter

▶ Hitting your target time

▶ Paying attention to your body

▶ Staying mentally focused

▶ Recovering from the marathon (and doing better next time)

. . . .

Most runners run races without giving much thought as to how they're going to run them. They just pay their entry fee and run, without any intention to their actions, hoping for a good result. But running a successful marathon takes knowledge, planning, and execution, not to mention a little courage. When you train smartly and effectively and develop and execute your race plan, you'll achieve your potential and run a great race that you can be proud of. In this chapter, I give you the best strategies and tips for you to do just that.

Staying on Track to Hit Your Target Time

Most people who run a marathon have some idea of what time they want to run it in. Even those who say, "I just want to finish," are much happier finishing faster than slower. The longer you're out on the course, the longer it's uncomfortable. Luckily, you can do a number of things to increase the chances of running the time you want, including pace yourself properly, consume carbs, stay hydrated, and keep cool. I show you how to do all of them in the following sections.

Use the early stages of the marathon to establish a rhythm. Focus on your legs and your breathing and try to get as comfortable with the pace as possible. You can even try to get a beat in your head to follow. The earlier in the race you can establish a rhythm, the easier it is.

Pacing your race properly

I used to coach a talented runner who ran the first mile of every race too fast, only to slow down dramatically during the latter segments and end up disappointed with the result. He thought he was better than his workouts, and he let his competitive spirit and pre-race adrenaline obscure his knowledge of his true fitness level. Watching him start off so well and get slower with each successive lap of the track was frustrating. Only after he understood proper pacing did he see the level of success we both knew he could attain.

The single biggest mistake runners make when they race is that they start out too fast, way above their fitness level. They either ignore their training or fail to learn what pace is realistically sustainable for the entire race. This is especially true in the marathon. You can't put running time in the bank. You end up losing more time in the end than what you gained by being ahead of schedule in the beginning. No matter how strong your will and motivation are, running too fast too early forces you to slow down during the race's subsequent stages.

In shorter races, like 5K and 10K, which you run faster than acidosis threshold (AT) pace, going out too fast puts you even higher above your threshold, making the effort more *anaerobic* (not using oxygen) and causing a high degree of acidosis in your muscles, which makes you slow down. Because you run the entire marathon below your acidosis threshold, you don't have the same metabolic problem of acidosis when you go out too fast. However, you have another problem. When you start too fast in the marathon, you use up the precious and limited amount of carbohydrate in your muscles and liver faster. The faster the pace, the more your muscles rely on carbohydrate for fuel. The sooner you run out of carbohydrate, the sooner you hit the wall and are forced to slow down. (Flip to Chapters 3 and 5 for more about AT.)

The best way to run your marathon is by running the second half of the race at a pace that's equal to or slightly faster than the first half. When you run the second half faster, that's called running *negative splits*. To negative split a race requires accurate knowledge of your fitness level, confidence to stick to your plan when others run the early pace too fast, and a good dose of self-restraint.

To achieve a specific time goal, the most economical racing strategy is to prevent large fluctuations in pace and run as evenly as possible until you near the finish line. Ask yourself within the first mile or two, "Can I really hold this pace the entire way?" Be honest with yourself. If the answer is yes, then go for it. If the answer is no, then back off the pace so you can have a better race.

Don't run your marathon at some arbitrary pace, throwing caution to the wind and hoping for the best. Most runners, especially inexperienced ones running their first marathon, choose a pace that's too far over their heads. From your training — especially your long runs, tempo runs, and marathon pace runs — you should have a pretty good idea of the pace you can maintain. To estimate your marathon pace, stride on over to Chapter 5.

Throughout the race, both your perceived effort and the distance left to run subconsciously dictate your pace. When it feels hard, you back off; when you know you have many miles left to run, you're not as willing to push the pace. It's always better to be conservative early in the race. That way, when it gets late in the race, you'll have the reserve to push the pace.

Surging past other runners

Surging involves picking up the pace during your marathon for a brief period, usually with the intent of passing someone or of breaking away from a runner who's running near you. A change of pace in a marathon, even when it's a change to a faster pace, can often make you feel more comfortable and give you a boost of confidence. Passing people feels good.

If you're an advanced runner, a mid-race surge is a great way to separate yourself from other runners, especially those who have a stronger finishing kick than you. Good times to surge are when you want to break away from other runners, at the top of a hill, and when you sense that the runner next to you is laboring.

Practice running surges in your workouts so you can execute them in the marathon. During your runs, pick up the pace for 20 to 30 seconds. Start the surge abruptly and end it gradually. If you run with a group of runners of similar abilities, you can make a game out of surging and practice it with the other runners. Run together for five to ten miles, and designate one runner as the pacesetter whose job is to surge at different points in the run. When the pacesetter surges, you and the other runners react to the surge and pick up the pace to match the pacesetter. Or, instead of having just one pacesetter, you can have each runner in the group surge whenever she wants to, and you and the other runners can react to the surge and cover the move.

Running hills effectively

Many runners slow down in anticipation of hills and while running them. But don't fret. Don't try to maintain your pace when you climb hills, and don't try to charge up them, either. Running hills effectively is all about maintaining your rhythm. If you maintain your rhythm, you'll make molehills out of the mountains. Follow these tips for running hills (and check out Chapter 5 for details on hill training):

- As you start uphill, shorten your stride.

- Maintain your posture — don't lean too far forward or back. Your head, shoulders, and back should form a straight line over your feet.

- Keep your feet low to the ground.

- Increase the cadence of your arms.

- Listen to your breathing. If it begins to quicken, you're either going too fast or bounding too much.

- Be light on your feet. Push off by flicking your ankles.

- If the slope of the hill increases, shorten your stride to maintain a smooth breathing pattern. If the gradient decreases, extend your stride. Try to maintain the same steady effort and breathing throughout the hill.

- Run through the top of the hill. When you reach the top, lengthen your stride.

- Accelerate gradually into the downhill.

- On downhills, let gravity pull you, but don't freefall and slap your feet on the ground. Stay in control, step lightly, and don't reach out with your feet.

Drafting off other runners to save energy

If you've ever run on a windy day, you've experienced how difficult it is to run into a head wind. You consume more oxygen running into a head wind, which increases your perception of how hard you're working. By *drafting* behind another runner, however, you significantly reduce both the metabolic cost and your perception of effort. Tucking in behind someone and letting him pull you along is much easier than maintaining the pace on your own. So, whenever you can, let other runners do the work for you as long as possible, especially if it's windy.

Listening to Your Body

In a marathon, it's important to listen to what your body is telling you. At times in the race you'll feel great, and other times you'll feel bad. To maximize the times you feel great and minimize the times you feel bad, you often have to act *before* your body gives you a warning sign. Check out the tips in the following sections to get started.

Consuming carbs to reduce fatigue

Running out of carbohydrate is one of the biggest factors that cause fatigue in the marathon. Because carbohydrate is your muscles' preferred fuel, when you run out, you'll feel sluggish and start to slow down. That sluggish feeling is called *hitting the wall* or *bonking,* which happens when you run out of gas. So you want to maintain blood glucose levels for as long as you can.

 During the marathon, your muscles use carbohydrate at a faster rate than you can replenish blood glucose, but the trick is to try to delay running out of glucose for as long as possible. If you consume carbohydrate during the race, you can delay fatigue. Pretty neat, huh? How you do it is a little bit science and a little bit art. Here are some guidelines:

- ✔ Consume carbohydrate that's quickly digestible and easy on your stomach, like gels, gummy bears, and liquid. Many sport nutrition companies make carbohydrate products for use in marathons, like GU Energy Gel, PowerBar Energy Blasts, and Clif Shot Bloks, all of which come in a variety of flavors. Experiment with them in training to see what works for you (see Chapter 6 for help).

- ✔ Begin ingesting carbohydrate about 30 minutes *before* you start to feel fatigued, about an hour or so after starting the race, so you can absorb it into your blood and use it for energy. Ingest about 100 to 120 calories (25 to 30 grams) of carbohydrate every 20 to 30 minutes or so to maintain blood glucose levels.

- ✔ Instead of consuming a whole energy gel packet at once, which is a lot for your stomach to process, consume half at a time and chase it with water to speed digestion. You want to create a steady stream of carbohydrate coming into your blood to delay fatigue.

- ✔ Practice consuming carbs on some of your long runs so you can experiment with how much carbohydrate your stomach can tolerate. That way, by the time you get to race day, you'll know exactly what to do.

Staying hydrated and cool

Dehydration can become a big problem in the marathon. You lose water by sweating much faster than you can replace it by drinking, so you want to do whatever you can to delay dehydration. Your performance begins to decline with just a 2 to 3 percent loss of body weight from fluid loss. As you lose water, your cooling mechanism also starts to fail, increasing your body temperature. Like consuming carbs to delay bonking from low blood glucose (see the preceding section), if you want to run a better marathon, you must stay properly hydrated. (And although it feels good on a warm day to pour water over your head, it's better to ingest the water instead to keep you cool.)

Listen to your body and pay attention to your thirst. Thirst is a very reliable indicator that you need more fluid. Running slows the absorption of fluid from your stomach, so you need to begin drinking early so the fluid is available later. If you can drink fluid with sodium, like a sports drink, that's even better, because sodium helps you retain water. As a general rule, try to consume 5 to 6 ounces every two miles. If it's hot or you tend to sweat heavily, drink more.

Drinking out of those paper Dixie cups along the marathon course while you're running can be a challenge. Half the fluid ends up on your hands and the other half goes up your nose. To make sure you get the fluid into your body, pinch the lip of the cup so that you expose only a small opening.

Don't go crazy with drinking during the marathon. Drinking too much water can lead to a dangerous condition called *hyponatremia,* which is a drop in the sodium concentration of your blood. Slower runners have a greater risk for hyponatremia because they run a longer amount of time and therefore drink more. If you drink a lot during the marathon, grab a sodium-containing sports drink from the aid stations instead of plain water.

Breathing correctly

Your marathon pace should be slow enough that your breathing is quiet and relaxed for most of the race. If you hear your breathing, chances are you're running too fast. Because runners often link their perception of effort to how hard they're breathing, when you breathe heavily, you feel like you're working harder. Slow down until your breath is quiet.

Controlling your breath, an ancient practice among yoga masters that's believed to clear the mind and provide a sense of well-being, can also be valuable in the marathon. I don't know about providing a sense of well-being while you're running 26 miles, but controlling your breathing can help you relax and focus on the moment rather than thinking about all the miles you've run or all the miles you still have left to run. Breathe with both your nose and mouth and from your diaphragm rather than from your neck or chest to fill your lungs with oxygen.

One trick to controlling your breath is to coordinate your breathing to your stride rate while you run, which helps you create a rhythm to the marathon beat, making your run feel easier. Doing so also gives you something to focus on during the race and guides your effort as the course terrain changes, like when you run up a hill. Take three or four steps per breath, exhaling as your foot lands on the ground.

Don't try to take deeper breaths to the point that breathing becomes effortful. The more active your breathing, the more oxygen your diaphragm and other breathing muscles need, which means less oxygen is available for your leg muscles.

Keeping Your Mind in the Race

Even though your body does the work of running a marathon, your mind often determines your success. It's easy to let your mind wander in the marathon; after all, the race takes a few hours, and concentrating on anything for a few hours at a time is hard. The following sections describe some ways to keep your mind in the race.

Being patient the first half of the race

One of the biggest lessons I've learned as a runner and coach is patience. (Being a classic New Yorker who likes things done yesterday, I still struggle with it every day.) In the marathon, patience is more than just a virtue; it's your ticket to being successful and preventing a disaster. The first few miles of a marathon — heck, the first 13.1 miles — don't feel that hard. They actually feel (or should feel) pretty easy because you're running at a pace that you can hold (or hope to hold) for 26.2 miles. Even though the pace feels easy, you have to hold back; you have to be patient. See the earlier section "Pacing your race properly" for more details.

Drawing on deeper emotions to run your best race

I have a friend who was an excellent high school and college runner who said she would always draw on deeper emotions in a race. Emotions can be very powerful.

Drawing on deeper emotions during a race stimulates the secretion of hormones, which can help improve your performance. Stress, both physical and psychological, is associated with an increased secretion of stress hormones, including *cortisol.* Cortisol increases when you run very long and stimulates the breakdown of protein in your muscles. Your liver uses the amino acids that come from the breakdown of protein to make glucose to give you more fuel during your race. Competitive and psychologically stressful situations increase cortisol even more, further increasing the availability of fuel when you need it most.

Hormones aside, there's also an inexplicable side to the powerful effect of emotions. They can bring you to places you never thought possible. My father died when I was 8, and my mother died a year and a half before the writing of this book. Sometimes, when I'm running a race, I draw on the deep emotions I have about losing my parents. In those moments, I'm in a place where no one knows, where no one can be but me. It's a place made up of anger, fear, emotional distress, and love. It's a cathartic experience. I draw on those emotions to fulfill my physical potential. It's so draining that I can do it only on certain occasions. When you get to the point in the marathon when it starts to become difficult, draw on deeper emotions and be amazed at the outcome.

Being positive and confident

One of the distinguishing characteristics of successful people — whether they're used car salesmen or Olympic champions — is their unrelenting ability to remain positive, even in the face of negative circumstances. You often can't control what happens to you, but you can control how you respond to what happens to you.

I have a friend who completed her first marathon in 6½ hours. After her experience, which she said was miserable, she told me that, prior to the marathon, her parents said they didn't believe she could do it. Instead of being excited for her, supporting her, and pumping her up, they put her down. Her parents' voice was with her the whole race, and she doubted herself. Her race turned out to be a disaster, and she swore she'd never run another marathon.

If you go into the marathon thinking you're not going to do well, you likely won't. Or if you think at mile 18, "Oh boy, I feel like crap and I still have 8.2 miles to go," you'll make things even more difficult for yourself. You need to recognize those thoughts and immediately refocus your thinking on the process. Remaining positive when things don't go as planned before or during your race keeps you calm and helps you run a good race. At the starting line and when you're in the middle of the race, remove all the negative thoughts and replace them with positive ones: "You can do this," "You're ready," — anything that makes you feel strong and confident. You owe that to yourself, and you even owe that to the runners with whom you're competing. After all, the word *competition* comes from the Latin word *competere,* "to seek or achieve together." You're in this together with all the other runners. If you think negatively and bring yourself down, you bring down the other runners. But if you think positively and raise yourself up, you raise up the other runners as well.

Counting steps (and other tricks) to distract yourself from discomfort

Although I usually advise runners to focus on what they're doing during a race and stay in the moment, sometimes you just need to get your mind off the task at hand. Counting your steps is a great way to do that. It helps you dissociate from the effort and focus on something other than the discomfort you're experiencing.

Count every time your right foot hits the ground for 500 to 1,000 steps. For the next 500 to 1,000 steps, try increasing the cadence slightly. Other tricks you can do to distract your mind include spelling words, singing a song in your head, calculating your pace, and counting the number of runners you pass.

Dividing the race into parts

Thinking of running 26.2 miles all at once can be overwhelming, so divide the race into smaller, more manageable segments, like each mile or each 5K, and focus on one segment at a time. If you're familiar with the marathon course, you can divide the race into sections based on landmarks, neighborhoods, or areas of the course.

If you're aiming for a specific time goal, focus on attaining that goal at each mile checkpoint. For example, if you want to break 4 hours, that's a 9:09 pace per mile. So concentrate on running the first mile in 9:09, the second mile in 9:09, the third mile in 9:09, and so on.

Don't let your head get ahead of you. You can't do anything about mile 24 of a marathon when you're running mile 3. Focus on getting to a certain checkpoint and don't think beyond that checkpoint until you've reached it.

After the Race: Recovering and Improving Your Performance

After you cross the finish line, pat yourself on the back (if your arm isn't too tired to lift). Whether it's your first marathon or your fiftieth, you've accomplished something very special that you'll remember for the rest of your life. You may even cry. Some people do. Of course, a lot of people, the majority even, cross the finish line thinking, "Why the heck did I do this?" But many of them return to do another one, after the salty sweat settles and they forget the ordeal. Revel in your accomplishment, and then use the tips in the following sections to recover and improve your performance.

Recovering from the marathon

Recovery after the marathon is similar to recovery after all your long runs, just more extreme, especially if you've never run the full distance before. How long does it take to recover from a marathon? Everyone is different. You should feel fine after about two to three weeks, but it could take longer if you've really stretched yourself during the race and don't pay attention to all the advice in this book. I've coached runners who feel fine within a few days.

After the marathon, you have to recover from

- ✔ **Dehydration:** You lose a lot of body water sweating for hours, especially in the heat.

- ✔ **Glycogen depletion:** Your muscles, once full of carbohydrate at the start of the marathon, are now empty. You've run out of gas.

- ✔ **Muscle fiber damage:** At the end of a marathon, your muscles are a mess. Pounding the pavement for hours, combined with the eccentric muscle contractions that actively lengthen your muscles while you run, causes microscopic damage to your muscles, making them very sore for a while. Expect walking downstairs to be difficult for a few days after the marathon.

- ✔ **Psychological fatigue:** Concentrating for hours on your effort leaves you mentally exhausted.

- ✔ **A suppressed immune system:** Running 26.2 miles, especially when you push yourself to your limit, can leave your immune system compromised. Combined with being dehydrated and glycogen-depleted, the effort leaves you vulnerable to catching a cold, flu, or other respiratory tract infection.

Use the tips in the following sections to recover after the marathon. For more on optimal recovery strategies, stride over (or, rather, walk slowly) to Chapter 12.

Right after the marathon

Immediately after you cross the finish line, you should

✔ Wrap yourself in a space blanket the volunteers hand you at the end of the race. This keeps you from getting a chill. If you don't have a space blanket, use a beach blanket or beach towel.

✔ Pick up your gear from the gear check and put on dry clothes.

✔ Walk (slowly) for a few minutes so you don't get stiff.

✔ Get off your feet, but not for too long. Sit on the grass and stretch your legs out for a few minutes before getting up to walk around a little.

✔ Consume about 200 calories of easily digestible carbohydrate (read: sugar). Chocolate milk, fruit, gummy bears, or a nutrition bar are good choices. Be careful about consuming too much so you don't get bloated.

✔ Drink at least 16 ounces of water or a sports drink to rehydrate.

In the first few hours after the marathon

Within the first hour after crossing the finish line, you should

✔ Consume 300 to 400 calories of easily digestible carbohydrate and protein.

✔ Soak your legs in a cold water bath to reduce inflammation.

✔ Elevate your legs to reduce swelling.

More than one hour after crossing the finish line, you should

✔ Go out to eat with your friends and family and have a meal high in complex carbohydrate and protein to replace muscle and liver carbohydrate and to repair your muscles.

✔ Drink enough water or a sports drink to rehydrate and replenish body weight lost in the marathon.

✔ Pop 1,000 milligrams of vitamin C to reduce inflammation and boost your immune system.

✔ Stay away from people with colds, as your weakened immune system makes it easier to catch a cold yourself.

In the week after the marathon

The first few days to a week after crossing the finish line, you should

- ✔ Eat and drink anything you want — chocolate brownie sundaes, beer, a New York egg cream. Have a little fun!

- ✔ Do whatever you want, but don't run! Take a walk, take naps, read a book, ride a bike, go canoeing. Your muscles will be very sore from the marathon, so the last thing you want to do is run. Both your body and mind need a break.

- ✔ Stay away from people with colds. Your immune system is still recovering.

Dealing with post-marathon blues

After a marathon, many runners experience depression. This is very common. There's so much buildup to the marathon — the choice to do it, the training, the planning, the travel, the anticipation, the excitement, the effort. And then it's over. Now what?

Anytime you plan for a big event, the aftermath can be a bit of a letdown. People get depressed after weddings, graduations, giving birth, and other life-changing events. I remember how anticlimactic it was after I completed my PhD. I looked forward to graduating for so long, and then, with just a single sentence from one of my committee members as she opened the conference room door after my dissertation defense — "Congratulations, Dr. Karp" — it was over. The initial excitement and relief was outstanding, something I'll never forget, but that only lasts for so long. It was time to get on with the rest of my life.

The best way to overcome the post-marathon blues is to come up with another goal or simply something else to do. The activity can be another marathon you want to run or something else entirely. Perhaps you want to learn another language, take a wine-tasting class, go on a trip, or write a book (but don't write *Running a Marathon For Dummies* — that's already been done). The world is full of possibilities.

Resuming running after the marathon

Although many runners have absolutely no problem taking off a week or more after the marathon is over (or sometimes never running again!), die-hard runners can't wait to start running again. If you're one of those runners, I urge you to resist that urge. Piling additional physical stress on a body that's already fatigued is asking for trouble.

Instead, you should ease yourself back into a running routine. In the following sections, I provide guidance on knowing when to start running again, increasing your mileage gradually, and improving your marathon strategy.

Knowing when to start running again

I usually advise the runners I coach to take two weeks off of running after they finish their marathon. The first week, they don't exercise at all, and the second week they cross-train with activities other than running to give their running muscles a much-needed rest. However, when you start running again is an individual choice. Many runners start running only a week after the marathon. Some even run the next day! There's no golden rule here; whenever you feel like you've recovered, you can start running again, although I do suggest taking at least a few days off.

If your goal is to run one marathon and you never, ever want to run another (or never want to run again, period), then you're done with this chapter. Move on to Part V or read some other part of this book. If, however, you're like a lot of other runners who catch the marathon bug and want to run better next time, keep reading.

Trying a "reverse taper" to increase your mileage gradually

If you continue to run (and I hope you do!), a smart way to plan your post-marathon running is to do a "reverse taper," starting with fewer miles per week and adding more miles over the following few weeks. Just like you reduced your mileage in the few weeks leading into the marathon (see Chapter 14), increase your mileage in the few weeks following the marathon.

For a four-week reverse taper, do

- ✔ No running the first week; cross-train if you feel like it

- ✔ 30 percent of your pre-marathon peak weekly mileage the second week

- ✔ 50 percent of your pre-marathon peak weekly mileage the third week

- ✔ 90 percent of your pre-marathon peak weekly mileage the fourth week

For example, if the peak mileage you ran leading up to the marathon was 40 miles per week, increase your mileage over the second, third, and fourth weeks to 12 miles, 20 miles, and 36 miles.

Sticking to what worked and improving what didn't

After you've gotten yourself back to about 90 percent of the running you were doing before the marathon (see the preceding section), you can start thinking about how to improve your performance for the next one.

Whether you have a good or bad race, you can learn things from each marathon that you can use to run a better marathon next time.

> ✔ When you have a good race, try to figure out what went right and why. Did you run even splits? Were you fully recovered going into the race? Did you do a good job of not giving up? Did you use a good hydration and carb-consuming strategy? For your next race, duplicate whatever it was that worked.

> ✔ When you have a bad race, try to figure out what went wrong and why. Were you fatigued going into the race? Was the training leading up to the race too hard or not hard enough? Did you start off too fast? Did you consume too little fluid and carbs during the race? Were there outside pressures or stresses that contributed to the outcome? If you can isolate why you had a bad race, you can help avoid another bad race for the same reason in the future.

> Apart from the weather, the biggest reason why people have a bad marathon is because they're not fully prepared and they overestimate what they're capable of doing.

Write down the good things and bad things from each race. Every marathon is an opportunity to learn. Variables like correct pacing strategy, the amount you need to drink, your strengths and weaknesses, and even the extent to which you're willing to be physically uncomfortable are all things you can learn with each marathon.

The easiest way to improve your marathon performance is to run more. If you're a beginner, follow the same 20-week program in Chapter 8 but add more miles to each week. You may even be able to go from the beginner program to the intermediate program in Chapter 9. That depends on your goals and how much more running you can handle. Every runner I've coached for the marathon has improved her marathon time by systematically increasing the volume and quality of training — more miles per week, longer tempo runs, greater emphasis on interval training, and more quality long runs.

Part V
The Part of Tens

The 5th Wave   By Rich Tennant

"You have to admit that we're more suited for a 2.62-mile duothon than a 26.2-mile marathon."

In this part...

From what to do (and what to avoid) on marathon race day to great places around the world to combine a vacation with running a marathon to the most curious of marathon questions, the chapters in this part leave no mile marker forgotten.

Chapter 17

Ten Things to Do on Marathon Race Day

In This Chapter

▶ Getting enough food, water, and rest for the marathon

▶ Wearing the right clothes and gear

▶ Pacing yourself and finishing the race with your best effort

*W*hen I was in high school, my electronics teacher had a silly saying to remind his students of how to handle electrical wires: "One hand in pockey, no get shockey." Like touching wires with both hands, there are lots of things you shouldn't do. For example, going down a slide headfirst, throwing a paper airplane at your high school teacher, and wearing leg warmers on the treadmill would all be considered by most as errors in judgment. (Okay, so I don't always make the best decisions.) In this chapter, I give you ten things you definitely *should* do on marathon race day; for additional guidance, check out Chapters 15 and 16.

Give Yourself Plenty of Time before the Marathon

Even if you're like me and you hate getting out of bed before the crack of dawn, you don't want to wake up too close to the start time of a marathon. Even if you're running the Turtle Marathon in Roswell, New Mexico (the smallest marathon in the United States, with just 47 finishers in 2011), you still need to give yourself plenty of time the morning of the race to do everything you need to do — eat, drink, get dressed, drive to the start, go to the bathroom, warm up, stretch, and mentally prepare yourself. So get up as early as you can, get food in you, and wake yourself up!

Eat Breakfast

You've probably heard that breakfast is the most important meal of the day. If that's so, then breakfast the morning of the marathon is as important as it gets.

Unlike shorter races, the marathon challenges your fuel reserves. When you wake up on race morning, your blood glucose is low because it's been about 9 to 12 hours since you've eaten. Because carbohydrate is your muscles' primary fuel when you run, you want to go to the starting line as full of carbohydrate as possible.

 One to two hours before the race, eat 300 to 400 calories of easily digestible carbohydrate and protein such as a nutrition bar, eggs, and toast with jelly. Stay away from fiber and fat. For more on the pre-race meal and a list of foods to eat, stride on over to Chapter 15.

Wear Familiar Shoes and Gear

 Although you may be tempted to wear some fancy new kicks in the marathon, especially after all the miles you've put in on your old shoes, one of the biggest mistakes you can make on race day is to wear brand new shoes. Even if your new shoes are the same type of shoes you've been wearing, don't wear them in the race. Promise me. (Seriously, you don't want blisters or any other foot discomfort.)

 If you've been training for a few months in the same shoes, you can buy new ones in preparation for the marathon, but buy them at least three weeks before the race and do at least one long run in them.

Although running shoes are your most important item, don't wear *anything* new in the marathon. That goes for clothes — including your shirt or jersey, shorts, spandex, socks, underwear, and sports bra — as well as anything you plan to carry on you in the marathon, such as a fuel belt, water, and gels. Practice wearing your clothes and gear well before the race on your long runs so you get comfortable with everything.

Avoid Cotton Clothes

Before I discovered synthetic fabrics, I used to wear cotton every day I ran. I figured I had enough T-shirts from races I'd run — why spend money to buy more shirts when my dresser drawers were already bursting with them?

But if you've ever run more than a few miles in a cotton T-shirt, you know why you should buy shirts made of a synthetic material like polyester. Cotton is one of the cheapest fabrics, but it's also the least breathable. It holds your sweat rather than allowing it to evaporate. Don't wear any cotton at all in the marathon. Wear lightweight fabrics that don't stick to your skin. And listen to your mother and wear clean underwear; just make sure it's not cotton.

Stay Off Your Feet before the Start

Twenty-six plus miles is long enough to run, don't you think? The last thing you want to do before running the marathon is to run (or even walk) another couple miles. You only have so much carbohydrate fuel to go around. Save it for the race.

If you're running a marathon near your hometown, have someone drop you off at the start line. If you're traveling to a marathon, stay at a hotel as close to the start line as possible (or close to the location where you'll pick up public transportation to get to the start). Stay off your feet as much as you can before the race begins except for the little bit of walking around to loosen up after you get out of bed and the short warm-up you do before the race. As a marathon runner, your legs are your most important asset. Protect them.

Consume Carbs during the Race

If you've been reading this book cover to cover (kudos to you!), one of the recurring themes you may have noticed is how important carbohydrate is in the marathon. That's because carbohydrate is your muscles' preferred fuel during exercise (wouldn't it be great if it were fat?).

Most people have enough carbohydrate stored in their muscles and liver to last a little more than two hours of sustained activity. The best runners in the world can therefore run the entire marathon without consuming any carbs because they take just over two hours to complete the race. Everyone else needs to consume carbs during the race to maintain blood sugar levels and delay the depletion of carbohydrate. For more on how much and what kind of carbohydrate to ingest during the marathon and when to ingest it, flip to Chapter 16.

Hydrate Frequently

Running a marathon without drinking water or a sports drink is like going to a wedding without a gift — it's just dumb. Hydration is very important because water is involved in the chemical reactions that enable your muscles to contract. Water also helps the flow of blood and oxygen to your muscles. If your body weight drops more than 2 to 3 percent during the race because of fluid loss, your pace slows down dramatically. Don't let that happen. Start drinking early and often. For more on specific hydration strategies, see Chapter 16.

Pace Yourself Properly

If you've ever watched a marathon and waited at the finish line for a couple of hours after the elite runners finish, you've likely seen what a catastrophe the race can be for some people, as they literally try to drag their bodies across the finish line. You don't want to be one of those people.

Proper pacing is paramount for the marathon. If you start at a pace that's too far over your head, it will come back to haunt you later in the race. I've seen too many runners run a strong first half, only to crash and burn in the second half, being relegated to walking and even stopping to stretch and hydrate. The most physiologically efficient (read: the least taxing) way to run a marathon is to run the first and second halves in the same time (or run the second half slightly faster than the first), with as little fluctuation in pace as possible throughout the race.

When it's hot, especially when it's hot and humid, be very conservative with your early pace. Start out slower than your goal pace and measure your effort against the climate.

Finish the Race

I used to coach a talented runner who didn't finish races when things weren't going well. He wanted to win all the time and would give up when he realized that he wasn't going to prevail.

An injury or illness is the only circumstance under which giving up is okay. Don't keep running if you're putting your health at risk.

Every marathon has moments when the effort starts to feel uncomfortable. Backing off from physical discomfort for self-preservation is a natural human tendency, but one of the characteristics that makes runners unique is their penchant for seeking out discomfort. Hitting a rough patch in the race is when you learn about yourself and what you're willing to do to meet your goal. Do you back off from the discomfort and slow your pace or walk, or do you address the discomfort and push through it? Running a marathon gives you a chance to discover the answer and, in so exploring, become the person you want to be. You want to walk away from your race feeling like you gave it everything you had. You want to be proud of yourself. So don't give up. See the race to the finish, which is at the finish line.

Focus on Your Performance, Not Your Time

When I first started running track and cross-country in school, and for many years after, I defined myself by how fast I ran my races. If I didn't run as fast as I wanted, I would get down on myself. I would mope around for days after a disappointing race. My identity was tied to my race results. Although I still get disappointed when I don't run as fast as I want as I chase my times from my youth, I've slowly and reluctantly realized that I'm not defined by my races. I'm still a great person if I don't run a 4:30 mile or a 2:59 marathon. And so are you.

One of the first questions people will ask you when you tell them you ran a marathon is, "What time did you run?" The answer is usually, "Not as fast as I wanted." Whether they want to qualify for Boston or break five hours, most runners go into the marathon thinking about a certain time they want to run. And most run slower than they want to.

Putting all your eggs in the time-means-everything basket is a great way to be disappointed if it doesn't work out. Although it's hard to run a marathon without some expectations, you're much better off if you focus on your performance rather than the outcome. The time on the clock is an outcome. If you focus on your performance, you have a much better chance of getting the outcome you hope for.

I always tell the runners I coach when going into a race that the most important thing is that they finish the race feeling like they couldn't have done any better on that day. Regardless of the outcome — the time on the clock and the place you finish — what matters most is that you walk away from the race and can honestly say that you gave it everything you had. That alone is something to be immensely proud of. That alone is worth the race entry fee.

Chapter 18

Running Amok: Ten Common Training Errors

*M*ost people run without giving much thought to what they're doing. They just run on their own or run with their friends, without any intention to their actions, hoping for a good result. If their friends run faster, they run faster. If their friends buy Nikes, they buy Nikes. If their friends follow a training program from *Runner's World*'s website, they follow the same training program.

As a coach, scientist, and runner, I've seen runners make lots of mistakes. Sometimes, those mistakes cause injuries. At the very least, they prevent you from reaching your potential. Why would you want that?

To guide you in your endeavor to run a successful marathon, in this chapter I point out ten of the most common training errors that runners make. Avoid all these errors and not only will you drastically reduce your chance of getting an injury but you also may cross the finish line of the marathon feeling like you want to do it all over again (no, that never happens).

Avoiding a Plan

Whether you're preparing for your first marathon or trying to qualify for the Boston Marathon, how you train has a dramatic effect on your performance. Although running just to run may make you fitter, training gives you the plan for success. Running versus training is like the difference between building a house by placing bricks here and there and having a blueprint laid out beforehand.

As the famous New York Yankees catcher Yogi Berra once said, "If you don't know where you're going, you might not get there."

 Too many runners don't have a good plan to run a marathon. That's why I wrote this book. Running whenever you feel like it with no specific purpose to each day's training is much less effective than following a planned program during which every day has a purpose. It's the difference between people who get bored or injured and end up failing and those who get to the start line excited to go after something they've been looking forward to for months.

For a lot of things in life, you can just wing it. Running a marathon isn't one of them. You need to plan for it. This book gives you great plans; use them and tell your friends to use them.

Doing Too Much Too Soon

Whether it's making a big jump in weekly mileage, lengthening long runs too quickly, or adding too much intensity with interval workouts, nearly all runners are guilty at some point of adding stress too quickly for the body to adapt (especially as they get older and wrongfully think they can handle the same amount or intensity of work that they used to do). And what happens when you do that? You guessed it — you get hurt. A muscle gets strained, a tendon gets inflamed, or a bone develops a hairline crack. In fact, doing too much too soon is the *main* reason runners get injured.

 Everybody wants results as quickly as possible, but you must give your muscles, tendons, and bones a chance to fully adapt to the amount and intensity of running you're doing before you do more. That may mean running the same number of miles per week and keeping the long run the same duration for a few weeks before running more miles and longer runs. It may mean taking more rest days or cross-training on days between harder runs. It may mean reducing your weekly mileage when you start doing interval training. The key is to systematize your training and introduce stress only a little at a time. To find out how to train smarter to avoid injury, stride on over to Chapter 13.

Doing Workouts Too Fast or Too Slow

Runners often do workouts too fast or too slow, which precludes them from maximizing their effort and time and obtaining the desired result. The problem is that they don't know what the desired result is. To determine the correct speed, you must know the purpose of each workout. For example, running too fast on your easy days adds unnecessary stress to your legs without any extra benefit. Because many of the physiological adaptations associated with aerobic training — like increases in muscle mitochondria and capillaries and an improvement in running economy (see Chapter 3) — depend on the volume of running you do each week rather than on the intensity of running, the speed of your easy runs isn't as important as the amount of time you spend running. Running faster isn't always better. You want to obtain the greatest benefit while incurring the least amount of stress, so run as slow as you can while still achieving the desired result.

On the other hand, if you run too slow, you'll just become a slow runner and never learn how to run at a faster pace. Interval workouts are supposed to be hard; easy runs are supposed to be easy. Running at specific paces for your easy runs, long runs, tempo runs, and intervals enables you to specifically target the physiological factors that influence marathon performance. To find out what paces you should run for each of your workouts, check out Chapters 5, 6, and 7.

Neglecting Long Tempo Runs

Long tempo runs (and their sister workout, marathon pace runs) are among the most important workouts of your marathon preparation. Too many runners, especially beginners training for their first marathon, focus too much on just the long run. If nothing else, complementing your long run each week with a long tempo run at a little slower than your tempo pace or at marathon race pace goes a long way (pun intended) toward preparing you for the marathon, both physically and mentally. Don't neglect the power of the long tempo, which trains you for sustained, faster-paced aerobic running and hardens you mentally to hold a solid aerobic pace for a long time. For specific tempo runs, see Chapter 5.

Doing Interval Training without Enough Aerobic Running

Many runners, especially faster ones, like to jump right in to interval training because it can be fun and it makes you fit fast. However, when training for a marathon, you need to do a lot of aerobic running first. Aerobic running causes many physiological and biochemical changes that you need to go the distance, like increases in mitochondria, capillaries, and enzymes, and the storage of more fuel (see Chapter 3 for more info).

Think of your training like a pyramid, with the base of that pyramid being your aerobic fitness level. After you build up a big base, you can put the interval training on top of it. It's just like building a house: Create the base first and then put on the roof. The bigger your aerobic base, the higher the peak of the pyramid. Focusing on the peak by adding more interval training will never make you as good of a runner as first focusing on the base. The more you attend to your aerobic running, the more you'll ultimately get from your subsequent interval training because the interval workouts won't fatigue you as quickly, and you'll be able to run more reps in each interval workout.

Because interval training puts a lot of stress on your tendons, ligaments, and muscles, doing too much of it can also lead to injury. So you must use it carefully. Flip to Chapter 7 for the full scoop on interval training.

Running an Inadequate Amount during the Week

Training for a marathon isn't just about one long run each week; it's about the total amount of running you do. Many novice runners don't run enough miles during the week to support the long run on the weekend. You don't want to run 4 or 5 miles for two or three days during the week and then shock your legs with a 15-mile run on Sunday. You may be able to get away with that once or twice, but do that week after week after week and you're setting yourself up to get hurt.

To avoid injury, don't make your long run such a large percentage of your weekly running. Ideally, your long run shouldn't be more than about a third of your weekly mileage. So, if your long run is 20 miles, you should run at least 60 miles per week. Obviously, the majority of runners don't run that much, so you need to be creative when training so that you don't accumulate so much stress in one run.

Don't misunderstand me — the long run should be stressful. After all, you're running for a long time and trying to make yourself exhausted so your body adapts. However, you don't want the long run to be *so much more stressful* than any other run during the week. It's always better to spread the stress around.

In addition to your long run, do a midweek, medium-long run that's about 65 to 75 percent of the length (or duration) of your long run.

Blaming Your Shoes for Injuries

With all the attention given to running shoes, you may be tempted to place the blame for all things gone wrong on your shoes. It's gotta be the shoes, right? Not usually. Although shoes influence the dispersion of forces and control the position of your feet when they land on the ground (as you find out in Chapter 2), and thus play a role in injury prevention, they're not usually the real reason why you get injured. Blaming your shoes for injuries only takes the attention off of where it needs to be — your training, which is typically the true culprit.

Always look to your training first to give you clues to your injuries. And read the second training error of this chapter, "Doing Too Much Too Soon."

Running Too Much on Soft Surfaces

Runners often ask me whether they should run on trails. Running on trails some of the time is fine to preserve your legs, but you need to accustom your muscles and tendons to the pounding on pavement, because most marathons are on pavement. Running on trails or grass to prepare for a marathon is like practicing tennis on a grass court to prepare for a tournament on a hard court. If you do most of your running on soft surfaces, the marathon will be a long day at the office because your muscles will experience a stress to which they haven't been accustomed.

 Do all your long runs on the road, as they most closely simulate the marathon. If you run the day after your long run, you can run on softer surfaces because your legs will be tired from the long run. The most important runs to do on the road are your long runs and tempo runs.

Ignoring the Conditions of the Marathon

Because of its length, the marathon requires practice. The longer the race, the more opportunity there is for things to go wrong. So the more you can simulate the marathon during your training, the more you'll reduce the likelihood that anything will go wrong and the better off you'll be. Be sure to address these issues:

✔ **Carbohydrate ingestion:** Don't use one product on your long runs and then use another product in the race. Do your homework and find out what kind of products will be offered on the course (you can usually find out from the marathon website). Practice your long runs using the same carbohydrate gels that you'll find at the aid stations on the course.

✔ **Climate:** If the marathon is going to be hot, try to run in the heat. If it's going to be cold, then run in the cold. This seems like a no-brainer, but you'd be surprised how many runners don't prepare for the race's climatic conditions. If you always run in cooler temperatures and the marathon is on a hot day, maintaining your pace and composure will be difficult.

Of course, there's always the unseasonable day that you can't foresee. Or can you? Whether it's global warming or Mother Nature, there seem to be enough unseasonable days that it's often hard to know what season it is! The Boston Marathon, for example, has a history of unseasonably warm days. It's in mid-April in Boston, after all. Prepare for the weather by running in similar climatic conditions so you're prepared to handle anything on the day of the race.

✔ **Hydration:** Ditto for drinking. Find out the exact sports drink that will be available on the course, and use that drink on your long runs. Stride on over to Chapter 6 for more information on fueling and hydration.

✔ **Topography:** If I had a dollar for every runner I knew who wasn't prepared for the hills on the marathon course, I'd have enough dollars for the very expensive entry fee into the ING New York City Marathon. Don't be one of those people. Many marathons post course maps and elevation profiles on their websites. Become very familiar with the course. If you live in a place that doesn't have any hills, make friends with a treadmill and do some hill workouts on it. (Chapter 5 has more info on doing hill workouts.)

Skipping Your Post-Workout Meal

Between running on your lunch hour and picking up your kids from soccer practice, you can easily skip eating after a workout. But not refueling after your run is possibly the single worst thing you can do to thwart your recovery, which makes tomorrow's run that much harder.

Make sure you refuel after your workouts with carbohydrates to replenish your fuel store and with protein to repair your muscles. To discover what to eat and drink after workouts and how much, check out Chapter 12.

Chapter 19

Ten (Or So) Great Destination Marathons

. . . .

In This Chapter

▶ Checking out top marathons around the United States

▶ Traveling to marathons in Europe and beyond

. . . .

Ah, vacation! When most people think about taking a vacation, they think of sunshine, palm trees, relaxing by the pool with an ice-cold margarita in their hands, perhaps horseback riding with the kids, and . . . running a marathon?

With marathons all over the world, running a marathon has become a popular vacation activity. What better way to explore new places than to run through them, right? Why run through the streets of your hometown when you can run through stunning scenery in an exotic, faraway place, and then hang out and take in the sights?

For those of you who like to travel, this chapter gives you ten (or so) of the world's top destination marathons, listed chronologically, with course and registration information for each one.

 If you want to run one of these marathons, you better make your plans early — many of them sell out many months in advance. Unless otherwise noted with specific qualifying or entry procedures, you can run in any of these marathons, provided you register before they fill up. Also, if you can't find some buddies who think running a marathon is the highlight of a vacation, you can travel with a group. Marathon Tours is one of the world's premiere companies specializing in travel to running events. Check them out at www.marathontours.com.

Walt Disney World Marathon

Want to take a family trip to Disney World? Why not run a marathon with Mickey Mouse while you're there? It's the most magical 26.2 miles on earth!

The marathon course takes you through all four Walt Disney World theme parks in Florida. You start at Epcot before dawn and run through the Magic Kingdom, Animal Kingdom, and Hollywood Studios before you finish back at Epcot. You'll enjoy plenty of Disney entertainment during the race and can even get a picture taken with the many Disney characters who cheer for you along the course.

The Walt Disney World Marathon is in January. For more information, visit www.rundisney.com/disneyworld-marathon.

Napa Valley Marathon

A more intimate marathon with about 2,500 runners, the Napa Valley Marathon is a quaint race in a very quaint part of the United States. If you like to mix wine with your running (and who doesn't?), this is the marathon for you.

The scenic course runs along the Silverado Trail on the east side of the valley and winds south from Calistoga to Napa alongside the many vineyards. Except for the last half-mile, the entire course is rural. Take in the views, but don't drink and run (okay, maybe just a little). After the race, stay at one of the charming inns and spend the next day wine tasting and relaxing.

The Napa Valley Marathon is in March. For more information, visit www.napavalleymarathon.org.

North Pole Marathon

If you like adventure, and I mean adventure, the North Pole Marathon may just be the marathon for you. Held in one of the remotest parts of the planet, the North Pole Marathon takes you to a place few people ever experience. Even Santa Claus and his elves move south for the winter! With just 35 male and 5 female finishers in 2012, completing this marathon puts you in very small company. Including the 2012 race, 215 people from 34 nationalities have completed the North Pole Marathon.

As for the course, well, it runs on water — frozen water — with just 6 to 12 feet separating you from 12,000 feet of Arctic Ocean. With extreme sub-zero temperatures and strong winds, this marathon isn't for wimps. Don't even think about running a personal best here! The men's winner in 2012 finished in 4:17:08; the women's winner in 6:06:36.

The North Pole Marathon is in April. For more information, check out www.npmarathon.com.

Paris Marathon

Ah, Paris! The City of Lights, the City of Romance, the City of . . . a Marathon? Yup, the most romantic city in the world has a marathon, and a popular one at that, with 35,000 to 40,000 runners.

The course starts on one of the most famous streets in the world, the Champs-Élysées, and runs a winding loop through the city, beside the banks of the River Seine, and past some of the city's greatest sites, including the Eiffel Tower, Notre Dame Cathedral, and the Place de la Bastille before finishing near the Arc de Triomphe. Volunteers hand out red wine and cheese to runners at the Eiffel Tower, about three-quarters of the way through the race — just enough time to numb yourself before hitting the marathon wall.

The Paris Marathon is in April. For more information, check out www.parismarathon.com/index_us.html.

Virgin London Marathon

Another of the world's most popular marathons with over 36,000 runners, the Virgin London Marathon runs around one of the world's most visited cities. London has something for everyone: history, culture, art, grand museums, dazzling architecture, royalty, and diversity. And don't forget the tea and crumpets! (Although I wouldn't suggest drinking the tea during the marathon.)

The course is largely flat and is nearby the River Thames, finishing near Buckingham Palace. During mile 6, you literally run across both sides of the world as you cross the prime meridian, the line that divides the earth's Eastern and Western Hemispheres.

Here are the four main ways to get into the marathon:

- ✔ **Enter the online lottery.** The lottery is drawn in October.

- ✔ **Run for charity.** You can find partnering charities on the marathon's website at www.virginlondonmarathon.com/ marathon-centre/enter-virgin-london-marathon/ charity-entries.

- ✔ **Run a qualifying time.** Qualifying times by age are on the marathon's website at www.virginlondonmarathon.com/ marathon-centre/enter-virgin-london-marathon/ good-for-age-entries.

- ✔ **Run as part of a tour.** If you live outside of the United Kingdom, you can apply for a spot in the marathon by contacting one of its approved tour operators for an application. Go to www. virginlondonmarathon.com/marathon-centre/ enter-virgin-london-marathon.

The Virgin London Marathon is in April. For more information, see www.virginlondonmarathon.com.

Great Wall Marathon

No matter how well trained you are, you'll literally hit the wall in this marathon. The Great Wall Marathon in China is the ideal way to combine an unusual running event with an exploration of one of the world's most astonishing sights.

The course, which starts a couple hours northeast of Beijing, is part wall and part villages and rice fields. The 5,164 steps of the Great Wall put your fitness to the test. The breathtaking surroundings of Tianjin Province compete with your tired muscles for attention. If you don't care about your finishing time and want an adventure more than a race, this marathon is for you.

Expect the race to take much longer to complete than an average marathon because of the extreme ascents and descents, which provide stunning 360-degree views of China's countryside.

The Great Wall Marathon is in May. For more information, check out www.great-wall-marathon.com/default.aspx.

Berlin Marathon

Another big marathon with 40,000 runners, the Berlin Marathon is one of Europe's favorite marathons and is considered one of the fastest marathon courses in the world, with the most marathon world records being set there. Berlin is a culturally cool city, a hotspot for fashion, art, design, and music. Famous landmarks such as the Reichstag, the Brandenburg Gate, Checkpoint Charlie, and what's left of the Berlin Wall make up a virtual three-dimensional textbook in a city where you'll find history staring you in the face every time you turn a corner.

The flat, very historic course is contained entirely within the city and starts and finishes near the Brandenburg Gate, one of the most well-known landmarks of Germany.

The Berlin Marathon is in September. For more information, check out `www.bmw-berlin-marathon.com/en`.

Dublin Marathon

The capital of Ireland, Dublin lies at the mouth of the River Liffey, near the midpoint of Ireland's east coast. Dublin is Ireland's largest city, and half of its population is younger than 25. This marathon is a popular destination spot, as over half of the runners travel to run it from overseas. Dublin is known almost as much for its people, who are lively even without the beer, as for its most famous export. The reaction of many thousands of Dubliners lining the city streets during the race has made the race known internationally as the "friendly marathon."

The mostly flat course is a single loop around the city, running through Dublin's historic Georgian streets. After the race, recover and imbibe with some amiable and witty Irish friends in one (or many!) of Dublin's numerous pubs. The most popular brewery in town (and Ireland's top visitor attraction) is Guinness Storehouse, the beer lover's Disneyland.

The Dublin Marathon is on the last Monday in October. For more information, see `www.dublinmarathon.ie`.

ING New York City Marathon

The largest marathon in the United States with over 40,000 runners, the ING New York City Marathon is the cream of the marathon crop. To paraphrase Frank Sinatra, if you can run there, you can run anywhere. The marathon is organized by the New York Road Runners, the largest running club in the United States.

The course begins on the Staten Island side of the Verrazano Narrows Bridge and runs through dozens of culturally and ethnically diverse neighborhoods in Brooklyn, Queens, the Bronx, and Manhattan, finishing in world-famous Central Park. You cross five bridges, including the Queensboro Bridge, which puts you onto First Avenue in Manhattan at mile 16, where you're greeted by thousands of screaming spectators, making it one of the most exciting streets to run on in the world. After the race, get off your feet and dine at one of New York's many famous restaurants, see a Broadway show, and ride a horse-drawn carriage through Central Park.

Because of its enormous popularity, getting into the ING New York City Marathon is harder than hailing a taxicab in Times Square on a Saturday evening. Here are the four main ways to get into the marathon:

✔ **Enter the lottery.** Each April, the New York Road Runners hold a lottery for runners who have submitted an application between January and April. If you're feeling lucky, it's because your name wasn't picked for three years in a row; if you've been rejected for three consecutive years, you're guaranteed to get in on your fourth try.

✔ **Run a qualifying time.** Think the Boston Marathon has tough qualifying times? Think again. If you're speedy, you can bypass the lottery altogether and get guaranteed entry into New York by running a fast half-marathon or marathon. Find qualifying times by age at www.ingnycmarathon.org/ entrantinfo/Guaranteed_Entry_Guidelines.htm.

✔ **Run for charity.** Raising money for a charity organization guarantees you entry into the marathon, as long as you raise the required minimum, which varies from charity to charity. Many of the participating charities offer their own marathon training program, with in-person coaching and online support for nonlocals. And you get a free T-shirt! For a list of participating charities, go to www.nycmarathon.org/charities_ index.htm.

✔ **Be a celebrity.** Each year, celebrities run the ING New York City Marathon (and other marathons) to draw attention to their charities or themselves (remember when Oprah ran?). Celebrities get to do anything they want. I know one celebrity who was taken by private helicopter to the start line!

The ING New York City Marathon is on the first Sunday in November. For more information, visit www.nycmarathon.org.

Athens Classic Marathon

This is where it all began. When the Athenian messenger Pheidippides brought news of the Greeks' victory from the battlefield of Marathon in 490 BC, little did he know what he had started.

The challenging course that's more than 2,500 years old begins on an ancient battlefield in the town of — where else? — Marathon, near the Aegean Sea, and climbs up toward Athens, about 360 feet above sea level. You finish in historic Olympic Stadium, the site of the first modern Olympic Games in 1896.

The Athens Classic Marathon is in November. For more information, see www.athensclassicmarathon.gr/marathon/fmain. aspx?lang=en-US.

Honolulu Marathon

Just in case running on ice in sub-zero temperatures in a remote part of the planet doesn't appeal to you, I've included one more destination marathon in a more tropical climate for those of you who like a little less arctic in your vacation: the Honolulu Marathon in Hawaii. With 20,000 to 25,000 thousand runners, it's the sixth largest marathon in the United States.

To beat the heat, the race starts at 5 a.m. (yes, you read that right!) on Ala Moana Boulevard, which is Hawaiian for "path by the ocean." And that's just what you get in this exotic locale known for its relaxed atmosphere, cheap noodle joints, and fancy Pacific Rim cuisine. Enjoy spectacular ocean views as you run alongside world-famous Waikiki Beach and Diamond Head and Koko Head volcanic craters before finishing at Waikiki's Kapiolani Park. After the race, soak your tired legs in the ocean and lounge on the sand. If you get there early, don't miss the concert and luau at the Waikiki Shell a couple days before the race.

The Honolulu Marathon is in December. For more information, visit www.honolulumarathon.org.

Chapter 20

Ten (Okay, Eleven) Frequently Asked Questions about Running a Marathon

● ●

In This Chapter

▶ Training with others and running long distances before the race

▶ Dealing with injuries, cramps, and illness

▶ Dressing for and fueling during the marathon

▶ Breaking through the marathon wall

● ●

*W*hen I was a kid, I asked my teachers some pretty dumb questions, such as, "Is Alaska a country?" and, "How do you spell letters?" (I used to think that you could spell the actual letters that make up words. Pretty dumb, huh?) But, hey, I ended up getting a doctorate, so all's good!

As a coach, I get asked questions about marathon running all the time. You'd be surprised how often the same questions come up (I guess that's why they're referred to as "frequently asked"). Like your teacher told you, there's no such thing as a stupid question. So, if you're one of those people who doesn't like to raise your hand in front of the class and ask a question for fear of being laughed at, this chapter is for you.

Should I Join a Training Group?

Many runners like training by themselves, especially if they're introverts or if they have busy jobs with constraints on their time. Unless you like running alone, are self-motivated and disciplined, and know what you're doing, joining a marathon training group is a good idea. You'll have people to run with, a coach to give you a program to follow, and nutritional support on long runs. You'll feel like you're a part of something bigger than yourself. For details on joining a training group, stride all the way over to Chapter 1; it's a long run from here, but you're marathon training!

Do I Need to Run 26 Miles in Training?

One major trait of the marathon that differentiates it from other races is that, unless you're a speedy runner, you won't cover the distance in training. That makes the last few miles of the marathon unexplored territory. But, hey, that also makes it exciting, right?

During training, time spent on your feet matters more than the number of miles you run. Obviously, the longer you run, the more prepared you'll be. But there's always a trade-off. The trick is to run as long as you possibly can without getting injured and without tiring yourself out so much that you can't run for the next week.

Because advanced runners run faster than beginners or intermediate runners, they cover more distance in the same amount of time. So an advanced runner may very well run 26 miles, or sometimes more, in training. My advice is to cap your long run somewhere between 19 and 22 miles or about 3½ hours — whichever comes first and depending on how many weeks you have to prepare. If you're planning your marathon to take longer than 3½ hours, I suggest you take a few 4-hour walks so you can get used to being on your feet longer without the same amount of stress on your legs. You can also include walking breaks in some of your long runs. For example, do some 4- to 5-hour run-walks, alternating periods of running and walking. With at least a couple of 19- to 22-mile runs on your legs and a few long run-walks, you should be able to complete 26.2 miles on race day, especially if you run a marathon with great crowd support that can motivate you.

In 2004, I did an interesting study for which I sent questionnaires to all the men and women who qualified for the 2004 U.S. Olympic Marathon Trials, asking them about their training for the year leading up to the trials. One of the questions I asked them was how long their longest training run was. The men averaged 25 miles for their long run, and the women averaged 23 miles for theirs. The long run ranged from 20 to 31 miles for the men (one guy even ran 52 miles!) and 18 to 30 miles for the women. So, clearly, some of the best marathoners in the United States run more than 26 miles in training, and none of them run fewer than 18.

Is Running Bad for My Knees?

If I had a nickel for every person who's ever asked me about my knees and commented on running being bad for your knees, I'd have enough nickels to pay the Kenyans' marathon appearance fees. People assume that, because running requires you to pound the ground with your legs, it must be damaging to your knees. But this is completely false. If you run correctly, you shouldn't be pounding the ground (flip to Chapter 4 to discover how to run with proper form). The research simply doesn't support that running is bad for your knees. People who run have no greater incidence of joint problems or osteoarthritis than people who don't run. On the contrary, running can be beneficial for your joints because it strengthens the surrounding musculature and increases bone density.

If you have a family history of joint degeneration — like if both your parents have had knee replacements or if you already have knee problems when you move a certain way or do certain activities — running can bring that genetic predisposition or those latent issues to the forefront. But running in and of itself isn't the underlying cause of your joint problems. As long as you have healthy knees, running won't cause your knees to go bad.

What Is This Pain in My Knee?

Training for a marathon is not without its fair share of aches and pains. The key is to be able to differentiate what's just an ache that will go away on its own and what's a real injury. If you feel something in your knee, don't freak out right away. It could just be sore after a long run and will be fine tomorrow. (As I note in the preceding section, running typically isn't bad for your knees.) The most common source of knee pain is *patellofemoral pain syndrome,* with pain behind, below, or around your patella. It can be caused by a number of factors and can be treated a number of ways, depending on the pain's cause. (For more, see Chapter 13.) If you feel pain below your kneecap, it could be patellar tendonitis, an inflammation of the patellar tendon (the tendon that your doctor hits with a rubber mallet to check your knee jerk reflex).

Regardless of the pain's cause, ice your knee after you run. Try running the next day, or give yourself one day of rest, cross-train instead, and try running the day after. If the pain doesn't go away within a few days to a week or if it gets worse, you may have an injury that requires further attention.

What Do I Do if I Get a Cramp?

Despite the common occurrence of muscle cramps, why they happen is still something of a mystery. A common misconception is that cramps are caused by dehydration or an imbalance in electrolytes. Drinking a sports drink on your long runs, although important to maintain hydration, won't prevent you from cramping. Muscle cramps are more likely caused by an increase in your running pace and premature muscle fatigue, which affects your nervous system's ability to relax a muscle after it contracts. Cramping is also associated with a family history of muscle cramps and a personal history of cramping and tendon or ligament injuries.

Long runs in particular can cause muscle cramping because they put more stress on your lower leg muscles. Cramps tend to occur when you run farther or faster than you're used to and occur more often in muscles that cross more than one joint, such as the *gastrocnemius muscle* in your calf (which crosses the ankle and knee) and the *biceps femoris* (one of your hamstring muscles, which crosses the hip and knee).

Side stitches, which have been given the fancy name *exercise-related transient abdominal pain* (ETAP), come from eating or drinking too close to running, especially food or drink that has a high sugar content. Side stitches can also come from the movement of internal organs inside the abdominal walls, which causes their connective tissue to pull on the diaphragm, which moves when you breathe. Side stitches affect nearly 70 percent of runners, typically occur on the right side of the upper abdomen, and are less prevalent in older and fitter runners.

If you get a side stitch while running, slow the pace down a little and take some deep, even breaths. Try bending forward while tightening your abdominal muscles and massaging the area with your fingers. For a muscle cramp in the middle of a marathon, keep running (if you can) for a few minutes and see if it relieves itself. If it doesn't, stop and passively stretch the muscle (see Chapter 12 for specific stretches). Because muscle groups work in opposing pairs, with one muscle group relaxing while its opposing muscle group contracts, you can also try to relax the cramp by voluntarily contracting the muscle group opposite the cramped muscle. For example, if you get a cramp in your hamstrings, try contracting your quadriceps, which should help your hamstrings relax.

Should I Run if I Have a Cold?

Exercise and your immune system have an interesting relationship. Moderate amounts of exercise on a regular basis strengthen your immune system and give you resistance against colds and other upper respiratory tract infections. However, this is one case in which more is definitely not better. Long and intense training can actually weaken your immune system and increase the chance of getting sick. Catching a cold or getting the flu immediately after finishing the marathon is very common because your immune system takes a big hit.

Consume both simple carbohydrates (sugars) and complex carbohydrates (starches) while you train. Carbs provide energy and also strengthen your immune system by limiting the rise in stress hormones following your workouts.

If you do get sick while training for a marathon, here's the golden rule: If the symptoms are above your neck, like a stuffed or runny nose, it's okay to run — just don't try to do a difficult workout or a long run. If the symptoms are below your neck, like a sore throat, coughing, wheezing, or a fever, you shouldn't run. Whether your symptoms are above or below your neck, do what your mother told you — pop some vitamin C, have some chicken soup, drink lots of fluids, and get plenty of sleep. And stay away from people with colds. If you can't avoid other people, wash your hands throughout the day, especially after shaking someone else's hand.

What Should I Wear in the Marathon?

On race day, wear comfortable shoes and clothes that you've already worn for your long runs. Don't wear anything new that you haven't already tried out or anything that can cause friction. Most people get by with shorts or spandex, a T-shirt or singlet, socks, and shoes. (For more about running clothes, see Chapter 2.)

What Should I Consume during the Marathon?

Cheeseburger and fries. Just kidding! Exactly what you should consume in the marathon depends on what your stomach can handle, but you definitely want to make sure you consume enough carbohydrate to delay glycogen depletion and hypoglycemia and enough fluid to delay dehydration. Both conditions cause you to slow your pace. Taking carbs and fluid at regular intervals throughout the race can make a huge difference in how you feel and perform. I know an Olympic marathon champion who drank flat soda during the marathon! For details about what, when, and how much to consume during the race, stride on over to Chapter 16.

Is Stopping to Walk Okay?

This is a loaded question. If you're a purist, the answer is no. When the marathon was founded, it was intended to be a running race, a test of running endurance. Once the domain of the running elite, the marathon has become something other than an athletic event, open to anyone and everyone. If you're a realist and your goal is to finish the race no matter how long it takes, then the answer is yes — walking is okay if that's what enables you to get to the finish line. Some runners walk as they go through the aid stations to make sure they grab a drink and are able to ingest it. Walking is also okay under certain conditions that would make running dangerous, such as hot and humid weather or if you're injured (or about to become injured if you keep running). Some people in the sport, who shall remain nameless, advocate walking breaks within each mile. I think you should do what's best for you.

What Is the Marathon Wall?

The *marathon wall* is the point in the marathon when your muscles have run out of glycogen, your stored form of carbohydrate, and you've become hypoglycemic because you've used up all the glucose in your blood. Because carbohydrate is muscles' preferred fuel, when you run out, you start to feel very fatigued and your pace slows down.

The marathon wall occurs in a different place for everyone — it depends on time, pace, and how much glycogen you have in your muscles before the race starts — but it usually occurs between mile 16 and 22.

To avoid hitting the marathon wall, make sure you train with enough long runs so your muscles get used to running for long periods. And consume carbs during the race before you start to feel fatigued to delay the inevitable depletion of muscle glycogen and blood glucose.

How Do I Meet My Family after the Race?

Of course you want to share the accomplishment of your marathon with your family and friends. But how do you find them at the finish? Many marathons can get awfully crowded at the finish line, especially the big ones like New York and Boston. Big marathons usually have a designated area beyond the finish line with lettered signs for families to meet you. When you cross the finish line, you walk through a chute specifically made for the race to the designated open area, where you can also pick up your gear bag. If your family name starts with a common letter, you may want to agree on another letter, like X or Y, to meet your family. Check the marathon's website for specific instructions on where to meet your family after the race.

Appendix

A Marathon Directory

*W*ith nearly 500 marathons in the United States to choose from and others around the world, deciding which marathon to run can be overwhelming. Here, I give you a month-by-month directory of the most popular domestic and international marathons, along with their websites so you can find all the information you need. Run one, run two, or run them all!

January

Houston Marathon
Houston, Texas
www.chevronhoustonmarathon.com

Miami Marathon
Miami, Florida
www.ingmiamimarathon.com

Rock 'n' Roll Arizona Marathon
Phoenix, Arizona
http://runrocknroll.competitor.com/Arizona

Walt Disney World Marathon
Orlando, Florida
www.rundisney.com/disneyworld-marathon

February

Austin Marathon
Austin, Texas
www.youraustinmarathon.com

Rock 'n' Roll New Orleans Marathon
New Orleans, Louisiana
http://runrocknroll.competitor.com/new-orleans

Surf City Marathon
Huntington Beach, California
www.runsurfcity.com

Tokyo Marathon
Tokyo, Japan
www.tokyo42195.org/2013_en

March

Georgia Marathon
Atlanta, Georgia
www.georgiamarathon.com

Kilimanjaro Marathon
Kilimanjaro, Tanzania
www.kilimanjaromarathon.com/index.php?q=con,1,%20
Home_Page

Los Angeles Marathon
Los Angeles, California
www.lamarathon.com

Napa Valley Marathon
Napa Valley, California
www.napavalleymarathon.org

Rome Marathon
Rome, Italy
www.maratonadiroma.it/default.aspx

April

Big Sur International Marathon
Big Sur/Carmel, California
www.bsim.org/site3.aspx

Boston Marathon
Boston, Massachusetts
www.baa.org/races/boston-marathon.aspx

London Marathon
London, England
www.virginlondonmarathon.com

Oklahoma City Memorial Marathon
Oklahoma City, Oklahoma
www.okcmarathon.com

Paris Marathon
Paris, France
www.parismarathon.com/index_us.html

Rotterdam Marathon
Rotterdam, the Netherlands
www.abnamromarathonrotterdam.com

St. Louis Marathon
St. Louis, Missouri
www.gostlouis.org/marathon-weekend/marathon.html

May

Cleveland Marathon
Cleveland, Ohio
www.clevelandmarathon.com

Flying Pig Marathon
Cincinnati, Ohio
www.flyingpigmarathon.com

Ottawa Marathon
Ottawa, Ontario, Canada
www.runottawa.ca

Pittsburgh Marathon
Pittsburgh, Pennsylvania
www.pittsburghmarathon.com

Toronto Marathon
Toronto, Ontario, Canada
www.torontomarathon.com

Vancouver Marathon
Vancouver, British Columbia, Canada
www.bmovanmarathon.ca

Vermont City Marathon
Burlington, Vermont
www.runvcm.org

June

Grandma's Marathon
Duluth, Minnesota
www.grandmasmarathon.com

Rock 'n' Roll San Diego Marathon
San Diego, California
http://runrocknroll.competitor.com/san-diego

Rock 'n' Roll Seattle Marathon
Seattle, Washington
http://runrocknroll.competitor.com/seattle

San Francisco Marathon
San Francisco, California
www.thesfmarathon.com

Stockholm Marathon
Stockholm, Sweden
www.stockholmmarathon.se/Start/index.cfm?Lan_ID=3

July

Deseret News Marathon
Salt Lake City, Utah
http://deseretnewsmarathon.com

August

Pikes Peak Marathon
Pikes Peak, Colorado
www.pikespeakmarathon.org

Quebec City Marathon
Quebec City, Quebec, Canada
www.couriraquebec.com/sites/marathon-en.html

September

Berlin Marathon
Berlin, Germany
www.bmw-berlin-marathon.com/en

Lake Tahoe Marathon
Tahoe City, California
www.laketahoemarathon.com

Rock 'n' Roll Denver Marathon
Denver, Colorado
http://runrocknroll.competitor.com/denver

Rock 'n' Roll Montréal Marathon
Montréal, Quebec, Canada
http://ca.competitor.com/montreal/montreal-splash

Sydney Marathon
Sydney, Australia
www.sydneyrunningfestival.com.au/enter/marathon

October

Amsterdam Marathon
Amsterdam, the Netherlands
www.tcsamsterdammarathon.nl/en

Atlantic City Marathon
Atlantic City, New Jersey
www.acmarathon.org

Baltimore Marathon
Baltimore, Maryland
www.thebaltimoremarathon.com

Beijing Marathon
Beijing, China
www.beijing-marathon.com/en/index.html

Chicago Marathon
Chicago, Illinois
www.chicagomarathon.com

Columbus Marathon
Columbus, Ohio
www.columbusmarathon.com

Detroit Marathon
Detroit, Michigan
www.freepmarathon.com

Dublin Marathon
Dublin, Ireland
www.dublinmarathon.ie

Hartford Marathon
Hartford, Connecticut
www.hartfordmarathon.com

Long Beach Marathon
Long Beach, California
http://runlongbeach.com

Marine Corps Marathon
Washington, District of Columbia
www.marinemarathon.com

Nike Women's Marathon
San Francisco, California
www.facebook.com/NWM26.2/app_193921220718307

Portland Marathon
Portland, Oregon
www.portlandmarathon.org

St. George Marathon
St. George, Utah
www.stgeorgemarathon.com

Twin Cities Marathon
Minneapolis/St. Paul, Minnesota
http://tcmevents.org

Venice Marathon
Venice, Italy
www.venicemarathon.it/home_en.php

November

Athens Marathon
Athens, Greece
www.athensmarathon.com

Monumental Marathon
Indianapolis, Indiana
http://monumentalmarathon.com

New York City Marathon
New York, New York
www.nycmarathon.org

Philadelphia Marathon
Philadelphia, Pennsylvania
www.philadelphiamarathon.com

Richmond Marathon
Richmond, Virginia
www.richmondmarathon.com

Rock 'n' Roll San Antonio Marathon
San Antonio, Texas
http://runrocknroll.competitor.com/san-antonio

Seattle Marathon
Seattle, Washington
www.seattlemarathon.org

December

California International Marathon
Sacramento, California
www.runcim.org

Dallas Marathon
Dallas, Texas
www.dallasmarathon.com

Fukuoka Marathon
Fukuoka, Japan
www.fukuoka-marathon.com/en/index.html

Honolulu Marathon
Honolulu, Hawaii
www.honolulumarathon.org

Memphis Marathon
Memphis, Tennessee
www.stjudemarathon.org

Rock 'n' Roll Las Vegas Marathon
Las Vegas, Nevada
http://runrocknroll.competitor.com/las-vegas

Index

Apple & Mac

iPad 2 For Dummies,
3rd Edition
978-1-118-17679-5

iPhone 4S
For Dummies,
5th Edition
978-1-118-03671-6

iPod touch For
Dummies, 3rd Edition
978-1-118-12960-9

Mac OS X Lion
For Dummies
978-1-118-02205-4

Blogging & Social Media

CityVille For Dummies
978-1-118-08337-6

Facebook For Dummies,
4th Edition
978-1-118-09562-1

Mom Blogging
For Dummies
978-1-118-03843-7

Twitter For Dummies,
2nd Edition
978-0-470-76879-2

WordPress For
Dummies, 4th Edition
978-1-118-07342-1

Business

Cash Flow For Dummies
978-1-118-01850-7

Investing For Dummies,
6th Edition
978-0-470-90545-6

Job Searching with
Social Media
For Dummies
978-0-470-93072-4

QuickBooks 2012
For Dummies
978-1-118-09120-3

Resumes
For Dummies,
6th Edition
978-0-470-87361-8

Starting an Etsy
Business For Dummies
978-0-470-93067-0

Cooking & Entertaining

Cooking Basics
For Dummies,
4th Edition
978-0-470-91388-8

Wine For Dummies,
4th Edition
978-0-470-04579-4

Diet & Nutrition

Kettlebells
For Dummies
978-0-470-59929-7

Nutrition For Dummies,
5th Edition
978-0-470-93231-5

Restaurant Calorie
Counter For Dummies,
2nd Edition
978-0-470-64405-8

Digital Photography

Digital SLR Cameras
& Photography For
Dummies, 4th Edition
978-1-118-14489-3

Digital SLR Settings
& Shortcuts
For Dummies
978-0-470-91763-3

Photoshop Elements 10
For Dummies
978-1-118-10742-3

Gardening

Gardening Basics
For Dummies
978-0-470-03749-2

Vegetable Gardening
For Dummies,
2nd Edition
978-0-470-49870-5

Green/Sustainable

Raising Chickens
For Dummies
978-0-470-46544-8

Green Cleaning
For Dummies
978-0-470-39106-8

Health

Diabetes For Dummies,
3rd Edition
978-0-470-27086-8

Food Allergies
For Dummies
978-0-470-09584-3

Living Gluten-Free
For Dummies,
2nd Edition
978-0-470-58589-4

Hobbies

Beekeeping
For Dummies,
2nd Edition
978-0-470-43065-1

Chess For Dummies,
3rd Edition
978-1-118-01695-4

Drawing For Dummies,
2nd Edition
978-0-470-61842-4

eBay For Dummies,
7th Edition
978-1-118-09806-6

Knitting For Dummies,
2nd Edition
978-0-470-28747-7

Language & Foreign Language

English Grammar
For Dummies,
2nd Edition
978-0-470-54664-2

French For Dummies,
2nd Edition
978-1-118-00464-7

German For Dummies,
2nd Edition
978-0-470-90101-4

Spanish Essentials
For Dummies
978-0-470-63751-7

Spanish For Dummies,
2nd Edition
978-0-470-87855-2

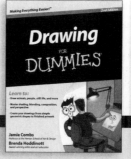

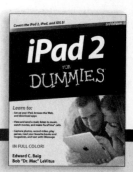

Available wherever books are sold. For more information or to order direct: U.S. customers visit
www.dummies.com or call 1-877-762-2974. U.K. customers visit www.wileyeurope.com or
call (0) 1243 843291. Canadian customers visit www.wiley.ca or call 1-800-567-4797.
Connect with us online at www.facebook.com/fordummies or @fordummies

Math & Science

Algebra I For Dummies,
2nd Edition
978-0-470-55964-2

Biology For Dummies,
2nd Edition
978-0-470-59875-7

Chemistry For
Dummies, 2nd Edition
978-1-1180-0730-3

Geometry For Dummies,
2nd Edition
978-0-470-08946-0

Pre-Algebra Essentials
For Dummies
978-0-470-61838-7

Microsoft Office

Excel 2010 For
Dummies
978-0-470-48953-6

Office 2010 All-in-One
For Dummies
978-0-470-49748-7

Office 2011 for Mac
For Dummies
978-0-470-87869-9

Word 2010
For Dummies
978-0-470-48772-3

Music

Guitar For Dummies,
2nd Edition
978-0-7645-9904-0

Clarinet For Dummies
978-0-470-58477-4

iPod & iTunes
For Dummies,
9th Edition
978-1-118-13060-5

Pets

Cats For Dummies,
2nd Edition
978-0-7645-5275-5

Dogs All-in One
For Dummies
978-0470-52978-2

Saltwater Aquariums
For Dummies
978-0-470-06805-2

Religion & Inspiration

The Bible For Dummies
978-0-7645-5296-0

Catholicism For
Dummies, 2nd Edition
978-1-118-07778-8

Spirituality For
Dummies, 2nd Edition
978-0-470-19142-2

Self-Help & Relationships

Happiness For Dummies
978-0-470-28171-0

Overcoming Anxiety
For Dummies,
2nd Edition
978-0-470-57441-6

Seniors

Crosswords For Seniors
For Dummies
978-0-470-49157-7

iPad 2 For Seniors
For Dummies, 3rd
Edition
978-1-118-17678-8

Laptops & Tablets
For Seniors For
Dummies, 2nd Edition
978-1-118-09596-6

Smartphones & Tablets

BlackBerry For
Dummies, 5th Edition
978-1-118-10035-6

Droid X2 For Dummies
978-1-118-14864-8

HTC ThunderBolt
For Dummies
978-1-118-07601-9

MOTOROLA XOOM
For Dummies
978-1-118-08835-7

Sports

Basketball For
Dummies, 3rd Edition
978-1-118-07374-2

Football For Dummies,
2nd Edition
978-1-118-01261-1

Golf For Dummies,
4th Edition
978-0-470-88279-5

Test Prep

ACT For Dummies,
5th Edition
978-1-118-01259-8

ASVAB For Dummies,
3rd Edition
978-0-470-63760-9

The GRE Test For
Dummies, 7th Edition
978-0-470-00919-2

Police Officer Exam
For Dummies
978-0-470-88724-0

Series 7 Exam
For Dummies
978-0-470-09932-2

Web Development

HTML, CSS, & XHTML
For Dummies, 7th
Edition
978-0-470-91659-9

Drupal For Dummies,
2nd Edition
978-1-118-08348-2

Windows 7

Windows 7
For Dummies
978-0-470-49743-2

Windows 7
For Dummies,
Book + DVD Bundle
978-0-470-52398-8

Windows 7 All-in-One
For Dummies
978-0-470-48763-1

Available wherever books are sold. For more information or to order direct: U.S. customers visit
www.dummies.com or call 1-877-762-2974. U.K. customers visit www.wileyeurope.com or
call (0) 1243 843291. Canadian customers visit www.wiley.ca or call 1-800-567-4797.
Connect with us online at www.facebook.com/fordummies or @fordummies